Martha McCannon Thomas

Captain Phil

A boy's experience in the western army during the war of the rebellion

Martha McCannon Thomas

Captain Phil

A boy's experience in the western army during the war of the rebellion

ISBN/EAN: 9783337197056

Printed in Europe, USA, Canada, Australia, Japan

Cover: Foto ©ninafisch / pixelio.de

More available books at **www.hansebooks.com**

*A BOY'S EXPERIENCE IN THE WESTERN ARMY
DURING THE WAR OF THE REBELLION.*

BY

M. M. THOMAS

NEW YORK
HENRY HOLT AND COMPANY
1884

TO MY NEPHEWS,

GEORGE W. THOMAS AND SAMUEL L. CORWINE,

I DEDICATE THIS LITTLE BOOK,

With the hope that they may always be animated by the love of Country, which characterized

CAPTAIN PHIL.

CLOVER HILL, March 1, 1866.

PREFACE.

IT is with some anxiety, and considerable hesitation, that I offer this volume to my young friends and the public. Almost every incident is a real experience; the dates, battles and marches, are matters of history. Faulty and incomplete as it is, yet it is very dear to me, for my heart has been in every line as I have written. If its reading help but one boy to love right, and hate wrong, and to hold his country and its institutions firmer in his heart, next to his God, I shall be satisfied and thankful.

CLOVER HILL, March, 1866.

CONTENTS.

CHAPTER I.
HOW I WENT TO THE WAR.
Attack on Sumter.—Family History.—A Fight at School.... 1

CHAPTER II.
THE DEPARTURE OF THE FIRST TROOPS.
The March to the Depot.—The First Night in Camp.—Joseph. 10

CHAPTER III.
LIFE IN CAMP.
The Uniform.—Joseph Dismissed.—Marching through Baltimore.. 17

CHAPTER IV.
AT WASHINGTON.
The Death of Ellsworth.—The President's Levee.—A Visit to Alexandria.. 24

CHAPTER V.
A DAY AT THE CAMPS.
Washington in a State of Siege.—The Return of the Seventh Regiment.—The Zouave Camp...................... 31

CHAPTER VI.
A DAY AT THE CAMPS—CONTINUED.
Exploits of the Zouaves.—Evening Service of the Rhode Islanders.—Concert......................... 39

CHAPTER VII.
FORWARD.—A NEW CAMP.
Contrabands.—Vivandieres.—An Ambush................. 45

CONTENTS.

CHAPTER VIII.
IN THE VAN OF THE ARMY.
Picket Duty.—The Fight at Vienna.—Foraging............ 55

CHAPTER IX.
HOW I BECAME A PRISONER
The Surprise.—Disguised.—In Camp Again 62

CHAPTER X.
AMUSEMENTS IN CAMP.
On Guard in a Storm.—A Scouting Expedition.—Writing Home.. 78

CHAPTER XI.
BEFORE BULL RUN.
The Advance.—Centerville Occupied.—A Skirmish......... 86

CHAPTER XII.
THE BATTLE OF STONE BRIDGE, OR BULL RUN.
Charge of the Black Horse Cavalry.—Pursuit of the Zouaves.—Panic.—Retreat to Washington....................... 97

CHAPTER XIII.
GOING HOME.
Washington after the Battle.—McClellan Summoned to the Command.—A Reception.............................. 108

CHAPTER XIV.
WESTERN VIRGINIA.
With General Rosecrans' Division.—The Pursuit of Floyd.—The Engagement at McCoy's Mills............... 115

CHAPTER XV.
FROM LOUISVILLE TO NASHVILLE.—AFTER BUCKNER.
At Green River.—Battle of Somerset.—The March to Bowling Green.—Loomis' Battery.—Buckner Taken Prisoner 123

CONTENTS. iii

CHAPTER XVI.
NASHVILLE AND PITTSBURGH LANDING.

General Nelson Reaches Nashville.—Reinforcing General Grant.—The Battle of Shiloh.—The Evacuation of Corinth.—The Pursuit of Bragg.—Kirby Smith in Kentucky.—Martial Law Proclaimed in Cincinnati.—Retreat of the Rebels.—General Bragg Threatens Louisville............ 133

CHAPTER XVII.
THE CHASE AFTER BRAGG.

The Battle of Perryville.—Going Over Salt River.—Bragg's Escape.—In Nashville —Buell Succeeded by Rosecrans.. 144

CHAPTER XVIII.
MURFREESBORO'.

The March to Murfreesboro'.—The Battle.—Retreat of the Enemy... 150

CHAPTER XIX.
AFTER THE BATTLE.

Frank Martin.—Women in the Army.—The Color Guard.... 162

CHAPTER XX.
CONTRABANDS IN CAMP.

Christmas in Camp.—Freedom.—Fetish.................. 171

CHAPTER XXI.
IN CAMP AT MURFREESBORO'.

A Spy.—Boys in the Army.—Seizing Horses............... 183

CHAPTER XXII.
MARCHING ON.

The Fight at Shelbyville.—The Occupation of Tullahoma.—Bragg's Retreat.—Across the Tennessee.—The Capture of Chattanooga... 192

CONTENTS.

CHAPTER XXIII.
CHICKAMAUGA.

The Battle of Chickamauga.—General Thomas's Victory.—General Garfield's Exploit.—Johnny Clem.—Military Operations in Three States at Once.................. 199

CHAPTER XXIV.
CHATTANOOGA.

A State of Siege.—Grant in Command.—General Sherman's Arrival.—The Battle Above the Clouds.—Pulpit Rock.—Storming of Mission Ridge....................... 215

CHAPTER XXV.
AT CHATTANOOGA.—IN WINTER QUARTERS.

Getting Supplies up the River.—Grant in Command of the Army.—Sherman Commander of the Department of the Mississippi.. 229

CHAPTER XXVI.
ROCKY FACE.—RESACA.

The Rebels at Buzzard's Gap.—The Assault of Rocky Face Ridge.—Johnston Withdraws to Resaca.—The Battle of Resaca.—The Pursuit of the Rebels.—Johnston Crosses the Etowah.. 256

CHAPTER XXVII.
KENESAW MOUNTAIN.

Allatoona Pass.—Death of General Polk.—The Siege of Kenesaw.—The Attack.—The Rebels Evacuate Kenesaw..... 269

CHAPTER XXVIII.
CROSSING THE CHATTAHOOCHIE.

The Battle of Nickajack Creek.—The March to Atlanta.—Hood Supersedes Johnston.—Battle of Peach Tree Creek.—Death of General McPherson.—Battle of Ezra's Church.—The Siege of Atlanta.—Capture of Atlanta............ 274

CHAPTER XXIX.
BEFORE ATLANTA.

The Flitting.—Burning of the City.—Living in Caves........ 286

CHAPTER XXX.

FROM ATLANTA TO SAVANNAH.

Leaving Atlanta.—Surrender of Milledgeville.—Contrabands.
—Crossing the Ogeechee.—Millen Prison Pen.—Crossing
Ebenezer Creek.—Savannah Invested.................. 292

CHAPTER XXXI.

THE CAROLINAS.—HOME.

Capture of Fort Mc Allister.—Surrender of Savannah.—
Preparations for the March.—In Camp at Beaufort
and Pocotaligo.—The March up the Savannah.—Through
South Carolina.—Crossing the Big and Little Salkehatchie.
—Crossing the South and North Edisto.—Burning of
Orangeburg.—Battle of Congaree Creek.—Crossing the
Saluda and Broad Rivers.—Entering Columbia.—Burning
Columbia.—Caring for the Destitute.—Crossi g the
Wateree.—Bridging Lynch Creek.—In the North State.
—Entering Fayetteville.—Fight at Averysboro'.—Battle
of Bentonville.—Meeting of the Armies at Goldsboro'.—
Lee's Surrender.—President Lincoln's Murder.—Johnston's
Surrender.—Passing Through Richmond.—In Washington.
—The Review.. 323

LIST OF ILLUSTRATIONS.

	PAGE.
THE DEPARTURE.	12
MOBBING THE PIE-MAN.	38
CLARY.	47
THE RETURN.	112
POSSUM.	125
THE PARTING.	204
MURDOCH RECITING TO THE SOLDIERS.	216
REFUGEES.	289
SACKING OF MADISON.	306
"OLE MARS."	320
"A FIGURE."	348

CAPTAIN PHIL.

CHAPTER I.

HOW I WENT TO THE WAR.

SUMTER had been attacked—we knew that. I sat in our room waiting my brother's return; he had gone down town to get the latest accounts by the night's telegraph.

Eleven—twelve—one o'clock struck. He did not come. I went to bed but was unable to sleep, excited by expectation and his long absence. I arose again, and opening the window gazed out. The night was cool, but the air was pleasant to me. There was no one in sight, and a dumb silence seemed to pervade the city.

I was picturing Anderson and his little band in their island fortress, and longing, with a boy's eager, impatient desire, to be with them; my heart throbbing and my breath coming quickly, as in imagination I saw the flash, and heard the boom of the cannon.

There were footsteps; near, nearer they approached, with a dull, heavy tread. I listened, looked out, saw three men coming up the street. Soon they were under the window, and paused at the door, speaking in low tones.

"Then you do not think Anderson a traitor?"

"I would answer for him almost with my life," was the reply, in my brother's voice. "We," he added, applying his night-key to the door, " will soon have times to try us all."

"God help the right!" was the rejoinder.

Anderson suspected of being a traitor? What could have happened? Suddenly turning cold, I drew down the window, and, facing the door, awaited my brother's entrance. He came up the stairs slowly, with a heavy tread. As soon as I saw his face I knew, ere he spoke, what he would say.

"Philip, my boy, Sumter has fallen!"

A heavy weight was at my heart, a choking in my throat, a swelling tide welled to my eyes; I could not help it, I sobbed aloud, covering my face with shame as I did so. For a minute or two my brother walked the floor without speaking; then, coming near, he put his arm about me and said tenderly: "God knows I envy you these tears, I should feel better if I could cry."

I had been ill, and for many weary months confined to my room. During that time how much had I heard, read and talked of Sumter, how much had I heard others talk!

Upon the mantel shelf was a model of Sumter which Capt. Schott had helped me to make as I sat in bed propped by pillows. How many lonely hours had I beguiled in carving and mounting the miniature cannon—how had I boasted of Sumter's strength, and scoffed at the idea of South Carolina doing it harm—and now—it had surrendered!

Should I live to be an old man I shall never forget the stinging pain of those moments—fierce indignation, pride, shame, anger, a crushing of hope, a thirst for revenge, tugged at my boy's heart and found relief in those bitter tears.

Ashamed of them as unmanly, I quickly subdued them,

and recovered myself; seeking to hide my emotion by asking question after question of my brother, which he answered, as he prepared for bed, in that deep tone which told how much he was moved.

Afterwards I heard the story of the brave seventy. I was all aglow when John read of their heroism, the dauntless bravery with which they had held out. When the account described the surrender, how they saluted and paid honors to the grand old flag ere they passed from the fort, I could not contain myself. Snatching Sumter from the mantel shelf and hugging it to my heart, I kissed our country's colors which hung there again and again. Burning to be a man, I upbraided nature that I was still a boy. My brother smiled in a troubled way at my enthusiasm, and said:

"We may have to leave all to defend that flag yet, Phil. The whole country must acknowledge its power."

To which I replied, "I am ready; I can do something."

"Yes, you might make a powder monkey."

That night I had little sleep; I passed it in restless tossings, with now and then a question when I knew John to be awake.

At dawn I slept soundly, and when aroused by the breakfast bell found my brother dressed and sitting at the window reading the newspaper. There was nothing to add to what I had already heard.

After breakfast he went to his business. I was to have re-entered school that day, but it rained heavily, and my going out was deferred until the morrow. I spent the morning taking the guns out of Sumter, and again replacing them; in thinking over what I had heard, and, by the aid of my mimic fort, going over the scene of the bombardment. Our landlady, who had been most kind to me in my illness—attending me through the day in my brother's absence—came in, and talked over the probabilities of a war, sighing heavily as she did so, for she had lost her father in that with Mexico.

John came to dinner. As there were a few additional particulars to be discussed, the gentlemen sat long at table. Again they left for their places of business, and night took them to the several newspaper offices to hear the despatches—so that Monday ended.

I had just passed my fourteenth birthday. My father died when I was eight years of age, and four years later my mother joined him. On her death-bed she gave me, with many solemn charges, into my brother's keeping.

I wish I could describe my brother John to you—he is so good and kind and brave and handsome. He is over thirty years of age, and was, when the war broke out, chief clerk in a large wholesale house. We are alone in the world. He is everything to me.

Our father was a Massachusetts man, and our mother a Southerner; but we were born in the West. My grandfather was one of the *minute men* of the Revolution. He lived on the road between Lexington and Concord, and was aroused from his sleep on the night of the memorable 18th of April, 1775, by the tread of an armed force passing his dwelling.

He saw the "Red Coats" and guessed their errand. Snatching his gun he passed through his back door, crossed the fields, calling up his neighbors by the way, and, accompanied by them, took a bridle path which by a short cut conducted them to Lexington, reaching it in time to warn the militia of the approach of the foe. He was one of those who drove the British soldiery back in their retreat over the same road.

My grandmother, seeing the British coming, took her youngest child in her arms, the other clinging to her skirts, and started through the fields to a neighbor's for safety. They saw her running and fired upon her, the ball from one of their pieces going through the high crown of her cap. She, however, escaped unharmed. After destroying all they could they set fire to the house. My father's uncle edited a paper at Worcester at that time, and the British set a price on his head, but he managed, notwithstanding, to keep it on his shoulders.

These and many other incidents in the early history of our country in which our family bore an humble part, my brother was wont, with pride and pleasure, to relate to me. His love of country was intense; he gloried as our father had in THE UNION.

The next morning I went to school for the first time in many months. Of course all our talk was of Sumter. Many a taunt had we to hear from the Southern boys, who jeered and laughed at its fall. I found the school nearly equally divided.

James Fontaine, a Mississippian, who for his bullying propensities we had named "South Carolina," was at the head of a set who glorified the South in everything; while his cousins, of the same State, took sides with the "Yankees." Since the fall of Sumter James had been unbearable, and that morning, for my benefit, was especially insolent and defiant. In study hours he drew on a slate a pack of lean hungry dogs, led on by a miserable cur, and labeling it "Anderson's Brigade," passed it round for scoff and comment.

I felt humiliated enough, and trembled so with passion I could hardly hold my book, or keep quiet until recess.

I stopped in the school-room for a while to speak to the teachers, and when I reached the play ground I found that Fontaine had formed a scarecrow of straw and paper, which he had placed against the wall with a flag in its hand, made and painted by him in school-hours. Yelling "down with the flag and Anderson the traitor," he urged his party to stone it.

Charley Thornley was a quiet fellow. He had stood this insult as long as he could. Now walking up to the figure he placed himself beside it, and seizing the flag, waved it above his head, and called out: "The boy who throws at this hits me, and must take the consequences."

With a huzza I sprang to his side, giving the scarecrow a kick that sent it flying. "Stand back, Phil," Charley said, "this is my fight."

As they all knew that Charley was a cool, resolute fellow, for a moment there was no movement among them, but presently "South Carolina" let fly, and struck him on the head. "Keep your distance all," Charley shouted, his eyes flashing as he grappled with the Southerner. We stood in silence waiting the mastery, for they were nearly matched. Charley got it, and throwing the braggart over one leg, he confined his feet with the other, tucked his head under his arm, and seizing a cricket-bat near, spanked him soundly. Such a shout! It made the walls ring, and quickly brought out Mr. Thatcher, one of the teachers, to inquire what was the matter. He reprimanded and ordered us in, but I saw the smile on his face as he turned away.

When dismissed we met in the play ground, and started a subscription for a flag, for we were determined that the Stars and Stripes should stream above the school house ere another day had passed. The secesh party were silent and sullen. The disgrace of their leader was the more bitter as the story got wind and the boys in the streets when they met one of them would make a peculiar and contemptuous gesture. accompanied by a prolonged whoop.

John did not come home to dinner. I had taken my tea, and was in our room studying my Latin lesson when he came in; he did not stop below but came straightway to our chamber and closed the door after him.

"How did school go to-day, Phil?"

He stood beside me and put his hand on my head. "Pretty well," I replied, and was about telling him what had happened, when he walked to the window and drummed on the glass. I saw he was deep in thought. Turning suddenly he said:

"Philip, there is to be war. The President has made a requisition for troops and I am going."

I made an exclamation, saying, "You will take me with you?"

"That is the trouble, my boy," and drawing me towards him, he added, "you are not old enough to be a soldier. I may be killed, then what will become of you?"

"I must go," I said passionately, "I must be with you; I cannot stay behind."

"Impossible! Suppose you should get sick; you are not strong now. You must stay here and do just as you would if I were with you."

"I will not stay," I sobbed, "I cannot; I am strong enough now; you promised mother we should not be separated."

"That is it," he said, sadly. "I feel it my duty to go; my father would have expected it of me, but to leave you, Phil—and you cannot join the army."

"Yes, I can; I am small of my age but I can be a drummer-boy; I drum quite well. Or I can go to wait on you."

"Do not add to my perplexities, Philip," was his only answer. He turned to the window and stood looking into the street.

A knock at the door startled us.

"Come in."

Dr. Grey, a friend of John's, and our physician, entered. After a word to me, he spoke to John of the President's proclamation, of the enthusiasm of the people, and the prospect of a regiment being off in a day or two. John informed him of his determination, and of his concern as to myself.

"Can't I go with him, Dr. Grey?" I interrupted. "I am well and strong now."—The probability of being left behind overcame me, I choked—stammered—stopped.

The doctor lowered his head in thought for a moment, then drawing me to him made an examination of my condition, thumped and jerked me, asked questions, criticised my teeth, looked at my tongue, shook me, then turning to John, said:

"I do not know that you could do better than to take him with you."

"How?"

"As camp follower—waiter—errand boy, any thing you will. Seriously, it could be easily arranged; there is no doubt Mr. B. will be colonel of the regiment; he is a life-long friend, and knows how you are situated. I really think that, with common precaution, camp life would physically be of great service to Phil."

"I can drum," I interrupted; "Charlie Greg is drummer for the Grays, and he is neither so large nor so old as I am."

The doctor laughed, eying me keenly the while. "They will have noise enough without your assistance, Phil. Drumming is not exactly what you need."

"The example, Grey; the loose morality, the temptations of a camp life, their effect on the character of one so young"—observed my brother.

"He will have your example, there, which he would be deprived of here, in this large city where there are quite as many temptations. With you he would have an experience, and an opportunity of learning what is not to be gained from books; in short, if he were my brother, he should accompany me."

I could have caught the doctor and hugged him, but I stood still holding my breath—watching John's face, and waiting his decision.

He took a turn across the floor, walked to the window and looked out for a second, then, with a great sigh, as though relieved, turned to me and said:

"I suppose it will be as good an arrangement as I can make, and if I can get permission you may go soldiering with me, Phil."

I sprang to him and threw my arms around him. I stumbled over the doctor's outstretched legs as I dashed through the door, leaped down stairs, and, rushing into the street, relieved myself by loud huzzas which brought the boys round me. I triumphantly told them that I was going to the war.

CHAPTER II.

THE DEPARTURE OF THE FIRST TROOPS.

THE following days were busy ones. John enlisted, and as he had no trouble about me, he made every arrangement to go with the first regiment leaving the State. His employers made him some handsome presents, and told him his situation would be open to him on his return. The next morning I went to the armory with him to see the men drill. The company was an old one, and the ranks were fast filling with new recruits. They expected to be off in twenty-four hours, and would be uniformed in camp or at the Capital.

I spent most of the day at the drill room, going through the exercises as the men went through them, or running errands for John. The city was all excitement, the streets full of men moving to and fro in eager haste, or standing about the recruiting offices; and even the women could not wait at home, but came out to see what was going on.

I felt the importance of my position, and I dashed in and out, only stopping to tell any acquaintance I chanced to meet, that my brother and I were going to the war; fully enjoying the astonishment and envy of my schoolmates.

Our last night in the city was spent at the armory, where squads were drilling all night, for we were to leave at six in the morning. Towards midnight the company was visited by several clergymen, who gave short addresses, sang a hymn, made a prayer, and presented each one with a Bible. The devotions over, I heard a man say, "I feel set apart for the work now." John came to me and bade me go into the office of his friend, Mr. B——, which adjoined the armory, and sleep on the sofa. He said he had packed a carpet-bag with all the wardrobe I could carry, and would call me in time. I slept soundly, and was awakened by his shaking me. I was quickly on my feet, and with pride and pleasure belted down the gray flannel shirt he had provided, finished my toilet by using the lawyer's basin and brushes, then hastened to the armory, where the men in high spirits waited the word of command. Lieutenant G—— was an intimate friend of John's, and by his side I was to march, John being in the ranks before me. The word given, the men filed out, filled the street, and marched to the place of rendezvous, where other companies fell in; and in order, attended by the escort, we took our way to the cars.

Although so early in the morning, the streets were crowded with people the whole line of our way; the sidewalks, steps, stoops, windows, were alive with human beings; hands waved handkerchiefs and threw bouquets; voices shouted cheers of encouragement and words of farewell.

It was a proud day for all. I held up my head and stepped as firmly as the best. "Bully for you, Phil!" I heard several times, as I stooped to pick up bouquets, of which I soon had a handful.

"Keep a stiff upper lip, boys," said Lieutenant G——, as we rounded into Broadway, and beheld the great crowd spreading as far as the eye could reach. "God bless the women," he added. "This is a glorious good-by, but don't break down." He vigorously wiped the dust from his face and eyes.

Shouts that deafened, flowers that covered us, greeted our turning the corner. Every man held a bouquet aloft, and many wore wreaths and garlands; one wreath, well-directed, struck John on the head. He colored as he waved in acknowledgment, shook it down, and wore it on his shoulders. So we reached the depot, the crowd there with difficulty making way for us to pass to the cars.

Now the men broke ranks, each seeking father, mother, sister or loved one, to bid the last farewell. Kissing, shaking of hands, tears and sobs followed; and "God bless you!" fell on the air, uttered by young and old, rich and poor. Many a stalwart man, from whom a bullet could not have forced a groan, cried outright.

I was standing on the platform looking for John, when I heard a familiar voice say, "Here he is now." In a moment I was surrounded by the boys of my school class, with Charley Thornley at their head, bearing in his hand a small flag ornamented with flowers.

"We have been searching for you, Phil," he said. "The boys wish to present you with this flag as a farewell token. The girls sat up half the night to make it, and have adorned it with flowers. We know you will take good care of it and do all you can."

I could not reply. I took the flag and waved it; the boys huzzaed, I blubbered, and was shaking hands with them when the shrill warning whistle interrupted, and the rush of men separated us. I wish I could keep the tears back on some occasions—it is so like a girl to cry. I would scorn to do it in sickness or pain, but when I am excited and moved they will come. John tells me never to mind, they will dry up quick enough. But I do mind.

The women seemed frantic; several of them stooped down, embraced and kissed me, speaking kind words,

THE DEPARTURE.

John took my hand, and we gained the inside of the car.

So we left our home for the war.

All along the road, at every station, the people had gathered to bid us welcome and to say "God-speed" to the first offering of our State to the nation. Banners crossed the track, bearing words of greeting; flags intertwined above our heads; green arches spanned the road; stirring music met us, and enthusiastic voices bade us "Remember our God and strike for the Union." It was like the triumphal processions I had read of in history—the tribute paid to a victorious Cæsar.

One of the new recruits took a seat beside me and made some complimentary remarks upon my flag. We soon got into friendly conversation, and I discovered that he had only joined the preceding night. He was a slender, delicate-looking lad of about seventeen, quiet in manner, but enthusiastic in the cause. His name, he told me, was Joseph Dale.

The excitement continued during the journey, and met us at its termination, where, weary and hungry, we arrived in the afternoon. Through some mistake there was nothing provided for us to eat, and we marched to our quarters, a race course on the edge of the city, and there awaited the next order to move.

Night came on—the first night in camp. Weary and supperless, the men threw themselves on the ground to sleep without any covering to ward off the chilly air. John managed to procure a loaf of bread, and divided it with Joseph and me. Then, spreading my traveling shawl on the earth, we huddled close and slept soundly.

The men made themselves as comfortable as possible; some grumbled good naturedly at their accommodations, others jested at their first war experience, but at last one by one the voices were hushed, and, worn by travel and excitement, all slept well in their novel quarters. The early light startled me from my dreams. Joseph was already awake. Giving ourselves a brisk shake, by way of righting our clothes, we started in pursuit of water for a wash. John met us with a cheery "Good-morning," and pointed out where we would find what we wanted. A quick sousing of our faces, a few passes of our pocket combs, and we were ready for the substantial and plentiful breakfast the citizens had provided.

Having taken a liking for each other, Joseph and I kept together. The men joked us on our camp experience, telling us we would soon wish ourselves back at "mamma's apron-string."

Joseph was the youngest of the company, and so delicate in appearance that he seemed altogether unfit for the rough life of a soldier. As I was known to be a hanger on, I was called upon to do many little offices for the men, which I cheerfully performed. Indeed John had said to me when talking of my going: "Remember, Phil, the only way you can serve your country as yet, is to serve those who serve it."

At which Dr. Grey had laughed and rejoined: "Yes, my boy, when a soldier wants a drink you must believe the Union is thirsty, and forthwith get it for him."

I am small for my age, and, from ill health, I suppose, and having always lived with people older than myself, have a staid old look and a precise way of speaking, they tell me, which attracts attention.

As I passed around several called to me: "Halloo, my little man, does your mother know you're out?" "Here pocket edition," etc., all said in a kindly tone. To some of them I replied, to others I did not.

Several of John's friends were commenting upon my

introduction among them, when one beckoned me to him with, "What do you intend to do for your country, Capting?"

"Keep the flag flying if I can't do anything else," I replied, waving mine.

"What is your first name?"

"Philip. I am Philip Wharton."

"Kneel down," was the laughing retort.

I dropped before him.

He took my flag, struck me on the shoulder with it, waved it over my head, and called out:—

"Rise up, Captain Phil."

And as "Captain Phil" I was always afterwards known in the regiment.

Our breakfast despatched, we again marched to the cars and were soon on our way.

Joseph and I became confidential. I told him all about John and myself,—and how I happened to be with the regiment.

He appeared interested in all I said. He told me he had neither father nor mother, and had run away from his aunt's house, determined to be a soldier.

I saw John was pleased with my companion; he made some inquiries, and learned he was nineteen, although he looked much younger. He expressed a wish to keep with us, and John told him he could join our mess. He seldom spoke to any of the men, and refused all invitations to drink or smoke.

That day passed much as the previous one had. We were everywhere received with the same enthusiasm, but the men were not so excited, and they slept between times. Joseph and I were sitting quietly on the same seat, when a rough recruit who sat behind us leaned forward and said:

"Aren't you getting a little homesick?"

"No," I answered, turning round and pointing to John, "I have my home with me."

"Good for you," he said, slapping me on the shoulder, "but I meant t'other one."

"Me," and Joseph straightened himself up. "Yes, homesick to meet the rebels."

"You'll do, both of you," was the reply as he sank back in his seat again.

I saw a drop like a tear on Joseph's cheek, and suppose this caused the query.

That night we made another stoppage, and the next day reached the camp where we were destined to stay many weeks.

CHAPTER III.

LIFE IN CAMP.

IT was several days before we got into any kind of regular routine, or began to feel at all settled. The troops were eager to go to the defense of Washington, threatened by the rebels, and grumbled much that they were not allowed to do so, chafing at the delay. The greater part of the regiment consisted of new recruits, who had to be drilled ere they were fit for duty, and then must be uniformed and armed.

We received regular rations of hard biscuit, salt pork, and coffee, no butter, but, twice a week, fresh meat was allowed. Soldiers' fare went hard with me at first, and all my money was soon spent for delicacies. We did our own cooking. Joseph and I volunteered for this duty; he had a natural talent for it, and taught me to make excellent coffee.

The regiment drilled six and eight hours a day. I always turned out with the men and went systematically through the manual, which soon began to tell upon me. I slept soundly, although my bed was only the *soft* side of a board, and I entered into every duty with zest. John had appeared anxious on my account in the commencement of our journey, but now he began to let me take care of myself.

Joseph was getting browned by exposure; he attained much proficiency in drill and bore himself well; when he came in after three or four hours' exercise, his eyes would be so bright and his cheeks so red that it was a pleasure to look at him. The men called him "Handsome Joe." Being neat and handy, and always ready to oblige, he was a favorite.

Many ladies visited us, and they did not come empty handed. They brought meats, pies, cakes, vegetables, pickles, and other nice things, which we enjoyed there as we never had at home.

I received so many of these favors that it soon became a joke among the men, when they saw a carriage approaching, to call me to hand out the ladies. My eagerness to obey brought upon me a sharp reprimand from John; I kept in the background after that. I was prouder of the bouquets presented to me than of anything else, and was always strutting about with one in my cap or jacket, which to tease me the men would sometimes snatch at. John tried to laugh me out of this "*puppyism*" as he called it, but I stopped him with an allusion to the wreath he wore on his shoulders the day we left home, and which hung over his knapsack in our quarters with my flag.

At nine every night the roll was called, before which I always read a chapter of the Bible with John, and said the Lord's prayer. At half-past nine the drum tapped and all lights were extinguished.

It was while in that camp that I made my first attempt at washing. Our flannel shirts and drawers were soiled; we could get no one to wash for us, so I determined to try to wash them myself. Going to a little creek some distance off, I waded in the water, and soaped and rubbed and scrubbed to my heart's content, then laid them on the rocks to dry. As John wished to indulge in a clean shirt, I, that evening, with considerable pride, produced the one I had washed, when to my astonishment he could not get it on, it was so drawn up and thick his efforts to stretch only tore it.

I told Joseph, who laughed and bade me never mind, he would show me how to wash. Next day, after morning drill, armed with the pot we made our coffee in, we proceeded to a retired part of the creek, made a fire, filled the pot with water, and put it on to boil. While it was heating Joseph proceeded to mend the tears and sew the buttons on, supplying himself with all he needed from his soldier's bag, some kind ladies having provided our regiment with them. He handled the needle so well, and appeared so thoroughly to understand what he was doing, that I remarked he sewed like a girl. He did not appear to like that, and answered that he had been apprenticed to a tailor once, but he did not care that every one should know it.

When the water was hot he made a soap suds and put the flannels in it, to take the *milling*, as he called it, out. After letting them remain there a while he and I stretched them, pulling them in all directions until they were almost dry, when they presented quite a different appearance from what they did after my washing. Being tired, we next threw ourselves upon the grass to munch a cracker. After a while Joseph wandered away, and I read a newspaper I had with me. He returned in a few moments and said: "I am going to take a bath, Captain Phil. There is a nice little spot around there," pointing to a bend where the alders drooped over and hid the stream. "You whistle if you see any one coming." I wondered why he should be so particular, but, remembering his shyness, his constant refusal to bathe with the men, and their saying that he must have been bitten by a mad dog, and must have hydrophobia, he dreaded water so, I made no remark.

He returned apparently much refreshed, and was full of fun and frolic. We had a nap; then collecting our things, went back to camp, reaching there just in time for battalion drill.

One morning news spread through the camp that the equipments and arms had arrived. All were on the alert. When I saw the men in their bright new uniforms I was, for the first time, dissatisfied with my flannel shirt.

I stood beside John when he put his uniform on, and arranged his haversack and handled his gun, with admiring envy. Observing my manner, he turned to me and said:

"What is the matter, Phil?"

I stammered "nothing;" then, looking up in his face with a half-laughing, half-soliciting expression, "I think I might have a uniform too."

"I thought that was it; but uniforms cost money, Phil, and I am poor, and the war will make me poorer."

I made no reply, but one of the men who stood by, said:

"You must put the livery on him, Wharton, or he will not be known as one of us."

John looked at me and smiled.

A few days after, as we were eating our supper, a large package was delivered to him. He put it aside. It was my turn to wash up and put the things away. Joseph helped me, as he always did. I washed my face and combed my hair when I had done, for John was particular about my appearance, and went and seated myself under the tree where he sat watching some of the men who were playing leap-frog.

"Here, Phil," he said, as I touched the earth, "is your uniform," and he drew the parcel from behind him.

I leaped up, cut the wrapper open, and there, sure

enough, it was, cap, boots and all. I examined them one by one, and to my satisfaction found that they were all of much better make and material than his. Going aside a little I put them on, stepped back and forth, looked up and down in admiration. Finally, I strapped the knapsack on my shoulders, and strutted back to John. Certainly I was never so proud in all my life as when I stood before him and exclaimed :

"Now I am a United States soldier!"

"You should have the tags and a gun and you would pass for the Little Corporal himself," said Lieuteuant G——, who had just joined John, and with him was enjoying my satisfaction, which was not complete until I had gone the rounds and exhibited myself in my new dress.

It was rumored that we were speedily to move for Washington, and all were in eager expectation of the announcement. One day I had been to the neighboring town on an errand for Colonel F——, which had kept me several hours from camp. On my return I observed groups standing round earnestly talking ; but as I had been told not to loiter, I hastened to Colonel F——'s quarters, although one or two of the men called me in passing. There was quite a crowd at Colonel F——'s tent, John among them. One said as I approached : "Here is Captain Phil, he can tell us all about her." Whereupon a half-dozen of them spoke at once, asking something about Joseph.

"Had I observed anything unusual about him?" "Had I seen him undressed?" "Did I know he was a woman?"

"Come here, Phil," said the colonel, and he repeated the questions.

I answered I had observed nothing unusual, and never dreamed he was a woman.

How the discovery was made I did not exactly understand; but it was made, and the regiment was amazed at it. The idea had never entered any man's head that the quiet, handsome boy, ever ready to do a service, and distinguished for his aptness in military drill, was a woman.

She would neither tell her name, nor give her reasons for enlisting, nor answer any questions about her former life. She only begged that she might be sent away where she could get women's clothes.

Many supposed her a spy, and she was told of the suspicion, at which she only laughed.

She desired to be dismissed, asserted she had faithfully performed the duties required of her since she had been in the regiment, and should have continued to perform them if she had not been discovered. She knew it was now impossible for her to remain.

They had her under guard preparatory to her removal from camp. The colonel requested me to go and see her, as she might make a confession to me.

She put out her hand when I went in.

"Well, Captain Phil, they have found me out. I thought *you* would have done so long ago."

I could not answer—could not believe her a woman.

"Do beg the colonel to send me to Cincinnati, Captain Phil. I have friends there," were her next words.

She would not reply to my questions except to say, "You are a good fellow, Captain Phil; but these officers don't know everything. I told you the truth when I told you I had no father and mother, and had run away from my aunt. If a man had been as miserable as I was he would have shot himself. I do not expect to see you ever again, Captain Phil. Keep this as a remembrance." She handed me her Bible. So we parted.

On the morrow orders came to march, and Joseph

was forgotten in the eagerness of all hands to press forward.

We were to go by way of Baltimore, and, in view of any trouble there, John thought of leaving me to follow him; but I protested so earnestly against it, insisting he was making a baby of me, that he yielded, giving me orders what to do in case of an attack.

With my uniform on I took my place by Lieutenant G——'s side, flag in hand, and, if not the tallest, I know I was the proudest MAN in that regiment.

We reached Baltimore in due season, strong and resolute, with guns half cocked, having orders to fire upon the mob if assaulted. The men left the cars and moved through the sullen crowd without molestation to the Washington depot (only greeted now and then with the cry, "Hurrah for Jeff Davis!"). They were soon on their way to the Capital.

CHAPTER IV.

AT WASHINGTON.

IT was twilight when, dusty and travel-worn, we reached Washington, where we found quarters provided for us, into which we were glad to go.

The next morning all were startled by the sudden announcement that Colonel Ellsworth was dead.

Our troops had silently passed over to Alexandria in the night, and he had been shot in an attempt to carry off the rebel flag floating from the Marshall House. With the flag in his possession he was descending the stairs, when Jackson, the proprietor of the house, saw and killed him. Jackson, in turn, met his death at the hand of Bromwell, one of Ellsworth's Zouaves. As the news spread, all was excitement. The men questioned its truth ; officers went out to ascertain its veracity, and returned with pale faces and set teeth, confirming the report. Ellsworth's men vowed deep vows of vengeance.

Ellsworth was my hero. He had exhibited his Zouaves in our city, when he made his rounds with them, since when I had been Zouave-crazy. The boys had formed a Zouave company, copying their dress and emulating their drill. Of this company I was a member. One of my promised pleasures in visiting Washington was to see the Zouaves face to face, with Ellsworth at their head, and to go to their camp. Our regiment was ordered to camp a short distance out of the city. The faces of the people we saw on our way there were gloomy. We had taken

Alexandria but had lost Ellsworth. His body was brought to the Navy Yard. The Zouaves were frenzied, and declared they would settle the account with interest on the first opportunity; henceforth their cry was, "Ellsworth and vengeance"—a threat the Red-Caps were not likely to forget.

After we were fixed in camp and our usual routine established, John, who was anxious that I should see all that was to be seen, gave me permission to accompany Colonel F——, who was going to Washington. He desired me to call upon Mrs. Leavit, an old friend of my mother's, who resided there, and present his compliments, stating his wish to do so in person as soon as he could get leave.

I went with the colonel to the city. He was an old friend; had known my father, and when he was in business John had been in his employment. Following his directions, I made my way to New Jersey Avenue, where Mrs. Leavit lived. She received me warmly for my mother's sake. When I told her I had accompanied my brother, who was a volunteer in the Union Army, she kissed me. I saw the sights with Mrs. Leavit, dined with her, and stayed all night at her house.

About two o'clock the next morning I was aroused by a magnificent band playing "The Campbells are Coming" in most stirring strains. I stretched my head out the window to see the "Highlanders"—the New York 79th —which had just arrived. Dressed in their beautiful costume, they marched steadily along, their arms glittering in the gas-light, the inspiring music rolling and swelling on the air, startling the people from their sleep, who thronged the windows in their night-clothes, and waved and shouted and clapped their hands.

Going down to the hotel I found the colonel full of business. He told me I must take care of myself that day. Not wishing to go back to Mrs. Leavit's, I found plenty to interest me as I wandered about the city.

About nine o'clock the colonel returned to his room and proceeded to make his toilet. He told me he was going to the President's levee. I gave him an account of my day, hoping he would invite me to go with him, but he did not appear to think of so doing. I rendered him all the assistance I could, but my hopes grew fainter and fainter as he proceeded, and when he turned for a final look in the glass, ere he pulled on his gloves, I resigned myself to my fate.

A sudden thought, however, seemed to strike him as he was about to leave the room, for, turning to me, he said:

"What are you going to do with yourself, Captain Phil?"

"I do not know—go to bed, I suppose, sir."

"Would you like to go to the levee?"

"Yes, that I would."

"Why did you not say so before, you young rascal? Make haste; I have not a moment to lose."

I lost no time, and we were soon on our way to the White House.

There were carriages and servants in waiting outside, music and brilliant lights within.

We entered the hall and managed to reach the room where the President and Mrs. Lincoln received.

About the center of the apartment there stood a tall, thin, angular, muscular man, whom I knew at a glance to be Mr. Lincoln. A few feet from him was a pleasant-looking lady, whom I also knew to be Mrs. Lincoln.

A gentleman near mentioned Colonel F——'s name, and the President shook hands with him, and made some remark; Mrs. Lincoln bowed courteously, and we passed on. I hoped Mr. Lincoln would notice me, but he did not.

People were constantly going and coming; most of the ladies were in bright, gay dresses, and many gentlemen were in uniforms. Visitors came in at one door, and passed out at the other, scattering through the rooms. The most prominent people, however, appeared to stay in the room with the President.

After sauntering through the great east room I contrived to get back to the one we had first entered. I wished to see more of Mr. Lincoln. No one noticed me, and I edged as near the President as I could get without being intrusive. I saw he liked the ladies and was a favorite with them. When they paused to pay their respects, a good humored smile lighted his face, and he had a pleasant word of greeting. Several times during the evening he laughed heartily. Once, I saw him pluck the sleeve of a gentleman who was passing, and say something which seemed greatly to amuse both.

I longed to have that great sinewy hand take mine and shake it, and feel those honest eyes looking down into mine. There was something so frank and kind in their expression, I felt I should love him.

I wished to know a little of the people about me, but Col. F—— had found friends, and was engaged with them, and I was left to take care of myself. Secretary Chase I had seen at home, and knew his Websterean head at a glance. Senator Wilson of Massachusetts, I also recognized; Mrs. Leavit had pointed him out to me at the Capitol, saying: " He is a pure patriot, Philip, and the soldier's friend." Gov. Dennison I also knew. But there were other senators and distinguished men, some of them wearing badges, whom I supposed were foreign ministers, that I should like to have had named to me. There were several plain men, who might have been farmers, walking about with their wives on their arms, the women looking shy and confused ; and a bright old Quaker lady to whom the President's manner was deferential.

As it happened, when Colonel F—— and I were making our way out we passed quite near Mr. Lincoln. Moving suddenly away from the group by whom he was surrounded he came against me. Placing his hand upon my head, he said kindly, while his weary look vanished and a genial smile came over his face:

"Whom have we here?"

"An incipient soldier. One of the Western defenders of the Capital," said Colonel F——.

"He looks like a brave one. Be faithful and true, my boy; you could not have a better cause."

Old Abe shook me heartily by the hand.

As we reached the door the band struck up "Yankee Doodle;" "Just in time," said Colonel F——, "that is the signal of dismissal."

I had little to say; I felt as I suppose my grandfather must have felt when he talked with General Washington, for John had often told me how he spoke of it, with a glow on his pale face, and a light in his dim eye, when he was a white-haired old man.

The next morning, instead of going directly to camp, Colonel F—— decided to inspect the scene of Ellsworth's murder, and was ready to mount his horse for that purpose when I got back from Mrs. Leavit's. I went with him. We found Alexandria deserted—the streets silent—the houses shut—sentries were the only signs of life, save two or three men, who scowled at us in passing. Not a woman or child did we see. A soldier, in answer to Colonel F——'s question, "Where is the Marshall House?" pointed to a dingy tavern, a sort of drover's inn, at a little distance. Riding up to the door we alighted, and Colonel F—— requested permission to see the spot where Ellsworth met his death. Three or four lazy, sullen-looking men were lounging about, one of whom pointed out the place on the landing where he was attacked, as he went down-stairs with the flag. Our attention was drawn to several doors in which bullets had lodged. The staircase and landing were much defaced, pieces of the wood having been cut off by visitors anxious to preserve them as relics. Our curiosity gratified, we returned to the lower floor. A Federal soldier, who had taken too much liquor, stood in the hall, and talked in a swaggering, defiant way of the "Zoo Zoos," and the vengeance they would take. The men only replied with fierce and gloomy looks, and set teeth.

Going back we stopped at the camp of one of the New York regiments and stayed some time. Walking around, I saw a little boy, of only about eleven years of age, eating his dinner off his drum's head. I went up and began to talk to him, and said : " You are very young to be in the army ;" he replied: " There are plenty of boys in the army as young as me—and I knew one boy who was killed." He then told me of Clarence McKenzie, of the New York 13th, who was killed at Annapolis, a little while before, by the accidental discharge of a gun in the hands of one of the soldiers. I asked him if he did not think he would be afraid in battle. He thought not, but he did not know ; he felt as big as anybody when playing for the soldiers. In answer to my question "If he did not want to see his mother?" he said: " Yes, sometimes, but father's here; he is drum major."

Showing our passes again at the Long Bridge we were soon clattering through the streets of Washington. A drove of mules and horses was being driven through the city for army use, and such rearing, dragging, plunging, never, I think, was seen before. Notwithstanding Colonel

F——'s annoyance at our entanglement in this crowd, I laughed until I could hardly sit on my horse at the attempts of an old negro to get out of the way of a refractory mule, one of a drove. The driver pulled and dragged, the mule shied first one side then the other, and then determinedly set his feet and backed. Sambo got across the street, edged himself against a house, and thought he was out of danger, when the animal backed on him, his heels flying at each blow from the driver. The darkey squirmed and dodged in the most ludicrous manner, holding his bundle up before him for protection, the drove preventing his getting out of the way. At length with the cry "Golly mighty, massa," as a blow reached him instead of the mule, he darted through the throng and down the street with all speed.

There was a carriage in front of the War Office as we passed. A tall, magnificent-looking old man, dressed in military clothes, was getting out, assisted by two of the clerks.

"Look, Captain Phil," said Colonel F——, "that is General Scott."

We drew rein. He halted to speak to one passing, then tottered to the door of the building.

I had seen "Old Chapultepec," as Captain Schott called General Scott. Perfectly satisfied with my visit to Washington, I returned to camp, and, as Colonel F—— ordered me, reported to John.

CHAPTER V.

A DAY AT THE CAMPS.

ONE day during this month Colonel F—— wished several commissions attended to, and proposed that John that I should be trusted with them. I gladly undertook the business. At the close of his directions the colonel said: "I intend to visit the Zouave camp next week, Captain Phil, and you shall accompany me."

Starting early, I reached the city betimes. After attending to the colonel's orders, which required considerable running about, I went to call upon Mrs. Leavit. She was glad to see me, and said:

"You are just in time, the New York Seventh returns home to-day. All Washington will be out to bid them farewell; you want to see the show, I know, so jump in, the carriage is at the door."

In I got, taking charge of the bouquets. Driving to the avenue we saw many carriages and people going the same way.

"Now, Philip, you must wave and cheer with all your might; the Seventh came to us in our extremity, and they were most welcome; they must have a brilliant farewell."

"I never was so glad in all my life," continued the little woman, half rising from her seat and gazing around her as the carriage halted: "I was never so glad to see men as I was to see the Massachusetts and New York regiments: I could have embraced each man separately," she laughed. "The Massachusetts Sixth had been attacked in coming;

the railroad was torn up; the road blocked. The morning came laden with fears that we would be in the hands of the rebels before night. Night found us trembling and watching for the dawn. We heard they had started; the time for their arrival came, and all hearts in expectancy turned to meet them. They came not; we had no word of them. Had they fallen into a trap of the foe? We could not tell; they could not communicate with us nor we with them. We knew nothing, and were alive to every fear.

"Word reached us that they were on the way; they came; the road was open; the city safe. Massachusetts and New York had come to the rescue. You should have seen the President as he welcomed them; his care-worn face was radiant with satisfaction—Hark!" she quickly added, as she held up her finger, "I hear the band —they are coming."

We listened; it was but a drum and fife.

"Those only," she continued, "could realize our joy who had shared our danger. It is a good thing to be a soldier, Philip;" she leaned forward and looked in my eyes as she laid her hand on my knee, "but a great thing to be a soldier defending your country, fighting for liberty and law—God bless all such."

She paused.

"How did you provide for the troops?"

"As well as we could, and there was no grumbling. They occupied the streets and the Capitol building, were quartered in the halls and lobbies, and I must say these were never better filled or more to my mind. Some of the men had left their homes in such hot haste they were in a sad plight. I came near stripping my husband's wardrobe helping them. Whenever I saw a sturdy yeoman from the hills of Vermont, or the old battle-fields of Massachusetts, my heart warmed to him, and I was impelled to stop and have something to say. I eschewed the Seventh," with another of her little laughs; "they needed nothing, had money and admirers enough; besides, I had seen a little of the world, and so had most of them." She turned quickly at a movement in the crowd. "Here they are, fine soldiers all, and did their duty nobly—I am sorry they are going."

There they were sure enough, and taking advantage of an opening in the line of carriages we moved to a better position.

Covered with dust, but with a gallant bearing, the Seventh came in, marching in perfect order, nearly every man having a nosegay at his button-hole. The day was hot, but the men were spirited and bright, and their appearance showed they had not been playing war. They were browned by the sun, and bore the marks of work and exposure.

The air rang with huzzas—women waved their handkerchiefs and showered bouquets,—men's hats circled in the air. In the midst of all the locomotive snorted in, the shrill whistle blew, the cry "all aboard" rang out—there was a cloud of handkerchiefs—a deafening shout—and the Seventh took to the cars, and, leaving a train of vapor behind, were whizzed off.

Mrs. Leavit drove away in the direction of the White House. There was a carriage standing before the President's mansion, and a lady was getting into it.

"That is Mrs. Lincoln, Philip," said my kind guide. She was the same lady I had seen at the levee.

Declining Mrs. Leavit's offer of a bed, I left her after dinner and went back to camp.

A few days after this, on a bright cool morning, I was rubbing my eyes, having been awakened by the reveillé and thinking it was earlier than usual, when John said:

"Make double-quick time, Phil. Colonel F—— is going to the Zouave camp to-day, and will be off early; report yourself at his quarters as soon as you are dressed; I have secured a horse for you."

"Have you seen him?"

"Not to-day, don't ask any more questions; a good soldier never questions, he obeys."

I made good time, and we were shortly on our way to Shooter's Hill, where the Zouaves had their camp. Much to my satisfaction no one accompanied Colonel F—— but myself.

It was a glorious morning; the sun was up, scattering the mists which had rested on the valleys, thus giving to our view a beautiful country. As we rode along dashing the rain drops from the trees, the colonel talked pleasantly to me.

When we reached the camp, the men were lounging about waiting the summons to breakfast. Some were in groups laughing and jesting, others stretched full length on the ground, apparently sleeping, while squads attended the fires and cooked.

"I say, Bill," said one sleepy looking specimen of humanity as we passed, "is that chicken done?"

"Almost," said a man who was stirring a pot over the fire,—"but, Dick, I don't think the old man's dog relished the bite he had of your leg last night; he spit it out like pisin. Joe was up there this morning, and says he hangs his head and looks sick."

"Ay, yi," yelled the group.

The man addressed raised himself, and, arranging a bandage about his leg, remarked:

"It burns like fire; I wish I had killed the beast; it may give me hydrophoby yet."

"Your flesh don't agree with him, sure, and, from all accounts, he is more like to die of manophoby than you of hydrophoby," said one who sat hugging his knees, and who suddenly ducked his head and rolled over and over down hill, to avoid a camp stool which came flying at him.

The colonel wore his uniform, but they took not the least notice of his presence. He glanced at me in a quizzical way out of the corner of his eye, as the conversation reached him.

One group were at their meal. A thin, wiry little fellow poured out the coffee; while doing so he made a motion as if he intended to scald the man next him, and said:

"Look here, Charlie, if this stuff is not better than that tobacco slop you gave us yesterday, I'll make you swallow it, pot and all."

On reaching the tent of the colonel's friend, we found him at breakfast, and were invited by him to share the meal, which I did with a relish, and with despatch too, for I was eager to get away to see more of the care-for-naught dare-devils outside.

The meal over, the colonel went with some officers to examine the fortifications, and I strolled where I wished.

Situated upon the top of a hill, the camp presented one of the prettiest sights I ever saw.

The soldiers in their red shirts and caps; the green trees and white tents, made a gay picture in the light of that summer morning. The valley spread out below in fields and meadows, scattered about in which were companies of soldiers belonging to the regiments near. The birds sang in the trees, the grasshoppers chirped in the grass, the bands played, and the sky was blue over all.

"Say, now, Sambarina," a brawny specimen called out, his mouth full, "are you sure this thing aren't pisened?"

"The Lord knows it aren't, massa." She was selling cakes.

"The Lord knows nothing about it, or you either."

The woman grinned from ear to ear.

"'Spec he knows as much 'bout me as you, massa."

"He don't know me at all; I never trouble him."

"I does, massa; I prays allys."

"What do you pray for? To be made white?"

"No, massa; I prays for you, dat dar may be a full heaven," she nodded expressively towards him, "and an empty hell," she nodded again. "Dat right, massa, aren't it?"

"Ki, ay, yi!" the group yelled with laughter.

The pie-eater turned a somersault, and in his peculiar way shouted:—

"S-a-y, git along, you hoavy old daughter of Cain, or I will make mince-meat of you."

She chuckled off.

Three or four boys were playing a game, and I paused to see what it was. One of them pointed to me, saying: "Look at that figure-head, Sam; is it man, mouse or monkey?"

I did not feel complimented, and my face grew red and hot.

"He's a fancy chap, I reckon," the one addressed replied.

"S-a-y, colonel, to what regiment do you belong?"

"To the good-mannered corps," I answered, "and there is not a Zouave among them."

"Ki, yi, ay! Take that, old fellow." They slapped Sam on the back until he writhed under it. One cried, "try it again, colonel;" another, "you must have breakfasted on razor soup, manikin;" while Sam muttered "he would like to put me through Baltimore."

We remained to see them drill. It seemed hard for them to submit to discipline, but they did, and in their exercises had not the loose, disjointed movement they ordinarily had.

The drilling over I continued my walk, waiting until the colonel had finished his visit.

My attention was attracted by a half-dozen men, (who had thrown themselves on the grass) suddenly starting up, and running down the hill towards a wagon which had just appeared below. I was midway of the declivity, and the first thing I knew, a voice called " Good-by, daddy," and a figure went flying over my head, alighting some three feet in front of me, somewhat after the manner the boys play leap-frog. Without a pause the red fez and shirt continued the descent toward the wagon, making frantic gestures and uttering wild cries.

Recovering from my astonishment, and not relishing being a stool for that kind of sport, I tried to get out of the way; but ere I could succeed the feat was repeated; this time, however, the Zouave dropped his fez, turned a somersault, caught it, clapped it on his head, and went whooping down the hill.

Beating a retreat from these acrobats, I ran with all my might toward the wagon, which seemed to be their object.

A man scrambled hastily out of the vehicle, as a half dozen red shirts, with cries of "put him through Baltimore," dashed into it, and, seizing bread, cakes, pies, hurled them to the surrounding crowd, screeching the while as though they were mad, or giving their yell whenever a pie hit a man on face or head.

In less than five minutes the wagon was empty, and the actors were going off with their spoil, unmindful of the supplications of the owner, who stood beside the old horse trembling and begging.

"Let's wash his face for him," said one, having a great soft custard pie in his hands.

"Teach him not to cheat the Zoo Zoos again."

"Here's 'blood and Baltimore,'" screamed another, as

he sprang forward and seized the man by the hair, bending his head backwards, while the first speaker slapped the custard in his face, grinding it in with his hand—filling his eyes—stuffing his mouth—plastering his hair, the lookers-on shouting and enjoying it. When it was all gone the operator gave his victim a box on the side of his head, which sent him reeling to a distance, and bade him "scatter;" an injunction he obeyed with what alacrity he could, followed by showers of soft mud, which were sent after him with yells which made both him and his horse tremble in every joint.

Highly pleased with their exploit, the party struggled up the hill, jumping on each other's backs, throwing each other down, whooping, singing, and swinging from the branches of the trees.

I gathered from their talk that this man was supposed to have cheated them in some transaction they had with him, and they had taken redress in their own hands.

When I gained the top of the hill, I found Colonel F—— ready to start. In a few minutes we were on our horses and off at a brisk trot. When I told him of the scene I had witnessed he laughed, and said :

"There is much in these men, but they are reckless and hate restraint ; are generous, yet cruel when roused. Ellsworth was the man for them ; they admired, feared, and loved him, and he disciplined them. To be a true soldier, Captain Phil, you must submit to discipline."

Riding further, he said : "We will take our dinner at the farm yonder. The farmer and I know each other, and I wish to see him. Afterwards we will go to the Rhode Island camp ; there you will see a very different set of men from the Zouaves."

Accordingly we soon pulled up at the farmer's gate, and were cordially invited by the owner to enter.

MOBBING THE PIE-MAN.

CHAPTER VI.

A DAY AT THE CAMPS—*Continued.*

THE farmer was a strong Union man. He received us kindly, and gave us a good dinner. When he heard where we had been, he said:

"The 'Zouves,' as the niggers call them, often come this way for vegetables, butter, etc. I like them, though some of them are hard cases. My old woman sometimes bakes cakes and pies for them; they are civil and good-natured to my family, and we have never suffered from them. They are great favorites with my niggers, who both admire and fear them. They have no mercy on the *snakes*, as they call the secesh; they plague and rob them on all occasions, and are cordially hated in return.

"Not long since," he continued, "a couple of them heard, through an old nigger, that a lot of ammunition was secreted in a house some miles from camp, whose owner they had spotted as one of the pisen ones; his place being the headquarters for the disaffected in all this region. The danger of the enterprise gave it zest; they determined on a seizure.

"Keeping their counsel, they stole from the camp at nightfall, soon reaching a point in the woods where the old nigger was secreted with a vehicle, which between bribes and threats they had compelled him to procure for them. Mounting the vehicle, they set off at what speed they could to the scene of their exploit; having frightened the blackey almost into fits with threats of vengeance if he betrayed them.

"The house was shut, and all seemed dark within. Prowling around it, they discovered a window on the lower floor, from a chink of which a light proceeded, and, drawing near, heard voices and the clang of arms within, as the speakers moved. One mounted to the shoulders of the others to look. The room was full of armed cavalrymen. The noise made by the accidental slipping of the Zouave, caused them, with crash and clatter, to spring to the window and throw it open. They saw only darkness; the Zouaves had dropped silently to the earth, and, breathlessly crouching, were overlooked by the foe above.

"Satisfied their fears were groundless, with threat and curse they closed the sash and withdrew.

"Waiting only to be reassured, the Zouaves proceeded to search for the horses of the men within. They found them tied in a thicket some distance from the house, and quietly cut their bridles. Going back, they scaled the piazza, and, noiselessly as cats, reached the second story of the building, where they groped until they found the room, of which they had an accurate description. Raising the window, they felt along the walls and floor until they came upon the bags of ammunition, of which there were a large number. The piazza ran the whole length of the house, at one end of which was this room, while at the other end, just beneath it, was the well. One went inside, while the other stood without, and, receiving the bags, traversed the roof and dropped them into the water. In their eagerness to finish the job, the last armful went with a dash, struck the house, and in a moment brought the whole party inside upon them. It was fight and fly, and they found they must fight first. With one bound they reached the earth, and stood side by side—killed two men, and threw a third down the well. At length, favored by the darkness, they gained their cart, lashed the old horse into a foam, and succeeded in reaching the camp in safety."

After dinner, while the farmer and the colonel smoked and talked on the porch, the old woman and her daughters entertained me within by asking me all manner of questions. Finishing his cigar the colonel was ready to start. We made a detour of several miles, visiting the posts of some Western regiments. Near the camp of one from Michigan we saw hanging from a tree the carcass of a lean, hungry, miserable dog, labeled "Jeff Davis." Within the lines of, I think, the 12th New York, suspended from a tiny gallows, was a mouse, and on a placard hanging from its neck, was written: "Traitors beware of the 12th."

We had been traveling leisurely, when, looking at his watch, the colonel said: "Do you feel like a hard trot, Captain Phil? I should like to be in at the evening service of the Rhode Islanders, and we shall have to ride for it."

I readily assented, and our trot broke into a gallop. In this style we neared the camp, and found ourselves in time for both parade and prayer.

Stalwart and brave, this regiment had the appearance of picked men.

As the sun set they drew up for parade on a grassy field near the camp. Never was there a more soldierly sight than they presented, as the sun's last beams glanced along the barrels of their guns, and glittered like diamonds on the points of their bayonets. Their hats gave them a cavalier look, notwithstanding their sober uniforms. I thought of the knights of old.

With the precision of veterans they went through the

exercises. These over, there was a pause, and dead stillness, followed by the heavy sound of grounding arms, and then they stood like statues. The faces of the spectators became grave, every whisper was hushed; the chaplain stepped forward with uplifted hands, the colonel uncovered his head, men raised their hats, women bowed their faces, and then the stillness was broken by prayer, followed by a hymn from the band accompanied by voices.

> " The sounding aisles of the dim wood rang
> With the anthem of the free ! "

was all I could think of, as with swelling heart I listened and wished for John's presence, for he would have enjoyed it. The benediction seemed to fall like dew, silently and softly from the heavens, on the heads bowed there; women wiped their eyes, and men turned aside as it closed.

The colonel intended to stay for supper, and I had permission to stroll about. The camp was in most beautiful order. Their houses were built in rows, forming streets, each street being named. Their quarters were adorned with flowers and green boughs and pretty little ornaments, and were as trim as a lady's parlor. The regiment was said to be one of the best appointed in the service. The men seemed to have everything, even to a French cook—at least I saw a Frenchman "*parlez vousing*" over his pots and pans, with a funny cap on his head from which was suspended a red tassel. He gesticulated, and scratched his pate, and hopped about in a fury because of some meddling with his dishes. Their cooking was done in good sheet-iron stoves, plentifully supplied with all necessary utensils; everything was in as much order as a man could keep it. As I passed round I saw a mess eating their evening meal. One of them had observed me with the colonel and asked me to join them, which I was glad to do. Coffee, with milk, light bread, and beef-steak, made a supper I enjoyed. Finding I was from the West, they asked many questions and appeared interested in all I told them.

After supper the men seemed to amuse themselves each after his fashion : Many read, one played a flute, several were drawing, one was rigging a ship, another carving a figure out of wood, while others sang, talked and laughed.

Leaving the camp, we had proceeded some distance from the lines, when we met, pacing along with a half dozen soldiers, a woman who wore the bloomer costume with a hat and feather.

The colonel told me she was a "daughter of the regiment," and that several accompanied the troops, resided in camp, and were considered almost a necessary part of the arrangement. I had always thought the daughter a young, pretty girl. The person we met was a middle-aged woman, and not pretty either.

The colonel was silent as we rode. Presently he said : " I should like to see my command as well cared for as that. But I tell you what it is, Captain Phil, the Western boys let none exceed them in love for the Union, and will fight for it, well cared for or not."

Next day I had much to tell, and I felt myself of considerable consequence, for the men surrounded me, asking questions concerning their fellow-soldiers. I was very important, and on Corporal T——'s modifying some statement I had made, I threw my leg impertinently in his direction, and said :

" Get along, you did not see it." Catching John's eye at the moment, its cold expression froze the conceit out of me.

That evening, when we were alone, he said I had

humiliated him by my impertinence, adding that he had brought me with him to improve my health, and give me an opportunity for other improvement ; that the moment he saw the least deterioration in either manners or morals, that moment he should start me home ; he gave me warning he was watching me closely.

I was so mortified I could not sleep, and before breakfast the next morning sought the corporal and begged his pardon.

"All right, Captain Phil," he said, when I made my apology. "We all get on a high horse sometimes."

I told John of what I had done, and he said : "It was what I expected of you, Phil." When he called me " Phil " I was satisfied ; it was " Philip " when he was displeased ; short and stern.

About this time I had my blood fired on hearing a regiment singing " John Brown," and seeing a thousand men march to time to this refrain, after the fashion of the psalm-singing Roundheads of Cromwell's time. " His soul is marching on" was always on my lips.

While we were in camp at that place President Lincoln and several of his Cabinet visited us. I was away at the time, and was disappointed at not seeing him. John told me he was so kind in his manner to the men and complimented them on their drill.

Many of the boys had but one shirt each. If one wanted a clean one, he would strip off that he had, wash it in the first creek, and dry it on his back. Often fifteen or twenty men went out together to do their washing, making a frolic of it, throwing water over each other, and jesting and laughing like boys in reality. I thought of Joseph on these occasions. We had heard nothing of him since he or she left the camp.

CHAPTER VII.

FORWARD—A NEW CAMP.

THE officers talked of a removal of camp further into Virginia. In a little while orders came to that effect, and soon, as Corporal I—— said, "we spurned the sacred soil beneath our feet like common dust."

Passing a tent where they were pulling up stakes, Private W——, who was singing at the top of his voice, hailed me with:

> "What miserable worms we be !
> And we can't calculate,
> With any kind of certainty,
> What is to be our fate."

"That is as true as gospel, Captain Phil. That Widow Bedott was a mighty smart woman. She could come it over a man, I know. My Sally would stand a poor chance if the widow was to try it on me.

"Now, you see, I don't know whether it is to be my fate to shuffle off with a dose of cold lead from a reb's rifle or die decently in my bed, with Sally crying over me. I hope the Grays will give me a chance before I do go, though; for I should not like to pass up yonder and have Father Abraham ask me what I had done for my country, and not be able to point to one traitor sent to his account. He might cast me among the rebs below, where I would have a pretty warm time of it."

Without waiting for a reply he began again:

> "What miserable," etc.

The place selected for the new camp was a beautiful spot, with a creek so near we had to walk but a few rods to have one of the finest bathing places in the country. Here discipline was much more strict ; scouting and picket guard duty began to be rather dangerous, and skirmishing was frequent.

The camp was regularly laid out, the colonel's, lieutenant colonel's, surgeon's, major's, and quarter-master's tents were in a line ; the colonel's in the center, after these came those of the captains and lieutenants ; then those belonging to the men, backed by the wagons ; the sutler's bringing up the rear.

The usual routine was—up at half-past four at reveillé, battalion drill from five to seven, at seven breakfast, company drill at nine. After dinner we had leisure until four o'clock, at which time battalion drill again for two hours, supper at half-past six, roll call at nine, tattoo at half-past, when all lights must be extinguished.

The sutler's tent was the great rendezvous for all idlers off duty. There the news of the camp was retailed by the crowd always about it. John had forbidden me to go there, except when sent. The Fourth of July came, and we prepared to celebrate it with a good dinner. We had procured ham and chickens ; a farmer's wife was to bake us a pudding, and I determined I would contribute a can of peaches, a large number of which were for sale at the sutler's tent, the luscious fruit pictured on the outside.

I made my purchase, and can in hand passed along to our quarters, the " boys " calling after me : " Going to celebrate the Fourth, Captain Phil ? " " Sly dog, Phil," etc., I had no idea what they meant, until our pudding was put on the table, and John proceeded to open the peaches. The laugh at my expression of blank astonishment was

CLARY.

loud and long when the can was found to be filled with whiskey.

Many of the surrounding farms were deserted by the white inhabitants, and the negroes alone left to take care of them. They came about the camp selling butter, eggs, pies, cakes, etc., for which they obtained enormous prices. Having plenty to eat and no master, and being kindly treated by our men, they enjoyed the only freedom they had ever known, and were happy.

We had much amusement with them. One evening near our supper time a woman, black as ebony, made her appearance mounted on a miserable, shaggy old horse, and carrying a basket of eggs.

As she neared us she tossed and bridled, simpered and hung her head, in the most ridiculous manner, as though she was mimicking and exaggerating the airs and graces of some young belle. Her manner, together with her grotesque appearance, attracted attention, and she soon had a crowd following her.

She was very ugly, had a large mouth, no teeth, a broad flat nose, high cheek-bones, and gray woolly hair, frizzed into some sort of imitation of curls. Her dress was a skirt of a species of light material, having on it flounces of blue, green and red shining muslin, the waist was black silk, low in the neck, with a cape made of a piece of dirty musquito bar, and her arms were bare. On her head was a faded pink silk bonnet, loaded with chicken feathers and soiled artificial flowers, and over all she held an old torn green parasol.

The horse was a worn out field animal, blind of one eye—lame of one leg—so thin we could count its ribs, and having a singular wheeze. She sat on a piece of torn, faded carpet, and guided her steed with a rope for a bridle.

As she passed, Jim, the captain's servant, a spruce dandy mulatto, came out of his master's tent and stopped to look at her with an expression of contempt and disdain on his face.

No sooner did she see him than she began to simper and repeat her fine airs. The men, almost convulsed, called to him to hasten and help her from her horse, that he had made a conquest, etc. But muttering something about "poor white trash's niggers," he retreated to his master's quarters.

She got off her horse, sidled, spread out her skirts and flirted her parasol in so comical a way that the bystanders fairly roared with laughter, which she evidently thought complimentary, for she nodded her head in acknowledgment and walked off, her short skirts showing her bare, bony ankles above her cowhide shoes.

"Come here, Caton, and see the black Meg Merrilies," called one of the men to him.

"My name's Clary," simpering and courtesying.

> "Clary, Clary, quite contrary,
> How does your garden grow?"

"I hab no garden, massa. I hab eggs."

Her eggs were soon sold. She kept tight hold of the basket, however, and would deliver none until she had received her money, counted it, and put it in the bosom of her dress.

Caton admired her bonnet.

"Yes, massa, I's allys in de fashion—poor white folks' niggers neber hab no fashions." She tossed and strutted, and spread her skirts and turned round, coming near upsetting her eggs as she did so.

"Where did you get that fine horse?"

"Massa Tom done gib him to me; field niggers allys walk, Clary allys rides."

"What's the price of shoes, Clary?"

She made no reply except to roll her eyes until only the whites were visible, and, getting on a stump, mounted her horse, pulling her scant short dress so tight in order to cover her feet, that she raised her knees nearly to her chin. We stood almost stifled with laughter, while she bowed and smirked, and took her departure, talking to herself as she went.

We afterwards heard she was "*streaked*," as the negroes expressed it—"a little out of her mind." She was harmless, and the person who owned her let her dress as she pleased. "But," added the man who told me, "she's no fool about money."

While on the subject of contrabands, I must not forget one belonging to our regiment. His mother, a free colored woman living in Washington, sold him to a member of one of the Rhode Island regiments for fifty cents. He presented him to our men as pet and plaything, and a smarter little imp never lived. Apple-headed, round faced, black and saucy, he was as imitative as a Chinese. In a marvelously short time he learned the Zouave drill perfectly, and, standing *à la Napoleon*, would put the men through it with the precision and gravity of a drill master. Thievish and tricky, he was a constant source of trouble as well as amusement. He was teased and petted, and although not eleven years of age, knew no home but the camp, where he was careless and happy.

Caton, of whom I have spoken, belonged to our mess; he was a fine active fellow, just eighteen years of age. He and I spent much of our leisure together, and visited the fields for berries, of which there was an abundance. The negroes drove a thriving trade selling the fruit in the camp. You could tell their whereabouts in the bushes by their songs and hymns.

>"O, there will be weeping,
> Weeping, weeping, weeping,
>O, there will be weeping,
>   At the judgment seat of Christ,"

was a prime favorite with the old slaves.

They also sang with great unction,

>"Where, O, where is the good Elijah,
> Where, O, where is the good Elijah,
> Who went up in the chariot of fire,
>   Way over in the promised land.
> By and by we'll go home to meet him,
> By and by we'll go home to meet him,
> By and by we'll go home to meet him,
>   Way over in the promised land."

And another:

>"Ole Massa Deaf
> He's a very little man,
> He goes from door to door;
>   He kills some sons
>   And he wounded more.
> Good Lord remember me,
> Good Lord remember me.
> Remember me as the years roll round,
> Good Lord remember me."

They had a great partiality for "Dixie." The story went, that a man named Dixie who had many slaves was very kind to them, and they believed that when he died he was taken bodily to heaven to dwell with the blessed; and, therefore, their heaven was "Dixie's Land."

I remember at home how puzzled I was at seeing the words "Dixie Land" painted over the door of a great stable where street railroad horses were kept. John explained that the heaven of the slave and that of the horse was the same—rest from labor.

Belonging to some regiments near were two vivandières, who went among the men with as much unconcern as though men themselves. They were true-hearted, kind, good women, bright and cheerful. One of them wore the bloomer costume, and she was very pretty. Their husbands were with the regiments. Generally they had little luxuries for sale, did jobs of mending, or washed for the men, always looking after any who were sick. We met one of them in the bushes gathering berries ; she put many questions to us, telling us her history in return.

Her husband and son were in the army ; she only wished she had a dozen sons to put there—she hated a secessionist as she did a rattlesnake, and would shoot one as soon as she would a burglar or mad dog. She charged us to do our duty, that our mothers might not be ashamed of us, and declared if the regiment ever faced the foe she would have a crack at them, for they had turned upon the country which gave them bread and protected them, and they would turn upon the mother who gave them life and suckled them.

Thus she concluded, and shouldering her basket of fruit she walked off.

One bright day Caton and I went to bathe ; after which we crossed a field to a spot where we thought we saw mulberry trees, but they proved to be trees of another kind. Taking off our shoes and shaking the loose dirt out, we walked down the pebbly bottom of a little stream which wound through the woods and meadows, to a place where it crossed a country road. We sat down idling with our feet in the water. Suddenly we heard the tramp of horses' hoofs on the smooth dirt road. Caton got upon his knees and crawled forward in the bushes in the direction of the sound. In an instant he fell back, his hand upon his mouth. I was silent, knowing there was danger; and following him in obedience to a sign he gave me, crept silently into a thicket. We had scarce gained its shelter when two horsemen rode directly past where we lay in ambush, and halted at the opening where we had been sitting. They were secesh officers in uniform, a captain and lieutenant, evidently reconnoitering.

Reining in their horses, they gazed around for a few moments, to make sure they were not observed, then proceeded to an eminence a few yards to the right and stopped. The lieutenant kept watch, while the captain, taking a glass from his pocket, raised himself in his stirrups, and swept the position of our camp and the surrounding country. They were across the road, but so near us that, parting the twigs, we could see every motion, and hear the sound of suppressed voices, but could not distinguish the words.

As we lay thus Caton raised himself noiselessly on his elbow, took sight, and, ere I knew his intention, fired once, and again. The arm which held the telescope fell, shattered, by the captain's side, their horses reared, both men wheeled about; another shot from Caton, and, with "By heavens, an ambush!" they galloped past our hiding-place and disappeared up the road.

Telling me to run for it, as they might return, Caton darted forward and seized the broken telescope as a trophy. We both plunged into the bushes which skirted the stream, bending low that we might not be seen, and thus we ran like hares for almost a mile, ere we paused to take breath. I never had such a race in my life. A half dozen times I was certain they were behind us, and once, when the limb of a tree caught in my cap and dragged it from my head, I was sure one of them had seized me ; with a deprecatory exclamation, which caused Caton, as he turned to see what was the matter, to stump his toe and nearly reach the ground head foremost, I increased my speed.

I lay panting upon the earth not quite sure of my safety, while Caton examined and exulted over his capture of the telescope, which indeed was a very fine and handsomely mounted field-glass.

Starting up after a minute, he exclaimed, "I ought to be killed for a coward; Captain Phil, we could have taken those men prisoners into camp as well as not!"

"How so; I had no arms?"

"No, but I could have fired at and disarmed the other; then you would have had arms and we could have had the prisoners. My thought was that they had a party behind; now I believe we ran from two men, and one of them wounded."

I was satisfied with the thing as it was, and said so. After a short rest we started for camp, finding we had strayed much further away than we thought, for which we had a sharp reprimand.

Caton took intense pleasure in exhibiting his glass, and telling how he hit the captain. For my part it was as near the enemy as I cared to be under the circumstances. It was some time before I got over the feeling I had when he fired, and I expected every moment to see the horsemen spring into the bushes.

A few days after, John and a couple of others were out in a clearing, when suddenly a body of horsemen bore down on them. They had only time to throw themselves flat on the ground, hiding beneath the branches of a newly felled tree, when the party came sweeping past Happily they were unobserved by their foes, whom they watched from their leafy covert.

The men delighted in these hair-breadth escapes, but joined in saying they preferred death to imprisonment among the rebels. I greatly enjoyed hearing the scouts relate their adventures, glorying as they did over the many times they had eluded the foe. They considered it a tame performance of duty unless they had "tricked the rascals."

The rainy days of our life in that camp were the most trying ones to me. Although I was well and strong, John would not let me expose myself. I had to keep under shelter. When he was on guard I had a sum to do, or problem to solve, to employ me during his absence.

The men laughed at me and called John the "schoolmaster," but he thought it best, and expected me to obey. I did obey, knowing that if I rebelled I should be sent home. I felt it was right, although it was hard to be laughed at, and made me seem more like a boy than I wished to appear. John was particular in the performance of his duties, and exacted no more of me than he imposed upon himself.

CHAPTER VIII.

IN THE VAN OF THE ARMY.

ANOTHER onward move. Several regiments were ordered forward, among them that to which John belonged. So we were the very outposts of the army, continually exposed to the attacks of the enemy.

The men gloried in their position. Skirmishing parties were out every day, and a man went on picket duty with many doubts in his mind as to his getting back.

Standing in an open field, or lying in the grass by a fence corner, behind a tree or clump of bushes, the picket guard kept watch, challenging every living thing which ventured within fifteen paces with "Halt," at the same time presenting bayonet with "Who goes there?" and an injunction to advance and give the countersign, which must be done "with arms thrown down and hands raised above the head."

If this demand was not instantly complied with the picket fired, and called for the sergeant of the guard, which call passed from post to post, until it reached that officer. He then hastened to the spot, to inquire into the cause of the outcry and take charge of the prisoner if there was one.

Sometimes the causes of alarm were laughable enough. One night not only were the pickets excited, but the disturbance spread to camp, and produced for a time some anxiety there.

It turned out to have been occasioned by a cow and her

calf, which upon being ordered to halt and give the countersign by an over-eager or over-frightened picket, and not obeying, were fired upon, whereat they had dived into the underbrush. The noise made by the calf was supposed to be cries of the wounded, and word went round that the enemy had attacked us.

Another time a man was caught who confessed he had been hiding in the woods, and had ventured near at night in hopes of catching the countersign ; he and others wishing to penetrate the camp for information. He was shot in the shoulder, and when he found he could not escape he placed his hand to his mouth and gave a warning cry, exactly resembling that of an owl.

One day John led in a boy about eleven years old, who had approached the post and thrown up his arms. When told to advance, he said his father had sent him with a message to the colonel and he could deliver it to no one else. He was taken to the colonel's quarters. He was not the least afraid. He said his father was a Union man and that the secessionists stole his horses. His business with the colonel was to inform him that in an old mill, a few miles off, the rebels had secreted a cannon and some ammunition which they had brought from Fairfax. A rumor having reached them that our troops were on the move, they concealed their treasure and ran, their movements being quickened by the sight of a skirmishing party near.

The colonel ordered some half-dozen men out, the boy acting as their guide, and a party of skirmishers in the advance. They brought the cannon and ammunition away.

Our pickets extended three miles from camp. They remained out twenty-four hours at a time, taking a day's rations with them. The posts were about two hundred yards apart, and two men, or more, were stationed at a post, one watching while the other slept. At night they generally advanced about a half-mile, the enemy doing the same, which brought them rather close sometimes, and caused a good deal of nervousness to those performing picket duty for the first time.

Caton told me privately that the first night he was out he thought he had the ague, his teeth chattered and he shook in his shoes all the time he watched. It rained, besides, and when the wind swept among the trees he was sure it was the rebels coming. It was so dark he could hardly see his hand before him, and he fancied there were strange noises in the air, and strange lights dancing in the marshes. His mind would run on his snug room at home, with its bright carpet and warm curtains, and the stories he had heard in his childhood of things natural and supernatural, which filled him with a dreadful awe. He tried to whistle, but he could make no sound; and every now and then he awoke his comrade from sheer fear and a desire to hear a voice. When ashamed to do this he challenged a tree, or a stump, or fence-rail, to convince himself he was not afraid. With the appearance of daylight all these feelings vanished. Caton was considered one of the most recklessly brave men in the company.

It was about this time we got the full particulars of the affair which happened on the 17th of June, at Vienna; John had a letter from a friend who was there. He gave him an account of the death of Daniel Sullivan, who was wounded in the arm and bled to death. The great tears ran down John's cheeks as he read the brave words he uttered with his dying breath. When told to "fall in;" he said, "I wish I could." And when a comrade asked how he felt, he raised his shattered arm with his whole one, and, saying "*Boys, I am for the Union still,*" died.

"Phil," said John, when he handed me the letter, "there must be something in country when a man will speak for it with his dying breath. Those are proud words and should be on his tombstone. I would be content to go like that." He knew Dan.

Several prisoners were brought into camp, who were taken while prowling around the pickets. They were sullen and dogged; evidently expected ill-treatment; would answer no questions, and seemed only anxious not to fall into the hands of the Zouaves.

Lieutenant G—— sometimes tired of camp fare and would go to a farm-house near and get a meal. His favorite resort was the house of an old secesh lady just outside our pickets, whose slaves, for a good price paid their mistress, prepared his chicken and pone bread to his entire satisfaction; the old lady sitting by him while he ate, and throwing in her spicy remarks gratis—by way of relish.

There was a thin little fellow in the company, a good soldier, devoted to the Stars and Stripes, but stingy and a *gourmand*. He was always wanting "something nice;" and if he captured a chicken, or came across any other luxury, he kept it for his private gratification.

This man, hearing of the lieutenant's occasional dinners, thought he would try the madam's larder. Stealing out of camp, he made a circuit not to be suspected, and went there. His mess, observing the pains he took to go alone, suspected and determined to trick him. Passing the pickets on his way back, picking his teeth after the full enjoyment of his feast, he was greeted with:

"Why, what is the matter, Smith?"

"Nothing."

"Where have you been? You look so strange about the eyes."

"Just over here;" and not wishing to explain he went on.

"Smith, hello! Why, you are sick, man!"

"Never was better in my life."

"Well, if I looked as you do, I would make tracks for the doctor."

Smith continued towards his quarters, between the remarks to which he had been subjected, and the quantity he had eaten, feeling decidedly uncomfortable. About to enter he encountered another of "the boys."

"I am sorry to see you so ill. Can I do anything for you?"

Smith darted to his knapsack and drew out his looking glass. He was pale with apprehension, saw it, and seizing his blanket lay down. His tormentor came near. "Have you eaten anything which has disagreed with you?"

"No," with a groan, and placing his hand on his stomach.

Another stepped forward.

"Depend upon it, he's poisoned. See, he bears it in his face; he is blue about his eyes."

"Yes, I know it."

"Gracious! gracious! that is it. She wished all manner of evil to us, and she has poisoned me." He groaned and writhed in real agony, telling where he had been, and begging some one to send for the doctor.

The doctor was brought. Some supposed he was in the secret. He administered a great dose of tartar-emetic, which made Smith fearfully ill, so that he was unable to go to drill, but lay tossing and moaning, perfectly satisfied that he had been poisoned. The sergeant was a friend of mine, and he told me the joke. It was a treat to the men to hear him tell of that dinner. He even warned Lieutenant G—— of the fate which awaited him if he continued to go there for meals.

The men resorted to all kinds of expedients to pass the time. I saw a tree which they had decorated with crackers, by boring holes in them and suspending them by strings. These crackers bore the addresses of the most prominent rebels, together with the compliments of the company, expressed in terms which were more strong than polite.

The poor dogs in this region were made to suffer for secession. The men caught them and plastered them with papers containing jibes and jeers, then tying tin pans to their tails, drove them, with kicks and blows, in the direction of the rebel camp. They made effigies of the secesh leaders, and hung or burnt them, and even fastened messages of insult and defiance to the scarecrows in rebel corn-fields, which the Graybacks returned in kind, for they despised the " Yankees."

Parties who had gone out would not unfrequently return laden with preserves, pickles and other dainties. These things were paid for *if perfectly convenient.* If not, they were put down to the credit or discredit of Uncle Sam.

If there was a chicken stew, or a roast of mutton, or a piece of fine pork served, and the question was put: "Where did you get it?" the reply always was, " We lit on it," which had a peculiar meaning, and was perfectly satisfactory and well understood by all.

If an officer's nose chanced to be regaled by a savory smell proceeding from a young porker tied between stakes, or a lamb (the fleece not far off) zealously watched by a hungry squad, his attention, at that particular moment, was almost always directed to an opposite direction, and there was no word or unpleasant remark from him, not even if a portion of the roast found its way to his own table.

CHAPTER IX.

HOW I BECAME A PRISONER.

A FARMER whose fields had been devastated by the movements of the troops, made complaint of his loss, and an amount sufficient to cover it, was, by General McDowell, ordered to be paid to him.

In gratitude, he told our mess he would supply them with milk and vegetables if sent for, for he dared not convey them to camp.

One morning I was sent for a bucket of milk. I received it, and was returning, when I happened to see in a field further on some bushes which promised berries. Hiding my bucket in the tall grass, I proceeded to examine the bushes. Getting a few berries—they only whetted my appetite—I searched for more.

On the edge of a cornfield, in the angles of a Virginia worm fence, I saw, I thought, a further supply. Forgetting John's caution about whistling when out from camp, I began "Yankee Doodle" as I trudged over a potato field which lay between me and the coveted fruit.

I found a prize, ripe and luscious, and was in its full enjoyment, with my back turned to the corn, when a man suddenly sprang from among the stalks, and laid his hand upon my shoulder. I knew, ere he spoke, that I was a prisoner, and felt cold to my toes.

"You belong to the camp over there, you young abolition rascal?" he said, eyeing me keenly.

I could not speak.

"How many men have they?"

I did not know, and I said so.

He put other questions concerning officers, prisoners, etc.; what they said of Manassas? when they intended to move? some of which I answered, others I could not. "Shake the truth out of him, if it is in him!" said a rough voice, and a coarse, thick-set man appeared from among the corn.

I trembled all over; knew that I did so; was ashamed of it, and tried to steady myself, but could not. Turning to the first comer, who had not an unkind look, I begged him to let me go.

He shook his head, "No, no, youngster, I let none off who wear this color;" he touched me on the shoulder. I thought of John, home, the camp, everything. My heart sunk and tears came into my eyes. The struggle to keep them back almost strangled me; the veins swelled in my throat, my face became red, but pride and the thought of appearing like a coward conquered. I would not be a puling prisoner. I forced back all my grief and stood calm, but what would I not have given to have been with John?

The second comer, who had eyed me harshly, now said:

"We had best get under cover, Morris."

They ordered me before them into the cornfield, the last speaker informing me that he would put a bullet through me if I attempted to run.

Morris questioned me as to the disposition of several men captured a few nights before, and from the threat his companion made: "If harm should come to Jake," I discovered that he had a brother among them.

Crossing the corn field we passed over some meadows, keeping close to the fences and coming out on the open road. They talked in a guarded way, but I gathered from what they said that they belonged to the army at Manassas. Although they were dressed in dark plain clothes they carried rifles.

As we proceeded we met several persons whom they stopped and conversed with, sending me out of hearing distance. Once, in consequence of information they received, they took to the woods. I caught the words "skirmishing party," and supposed they were afraid of falling in with one.

Late in the afternoon we reached a farm house hidden among the hills, and approached by a bridle path. The space before the door was inclosed in a worm fence and overgrown with weeds. Turkeys roosted on the top rails of the fence, and pigs huddled in the angles. A dog kennel, before which was chained a ferocious looking dog, occupied one corner. Beside a moss-grown well, rolling on a log, were two small negro children, dressed in coarse, dirty cotton shirts, which barely came to their knees.

As we reached the gate the dog gave a low growl, and, slowly raising himself, attracted the attention of the blacks, who tumbled over each other in their efforts to get to us. Morris ordered them to the kitchen. They retreated backwards, their fingers in their mouths, every now and then stumbling over something in their way, until they disappeared around the corner of the house calling "mammy, mammy." This cry brought a negro woman with a skillet in her hand to the door of a hut near by. Altogether it was about as dreary a place as I had ever seen.

Crossing the yard we went into the house, which consisted of three rooms on the ground floor and one above. In the first room we entered were two girls, one black and one white, each appearing to be about eleven years old. They were sitting upon the floor building houses with corn cobs.

"Where is mother?" was Morris's salutation.

The sound of his voice brought a lady of about fifty from an adjoining room. He introduced me to her, saying:

"Here is a prisoner, mother; I deliver him to you for safe keeping. Now let us have something to eat, for I am starving."

I raised my eyes to the old lady's face and felt them moisten, as she said:

"Poor boy! he is so young."

The girl put a chair beside me and said, "Sit down."

"Poor boy! Yes, that is the way with you women always," said Morris as he went out.

The old lady went to the door and gave her orders, then seated herself and gazed steadily at me.

With a deep sigh she presently asked:

"Are all Lincoln's soldiers as young as you?"

I explained that I was no soldier. She put other questions to me to which the girl listened eagerly, as did also the owners of several woolly heads peeping in at the door. Every few minutes the mistress would stamp her foot, saying, "Off to the kitchen with you." These imps scampered back only to return ere the words had well died away.

"One ob Massa Linkum's gang," I heard one say, "he'll cut your head off, Jack."

"Whar's his tail?" said another.

Supper was ready; I asked permission to wash my hands. They pointed to the well, and a negro girl brought me a not very clean towel.

There was hot coffee, hot biscuit, broiled bacon, apple

sauce, and roast potatoes on the table. I could not eat, although told to do so.

The meal over, Morris called for Ben. A burly, good-natured negro presented himself, and was told to bring round the horses. They were brought, and I heard Morris charge him to keep a strict watch on me. "Mind," was his injunction, "if he gets off, I will nail your ears to the barn door."

From what I afterwards heard, these men were not regular soldiers, but were employed as spies, and I believe were accomplices of the man taken by us a few nights before.

It was the saddest evening I ever spent in my life. I longed for night and bed. It was not yet dark, and as I sat looking out the window, a saying of John's came into my mind—"Make the best of the circumstances which surround you."

I turned and made an effort to amuse Carrie, for so they called the little white girl. She was quite as tall as I was, and was astonished when I told her my age. We were soon good friends.

She said I did not look as if I was so very bad, and asked why I was among the Lincoln soldiers? At this the old lady burst out about our cruelty and injustice, declaring we had come to plunder and rob, and drive them from their homes; that we were like the Egyptians whom the Lord smote. I did not reply.

I asked to go to bed. "I reckon you can get along in the dark," she said; "the moon shines in the room."

"Certainly," I replied, "but will you not let me read here?" Taking my Testament from my pocket, where I happened to have it, I proceeded to do, what I had promised my mother if possible never to omit: read a chapter. The old lady laid down her knitting and watched me for a few moments, then requested me to read aloud. When I finished she called Ben, and giving him the candle told him to see me to bed and bring it back. The negro led me up-stairs into a comfortable room and waited until I took off my shoes.

"That will do, Ben." I was about to throw myself down with my clothes on.

"I must hab youse clobes, massa, for fear youse git off in the night."

"I do not know what they want with me, Ben; I am no soldier, only a boy."

"Plenty no bigger dan youse soldiers down yonder," pointing, as I supposed, in the direction of Manassas. "Massa Morris say, he'll keep all he kin ketch to make up for some Massa Linkum tuck."

"What will they do with me, Ben?"

"Make you dig in de ditch, I reckon; de niggers dig, but dey git sick, so dey put de poor white trash at it."

"Where is your master, Ben?"

"Ole massa dead; was frown off his horse jumping a fence; he great horse racer; lib in a big house, de stable better dan dis place; but he war 'solvent, and all de niggers was sold, 'cept my wife and me; and ole missus' brudder gib her dis place to come to, wid de childers; it's nigh gone ten years since ole massa dun got killed."

Seeing I was undressed, Ben took my clothes and left me, fastening the door with a chain after him. I never believed I could feel so miserable. I knew John was sleepless on my account. I shuddered when I thought of being taken to the rebel camp, and determined to make my escape. Feeling uncomfortable on the feather bed, I lay down on the floor, where Ben laughed to find me in the morning. Dressing myself, I went down and washed at the well; breakfast was ready, the morning bright; I felt hopeful and ate heartily.

After breakfast I tried to amuse myself with Carrie and the negro children, but the day dragged; if I went out doors I was watched, if I sat still curious eyes were upon me. About eight o'clock the old lady came in, and sitting down to her knitting questioned me about my family. I told her my little story. How John and I were alone in the world—all in all to each other. I saw she was touched, then I begged her to let me go. She shook her head; I turned to Carrie and asked her to beg for me; she jumped on her mother's lap, and putting her arms around her said: "Let him go, mother; how would you feel if it was I who was kept a prisoner from you?"

"But," she dropped her knitting in her lap, "Morris will be very angry."

"Let me go," I pleaded; "my mother was a Southerner and she would have let your son go, I know."

"Well," she said, "I am a mother, and I hope a Christian, if I am a secessionist, and for your mother's sake I promise you your freedom. It don't seem right to a Virginia lady to keep white blood in bondage; but if you were really one of Lincoln's soldiers I would keep you if I had to guard you myself."

I could scarce express my gratitude.

"You must wait until to-morrow, when Ben has to take a load to the Run and only old Zeke will be about the house."

"Suppose Morris comes to-day, mother," said Carrie.

"He will not be back until Saturday."

Greatly relieved, and excited at the thought of getting away, I entered into all Carrie's amusements.

Towards evening I went out to take a walk. Passing the kitchen, a log hut which stood some ten feet from the house, the cook spoke to me. Pausing at the door to reply, curiosity detained me for a better look within.

The bed, which seemed of rags, occupied one side of the room, a door and window another, while a third was taken up with an enormous fire-place, in which huge logs of wood lay smouldering. Supper was in preparation; an oven, broken at the side, the top covered with live coals, stood on the hearth; near it was a coffee pot; directly in front of the fire, propped by a "rock," was a board like a boot-jack, supporting a roll of corn bread, which, with one end resting in the ashes, was browning, and across the chimney was a crazy old crane, from which hung several pots and kettles.

A six months' baby lay upon the bed, from under which protruded an old basket filled with onions and dried herbs, two or three old shoes, a hoe, and some broken crockery and rags.

Sitting on the hearth, in his one dirty garment, over a pan of potatoes, which had been boiled, then thrown into water, and off which he was rubbing the skins to have them ready for supper, was a blear-eyed little negro boy.

The sight was a novel one to me, accustomed as I had been to Mrs. B——'s scrupulously clean kitchen. It did not increase my appetite for supper.

Carrie and the negro girl were trying to sew when I went in, but did not appear to make much progress. I made them laugh heartily by taking the garment from their hands and sewing on it myself. I told them of Joseph, and my astonishment at his sewing. I also showed them my shirt, made by the sewing machine. The old lady asked many questions concerning the machines. She had heard a great deal of them, but was out of the way of seeing such things. I described to her, as well as I could, Wheeler & Wilson's machine. Our landlady had one; I kept it in order for her, and often sewed on it; indeed, I was quite a good machine sewer. She seemed astonished at the quantity of work they turned out, and remarked that she did not believe that the slaves could be taught to use them.

When I went to bed Carrie whispered that she was sorry that I was going next day. I could not express regret, but I thanked her for her kindness. I wanted to sleep that I might awake and find it morning.

I needed no rousing, but was awake when Ben brought my clothes. I saw, impatiently, at breakfast, his lazy ox team start, and soon as the meal was over reminded the old lady of her promise.

She took me into her room, drew the window curtains, and shut the door; then, pointing to a frock of Carrie's lying on the bed, said;

"You must put that on; I have no boy's clothes; you could not go a mile in those you wear without being taken again."

Opening my shirt at the collar, I spread it back, and put the dress on over my blouse. Carrie was much stouter than I. I was just fastening it, when the latch of the door was raised and Carrie begged admittance. I did not relish her presence just then, but her mother let her in.

"O," she exclaimed, "he must have a skirt and a hoop. Here is this old one which you said I might give Milly."

Her mother objected.

"Why, mother, even the niggers wear hoops on Sunday. I never go from home without one."

She had her way, and put it on me. I could not manage it at all; it popped up before and behind, and I felt as if I were going to fly. Carrie clapped her hands and fairly danced. When she had parted my hair in the middle, and tied an apron over my striped calico frock:

"There!" she said, pushing me towards the glass, after she had tied my sun bonnet on. "Look at yourself."

I stepped forward and tried to pull the hoop down. She threw herself upon the bed and laughed at me. I felt uncomfortable enough, but I never should have recognized the figure that met my view when I looked into the glass as being myself.

"See, only see, mother," she capered about in ecstasy. "Morris himself might meet him and never know him."

Suddenly she threw up her hands and exclaimed: "Good gracious, mother, he has no drawers on."

I looked down at my feet; there were my blue woolen pantaloons conspicuous below my short dress.

She produced a pair of white drawers and told me to roll up my pantaloons, which I did above my knees; then with her aid, holding the hoops, and interrupted by bursts of laughter, I got them on. She would not permit me to take the hoops off.

My disguise was complete—but no, my boots would betray me. What was to be done? Cut them down. A pair of shears was produced. I cut the boots, slit and laced them up like buskins, to show my stockings, which were white and happened to be passably clean. So we hoped my feet would not attract observation.

The old lady gave me a basket, in which was a paper containing some bread and meat, and told me to wait a minute while she looked around.

She came back and said Zeke had not returned from mill; Viney was spinning in the smoke-house, and she had sent the little niggers to the corn field; now was the time for me to start. She gave me particular directions as to the way I was to go, making me repeat them after her. If I should meet any one who questioned me I could say I had been visiting, and she told me the names of some of the families about. Carrie was to go with me to the lower orchard fence, and point out the road to the old mill. As I bade her good-by and thanked her, she said:

"Should any of our men fall into your hands, tell your brother to remember what a Virginia woman did for you."

I heartily promised for him that he would.

We crossed the orchard, from the bottom of which the old mill could just be seen in the hollow. Going a little further, Carrie paused at the meadow fence to say good-by, but staid to see me over it. Mounting the rails I forgot my hoops, made a jump, and hung suspended by a large splinter of the top rail, looking for all the world like a great crab. Carrie dropped on the grass, put her face in her lap and laughed till the tears came, before she could move to my assistance. At length she helped me down, warning me to be more careful in future. I turned to go, and had made a few steps forward, when the thought of how kind she had been came over me. Putting my hand into the dress pocket where I had dropped it, I took out my gold collar-button, which had my initials on it, and begged her to keep it in remembrance of the kind acts she had done. She hesitated, but finally accepted it. I drew closer to drop it in her palm, stooped and kissed her, then walked quickly on. When I turned and looked back she was not to be seen.

I felt conscious and awkward in my new dress, and being afraid that if I met any one I should betray myself, I kept as closely as possible under cover.

The old mill was about a mile distant. My directions were to keep to the left, taking a bridle-path down the valley until I came to a red brick house. I was then to turn to the right, and on reaching the forks of the road to take the right fork; follow this until I reached a sycamore tree blasted by lightning, which stood at the head of a ravine, turn up the ravine and I would come out on the public road about a mile from the spot where Morris had captured me. I repeated these directions as I trudged along in the road leading to the old mill, which was an old ruin partially destroyed by fire, and stood by a brawling little stream in the valley. I had almost reached it when I thought I heard voices. I paused to be sure, but concluded I was mistaken, when I distinctly heard a voice coming from the direction of the mill. I instantly left the path and struck into the woods among the underbrush. Lying down I listened.

Then, determined to find out who it was talking, I took off the abominable hoop, which had tormented me ever since I started, tripping me by catching in everything, and without making the least noise, went forward, stopping every few minutes to hearken.

Hidden by the grass and shrubs, I got close to the wall of the mill, and creeping along reached a corner where the boards had been torn away. The voices were within. I stooped and cautiously looked in, when lo! directly opposite me sat Morris, the man who was with him when he took me, and another man.

I fell back in a cold perspiration, and with a rustling which I supposed would bring them to the spot, but they did not notice it. It was several minutes ere I had courage to look again. Morris sat with his elbows resting on his knees, his chin in his hands, while his friend stood by whittling a stick. The third person leaned against a wall, intently engaged in pushing the dirt back and forth on the floor with his foot as he talked.

"No one who did not know it was here could have found it. There is a traitor somewhere," he said. "Jake told me they took it down t'other road. He heard a noise, and climbing a tree for a look out, saw them."

"What time was it?" questioned Morris.

"Early in the morning."

"What was he doing here then!"

"Don't know."

"Perhaps the little chap we took over yonder could tell," said Morris's friend.

I again sunk into the bushes, for I knew they spoke of me. I supposed too they talked of the cannon and ammunition, for this was the mill where they were secreted. When I looked again Morris was up and going. He said:

"We must be off now. We can have it all arranged to-morrow night. Joe went so near last night he heard them talk. He crawls as noiselessly as a lizard, and is as wary as a fox. He thinks we can pick off half a dozen if we can do nothing more."

They left the mill, and I saw them going up the valley at a brisk trot. Their horses had been tied some way off in the woods.

When quite sure it was safe, I stepped from my hiding place and went to the spot where they had been sitting. I found a piece of crumpled paper which I smoothed out. On it was a rough but true sketch of our camp, the outposts accurately marked, and beside one or two of these was a peculiar figure.

I put it in my pocket and hastened on, a little nervous at the thought of having been so near my captors.

I soon reached the red house, which I skirted, and went ahead, looking out for the forks of the road. I had walked a mile or more, supposing every minute I should reach them, and fearing I had made a mistake, when I heard some one whistling, and saw coming round a turn in the road a negro boy riding a bare-backed horse and carrying a bag before him. "Sarvent, miss," he said, pulling one of his locks of wool, for he wore no hat. I started at first at his address, but looking up boldly returned:

"The road forks near here?"

"Just beyond the bend, miss."

I went on with a lighter heart, soon gained the forks, took the one to the right; then came to the tree struck by lightning which marked the ravine.

It was cool and shady in there. I was tired and hungry, so down I sat to rest and eat. After my meal I started up the ravine. The distance was greater than I hoped, but after a while I saw the high road and soon reached the fence. Looking up and down, there was only an old man driving a couple of oxen to be seen on the highway. I waited until he went past, then climbed the fence and gained the road, pushing on.

There seemed to be but few persons going my way. I met two ladies in a carriage, a black man driving them; a man with a cow, and one or two others on horseback.

It began to get late; I strained my eyes to see the farmer's house near which I thought I must be, but saw nothing of it. Fearing I had passed it I paused in perplexity, when two horsemen came dashing round a turn in the road and nearly ran over me. My heart stood still, and I was near fainting; for they were Morris and his friend. They rode on, however, without pausing, Morris only turning his head to see if I was hurt.

An old farmer followed them at a jog trot. I had recovered from my fright and ventured to ask him if Mr. —— lived near.

"You passed his fields a quarter of a mile back. They come to the road right where the two big trees stand."

"I did not see the house," I said, turning to retrace my steps.

"Bless you, no, thar's a good smart piece of woods

before you come to that; the house is in a hollow; but you seem tired, git up behind and I will give you a lift." He backed his horse to the fence.

I thanked him, but declined.

"Well, you can't miss it now; you'll stay thar to-night, I reckon; bad times for gals to be out alone. Mr. ——'s an abolitionist, they say."

I saw how I had made the mistake. I had forgotten that the public road did not run past his house.

That quarter of a mile was a long one, but at length the trees were reached, and I plunged into the woods, and after a brisk walk saw the house just beyond.

The landscape began to grow familiar. I knew the direction in which the camp lay, and hoped to reach the pickets before dark.

I pressed forward. After some fifteen minutes' fast walking, just on the edge of a field I was stopped with "Halt!" and saw Caton, who had heard my step and stood up from the log where he had been sitting. I heard him say, "Davis, here's a girl;" at which Davis also presented himself.

I saw they did not know me. I drew nearer, and putting forward my basket, said: "Want to buy some eggs?"

Caton felt in his pockets.

"I never have a penny, and always owe the sutler every cent I get. A boiled egg is a good thing, Davis."

Davis had no money either.

Becoming impatient, I tore off my bonnet, with:

"You do not know me?"

They looked in bewildered surprise, then Caton exclaimed: "Captain Phil!"

Assisting me over to their side of the fence, they turned me round and round, laughing at my appearance, and asking questions. John was not well, they said, and in great trouble about me. I broke from them and hurried to the camp, still over two miles distant. The gleam of the fires, however, seemed to shorten the way. I reached the tents just as the men were at supper. Corporal F—— happened to see me first, and, surprised to see a girl in the lines at that hour, came to me. He went with me to John. As I drew near John was in the act of raising a cup of coffee to his lips. I stood still beside him ; he looked at me in the waning light ; I smiled, he put up his hand and threw off my bonnet.

"Thank God ! it is Phil." He took me in his arms with a warm hug.

Such a noise as the men made when they heard my story. Not a little elated, I had to make the rounds, show myself in my new rigging, and tell the tale of my capture.

I took the paper I had found to Colonel F——, and told him what I had heard. He thought it of sufficient importance to double the guard.

Very glad was I to get back, see John's kind face and hear his voice. I was " out of Egypt," and I should endeavor to keep out in future.

The following night an attack was made upon the pickets, but the party was repulsed, and the strange man I saw with Morris at the mill was taken prisoner. I knew him at a glance.

My dress and bonnet were hung up as a memorial, John saying that if ever opportunity offered I was to send Carrie a token of my appreciation of her kindness. I did not tell him about the button. I felt quite a hero, and am afraid I strutted and swaggered considerably, very proud of having been a prisoner.

CHAPTER X.

AMUSEMENTS IN CAMP.

THE weather set in wet and gloomy. We had three or four days of incessant rain, and everything was saturated. During this wet season it came John's turn to stand picket guard. When he and Johnston, his comrade, came in next morning they presented a doleful appearance. Wet to the skin, their shoes clogged with mud, their trousers daubed, their hair stringing about their clay-stained faces, they looked about as uncomfortable as any two men could look. John quietly went to work to put himself in better condition. Johnston had a cup of coffee, then proceeded to give an account of his night out:

"Our position was at the far end of a ploughed field, with a sloping pasture on the other side of the fence, and not a stump or tree nigh; our only shelter being some berry bushes in the fence corner. The rain came down in floods as we paced back and forth and tried to 'keep our powder dry.' Soon the field was a sea of mud, and the water ran in a torrent through a ditch made to drain it. It was as dark as Egypt; a man might have slapped you in the face and you not know where the blow came from. Presently my feet slipped—splash! dash! I found myself in the ditch, anchored as fast as a Mississippi steamer on a snag. I squirmed and tugged to no purpose; the more I tried to get out the deeper I got in.

"Wharton came to my assistance, and took my rifle, while I put both hands to it and managed at last, on my knees, to reach the level field. While drawing myself up by the long grass which grew on the sides of the ditch, the roots gave way several times, and plunged me to the bottom, sousing me. I was minus a boot, but it was no use looking for it then. Feeling wrathful and savage, I wished with all my heart a secesh would come along and let me have a pop at him, though how I should see him I could not tell. I felt my way to the fence corner and retreated among the bushes.

"I had been there but a minute when something sharp struck me on the leg. I put out my hand to find what it was, and caught hold of—what do you think? A pair of horns. I hope I may never see home again if I did not think the devil had me. I shrunk back into as small a space as I could, and gave a groan. Wharton heard and asked what was the matter. He had a match, and somehow managed to light it, after a dozen trials, and groped his way toward me, sheltering it with his coat. In a minute he fell back with a low laugh. I had run foul of an old billy goat, which had strayed in the pasture and taken shelter behind the bushes.

"You need not laugh," he said, as the mess roared, "there was no fun in it, I can tell you. As soon as it was light I tried to find my boot, which I at length did by the aid of a fence rail. Of course it was soaked with water and filled with mud; but as there was no remedy, I put it on, and with the water oozing out at every step paced back and forth until time to change guard.

"Now, if that is as pleasant as occupying a comfortable bed, or having a cozy talk with one's sweetheart— why tastes differ, that is all."

The next day the sun came out bright and warm.

Lieutenant G—— received an order to take four men and go out on a scouting expedition. John was one of the men, so I went too.

Keeping under cover of the woods, sometimes creeping through the brush, and again plunged to our knees in water in swampy meadows, we reached the designated place and gained the information desired. Returning, we halted in a little valley watered by a noisy brook, which had overflowed its banks, and seated ourselves on the trunk of a fallen tree to eat our rations, talking the while in whispers to one another.

Presently one of the party pointed to a hill, which, bare of trees, rose immediately before us. Following the direction of his finger, we saw from behind it light wreaths of blue smoke curling in the air.

Seizing their guns, the men waded the stream, stumbled through the high grass on the other side, and on their stomachs dragged themselves by hands and knees to the top of the hill. Seeing their object, and being unencumbered with arms, I gained it first, and, lying flat, raised my head and looked on the other side. A party of some twenty-five horsemen, their animals picketed at a little distance, were bivouacked on the green meadow near, while further off two negroes were busy about a freshly kindled fire, evidently going to prepare a meal. Our men had paused half-way up to take breath, so, rolling over, I told them in a whisper what I had seen, for the foe were so near we could hear them talk, and see that they were completely armed. Cautiously looking to their rifles, bending to the earth, and dragging themselves up with one hand, our little party reached the top and gazed below at the Graybacks.

Lounging upon their blankets, which were spread upon the wet grass, they smoked and played cards in the sunshine, occasionally calling to the negroes to "hurry up the cakes."

The "boys" burned to have a crack at them; but it was forbidden as hazardous, and we had been charged to run into no unnecessary danger. So, after a survey, they noiselessly and unwillingly withdrew, and bent their way back to camp.

There was a man in the camp who had the longest and thinnest legs and the largest pedestrian digits, as Captain Hull called his feet, I ever saw; a tall, supple fellow; he could twist and twirl himself in all directions as though made of India rubber. His nick-name was "Shanks." It was given him because of a peculiar and comical way he had of throwing out one leg, as if about to dance, before answering when his name was called.

Good-natured and full of fun, it was the delight of the men to get him out for a *hoedown*. In dancing he used his hands almost as much as his feet, and timed his movements to his own voice in singing.

One night the boys had collected outside in the moonlight, some lying on the ground and some leaning against trees and tent poles, when "Shanks" suddenly dashed among them, and with a funny song began with spirit one of his wildest and most grotesque dances.

In a moment there was a circle formed around him, clapping and cheering. He gave them "Uncle Ned," "O Susannah," and a half-dozen other melodies, every now and then springing out of the ring and seizing one of the boys by the waist, and whirling him until he was out of breath before he let him go. At length, tired out, with a gesture and grimace he turned a somersault and threw himself on the earth to rest, amid loud huzzas.

The laughter having subsided, there was a silence of a few minutes. Somehow "Shanks's" singing even his funniest negro songs always made me feel sad. Suddenly he broke out with the "Soldier's Dream." His voice was clear and beautiful. Several of the men joined in, but as he proceeded they dropped off one by one. A subdued feeling seemed to creep over them. He continued on alone, amid a dead stillness. When he came to the lines

> "My little ones kissed me a thousand times o'er
> And my wife sobbed aloud in her fullness of heart,"

two or three coughed violently and there was a good deal of sneezing.

"Keep to your buffoonery, Shanks," said I,—when he had finished. "You have neither wife nor child, and yet you try to make *spoonies* of those who have."

Shanks bowed and cut a pigeon wing, then seizing the speaker by the waist, despite his struggles whirled him around until he was dizzy. Letting him suddenly go he made another somersault, and ere the poor fellow could get up the taps sounded, and all dispersed laughing to their quarters.

Before he went to sleep John took his withered wreath from the post where it hung, and held it in his hands for a few moments: I wondered if he felt "*spooney*."

A crowd always gathered about the scouts and skirmishers, to hear of their exploits when they came in. One day a party who had been absent twenty-four hours beyond their time, and had been given up as captured, came in mounted on fine horses and driving others before them. They had lain out all day in the grassy swamp while the enemy in treble their force bivouacked in their path. Determined to do something, they resorted to stratagem. Fastening their caps and coats amid the tall grass, they left one of their number to give the signal. Then passed around the foe, dragging themselves through the marsh, and creeping on hands and knees over the briers and underbrush. Careless of scratches from thorns, they kept on their way as silently as snakes, until they got between the rebel party and their horses, which they had picketed at a distance from where they rested, a guard watching while they slept.

This manœuvre accomplished, their comrade in ambush fired on the guard and took to cover, firing again as he did so. Springing to their feet the rebs banged at the caps and coats just visible through the grass, in the direction from which the shot had come. Our boys giving them a volley from behind, mounted their horses. Attacked side and rear, they were afraid of being surrounded, and, seeing their horses gone, took to the woods leaving two of their number dead behind them.

It was amusing to see some of the men writing home. Any thing that would hold a piece of paper did duty as writing desk, it might be a knapsack or a pot lid. One poor fellow in our mess had left "a girl behind him." When he attempted an epistle to her he took to the woods, out of sight of his comrades, and, stretched at full length on his stomach, his paper under his face, he would rest on his left elbow and try to write; scratch his head and try again, as though the scratching process brought words and ideas.

Most of the men I knew, however, wrote regularly, and several of them kept journals.

There were in the company a couple of Irishmen whom I had known before we joined the army; one of them was porter in a store, the other drove an express wagon. Occasionally they desired letters written, and would call upon me to perform the duty for them.

When Mark wanted to write to Biddy, "His fingers were so stiff, faith, he could not hold a pen."

He never had the least idea of what he wanted to say, and if I asked him would answer: "And sure, Captain Phil, you know best what to write."

When I suggested any thing: "Indade and that's the very thing, sure and it's a beautiful letter you write, it is; the praist himself can't make a better fist at it."

Patrick was married; his great anxiety was that Mary would think he was dead, and then marry Luke Morgan. "Be sure to tell her, Captain Phil, not to believe it till I write it myself. It was a beautiful writing I did till the fever took it all out of me."

The merry time of our life was from tattoo to taps. Then—no matter what hardships the day had brought—all was fun and jollity.

There were dancing, singing, card playing, jumping, wrestling, and games of all kinds. Some sat quietly criticising the actors in the various scenes around them, making occasional quaint remarks; others read.

Sometimes a fiddle would scrape "Yankee Doodle," and enliven the scene. For

"Yankee Doodle is the tune,
Americans delight in;
Good to fiddle, dance and sing,
But best of all for fighting."

A favorite amusement was target shooting. Drawing upon a board the figure of a man almost always labeled "Jeff Davis," "Beauregard," or the name of some other rebel leader, the heart or other vital part was marked and the men fired, the object being to come as near the mark as possible. I generally joined in this, and although I had never drawn a trigger before I left home, was getting to be quite an expert shot.

I suppose there is hardly a boy in the country, now, who

does not know more than I did about fire arms when the war broke out. Muskets, rifles, pistols, all presented the same picture to my mind, but I soon learned the difference between them. At first, the rifled and smooth bored muskets bothered me not a little, but I discovered that the rifled had a succession of thread-like grooves like a screw turning in the barrel, which forced the bullet round and round and gave it more power. The Minie rifle is named from the Minie bullet, which was invented by Captain Minie, a Frenchman. The ball is hollow over a third of its length, and has a small piece of iron in the hollow ; is long and has jagged edges ; it is greased before it is used, that it may pass smoothly through the barrel. Muskets and other guns are made with rifled bores and the Minie ball is used in them. Sharpe's rifle is loaded by sliding part of the barrel off. The ball and cartridge are put in the opening thus exposed and the slide is returned to its place again : this is called breech loading.

CHAPTER XI.

BEFORE BULL RUN.

FOR some days a forward movement had been expected, and the men were restless in their eagerness to meet the enemy.

At length one warm morning orders were issued, and notices appeared upon the stanchions of certain tents, that the officers were to hold the men in readiness to march at a moment's warning. Intense excitement prevailed; all hoped our destination was Manassas. There was no thought of defeat. We were marching to victory.

The orders came on the 17th of July, a telegram from General McDowell's headquarters commanding that all divisions and brigades move forward at two o'clock.

The men shouted wildly when the announcement was made, and proceeded hastily with the work of preparation. Three days' rations were given out, shoes distributed, arms cleaned, tents taken down, wagons loaded and everything put in readiness for instant departure.

John went quietly to work to get himself in trim. I saw he was anxious and knew it was on my account, for I had watched him talking with Lieutenant G——. I assisted him without a word, at the same time putting up my own things. I was fearful that, in prospect of a battle, he might order me to stay behind; and in that case I really think I should have mutinied, and, for the first time in my life, refused to obey him.

While I was thus thinking, an old and intimate friend

of John made his appearance, and stopped to speak to him. I had known him ever since I could remember any one. He told John he was to accompany our division as a reporter for one of the newspapers, and, after they had conversed a while, said :

"What are you going to do with Phil?"

"I do not know," was the reply; "I do not feel justified in letting him go into danger when he can do no service."

"Let him accompany me, he can have Harris's horse; he, poor fellow, cannot get out of his bed, having sprained his arm and ankle in a fall he got yesterday. I do not expect to be in the fight, but if Phil will obey orders make me his captain."

I did not relish this arrangement, but was afraid to object; so when John told me that he put me in Mr. D——'s charge, I acquiesced and gave the promise to keep close to Mr. D——'s side required of me.

Everything was in readiness at the time appointed, and the division moved forward.

Before his regiment fell into line, John took me into his arms, embraced and kissed me, charging me to take care of myself for his sake; for if anything should happen to me, he would never forgive himself for allowing me to come.

Then he told me that if he should be killed, Mr. D—— would hand me a letter he had given him for me; in this letter he had offered me his best advice and counsel with regard to my future. He had long since insured his life for my benefit, and, in case of his death in battle, there would be no trouble about the payment, he having secured that by increase of premium.

His last words as he shouldered his musket were:

"Be a good man, Phil, and stick to the flag while a shred of it floats."

And I cried like a girl as for answer, I waved my little flag which was to go with me.

"Take courage, Captain Phil," said Caton, as he tightened his straps over his shoulders; "I am sorry for you, Phil. If those fire-eaters prove more troublesome than we think, there is a chance for you yet."

John's last words made me resolve to obey his injunctions strictly.

So soon as the word was given to move I went with Mr. D—— to a hill at a little distance which overlooked the whole scene.

"Now, Phil," he said, "you see the advantage of not being under orders, military orders I mean; we can view the whole march at our pleasure and yet be in at the fight."

It was the grandest sight I ever saw. The scenery was magnificent—hills and valleys with dense forests and smooth plains lay near; while away the blue mountains raised their peaks to the sky, and as far as the eye could reach a great, broad, black belt, shimmering with bayonets flashing in the sun, wound, like a huge, dark river, through valleys and over hills, its billows crested with floating banners, and its huge waves timing their movements to the exhilarating strains of martial music.

I watched them on their winding way, almost wild with excitement.

Penetrating the music, or heard in the pauses, came the voices of the men, singing "America," "Dixie," "The Star Spangled Banner," "Hail Columbia," etc. It reminded me of the line: "treading to death as to a festival."

Mr. D—— could not stay in one place. He made a few notes, and calling me to follow, ran down a hill to a farm house where were our horses. Mounting them, we took to the fields, getting as close to the column as possible. For a time we kept alongside the First Division, which constituted the right wing and was under the command of General Tyler. As we passed "our company," I saw John, grave and silent, marching with his head erect, and his wreath over his shoulders. The men recognized me as I rode to the front, and one called out: "Tell them we are coming, Captain Phil;" another, "The avengers of Sumter are on their track." All along, as the spectators passed, the cries were: "We carry the mail from Washington to Richmond."

"Ask the price of hemp in the Southern capital!"

"Tell Jeff, we bear him General Scott's compliments," etc.

The 69th New York, Irish regiment, were in the third brigade, and could scarce contain themselves. They whooped and hallooed and sang and laughed.

When they had to halt, as they frequently did, that the obstructions put by the rebels in the road might be removed, they wrestled and played with each other, and gave the most unearthly yells, which almost startled me out of my saddle.

The way was narrow and rough, and the march slow. A band of skirmishers and pioneers were sent ahead with axes to clear away the barricades, trees in large numbers having been cut from the hillsides to form these hindrances.

There was not much progress made this first day. At night the men lay down in the wet, swampy fields and meadows, the heavy fog drenching them to the skin. They arose at daybreak with light hearts, wringing the water from their clothes and blankets, while rejoicing in the prospect of encountering the foe.

The division was on the move by half-past five, but

Mr. D—— and I, who had spent the night in a barn belonging to a farmhouse near by, waited at the farmer's for breakfast, preferring hot cakes and coffee to an early start, satisfied to come up with them later in the day.

The road was more obstructed than that already passed over; the sun hot, the dust stifling, the advance slow and trying to the patience of the men. Every little while, when a halt was called to clear away, the soldiers would leave the ranks in search of water, for they were tortured with thirst, and there was nothing to quench it.

I rode into the farmyard of every house where there was a prospect of obtaining water, with my saddle hung with canteens; but most of the dwellings were deserted, the well chains and buckets gone, and we had no means of supplying others.

The rebels ran as we approached, and the few women and children we saw appeared frightened almost to death. They crouched as we came near, as though trying to elude our blows. We took several prisoners. One, a rebel officer, was caught by a private in the 69th, who had strayed off in a vain search for water. The officer looked crestfallen, and the soldier appeared as though, if it were not for the consequences to himself, he would have liked to have taken vengeance on him for his disappointment.

The advance discovered some earthworks, and orders were given to form for battle; but, seeing the movement, the rebels retreated, leaving canteens, blankets, etc., behind them, which were soon in the possession of our men.

I had several opportunities this day of seeing John, for Mr. D——, intent on gaining all the information in his power, dashed here, there and everywhere, and, unless forbidden, I always followed.

I was sitting under a tree which stood a little distance from the road in a field with Mr. D——, when Ayres's battery went thundering by to the front, the column having halted.

"There is a battle on hand, Captain Phil," said he; and gathering up his notes, we started forward. We were informed that the advance had reported a formidable battery within half a mile of Germantown, in the vicinity of which we were. Preparations were made for an attack, but the rebels disappeared as we approached.

As we entered the little village it was in flames; some lawless members of one of the regiments had set fire to and plundered some vacant houses. This caused an order from General McDowell, that any soldier discovered setting fire to a house should be shot on the spot, and those found stealing be sent back, under guard, to Alexandria.

Mr. D—— went into the yard of a pretty little dwelling, which had been burned down, in search of water. I followed, and looked about while he took a hasty sketch of the premises. Hearing a groan from a shed which stood near, I peeped into it, and saw two men lying there ill of the measles. One of them saw me and begged for water. I called Mr. D——, and he examined them. They were rebel soldiers, wrapped in blankets, and were unshaven and dirty in appearance. We replied to their questions, gave them water, assuring them they were safe under the protection of the Stars and Stripes, which waved over them only a few rods further on.

The halt was ordered for the night in a broad valley surrounded by woods and having plenty of water. It was more sheltered than the camp of the night previous. I remained with John, sleeping on the ground with my head and shoulders well wrapped in a blanket. I never rested better, although I could almost wring the water from my clothes in the morning.

There was an alarm during the night, and all sprang to

arms. Near us the whisper went "Be silent and steady, boys." The trumpet rang out, the drums sounded, and the word of command came clear and firm from the different leaders over the field, although they could not see the faces of their men.

Standing still, waiting, but on the alert, it was discovered that the alarm was caused by some confusion among the cattle, consequent on several getting loose. There was a rattle of steel as the thousands sank down again. While listening to the baying of the dogs, I fell asleep.

The reveillé started us betimes next morning. "We shall have a taste of the work to-day, boys," said an officer, passing a group shaking themselves into trim.

"The sooner the better," was the reply.

In a short time all were *en route* for Centerville, a breakfast of coffee and bread having been hastily swallowed.

The black stream of infantry slowly moved again ; the cavalry took their places in the line ; the white covers of the wagons gleamed in the sun ; the ambulances with their sleepy conductors crept by ; while the beeves, following in the rear, were with difficulty kept together by the drivers, who shouted and yelled themselves hoarse in their efforts to confine them to the road—so, through thick woods the division took its course.

As we rode along the column the mists arose and dispersed before the sun, and Mr. D—— drew my attention to the several regiments.

The 79th were stern and calm. Pointing to them, he said : "They have made up their minds to the issue, be it what it may."

The green banner of the Irish regiment fluttered in the breeze as they went cheerily onward, their band playing the merriest tunes. Some of them were without coats or blankets, having thrown them away the day before, when they dashed through Fairfax.

The Ohio boys trod bravely, young as many of them were, particularly the Zouaves. They clutched their arms like men eager for the fray, and bore themselves proudly with a firm step. "No danger but we will have a good account from them," was Mr. D——'s comment.

As we passed the New York 2nd, at some little distance, for we were not allowed to ride close, the band struck up. I observed a very small boy among the drummers, and dashed nearer to get a better view of him. I must confess I was envious, he appeared so joyous, and beat his drum with so much spirit among those gallant men.

"They speak well for the West;" Mr. D—— pointed to the Second Wisconsin and some Iowa troops, "and when they have the opportunity will speak for themselves."

We reached Centerville about noon and encamped in a valley on one side of the highway, the Fifth Division being on the opposite side, separated from us by the road. The village had been abandoned by the rebel men, the women and children only remaining. The deserted huts of the rebel troops dotted the hill sides. I went over the grounds with Mr. D——. There had been no resistance to our force entering Centerville and now the Stars and Stripes floated there.

General Tyler and staff took up their quarters with a secession family, living in a comfortable old house in the neighborhood, not as welcome guests though. I heard an officer laughing at the objections made by the old lady, all of which the general politely but firmly put aside, concluding with, "I intend to pay for the quarters, madam, and must have them."

As we looked about us Mr. D—— pointed to some Massachusetts and Connecticut troops, ordered in the direction of Bull Run for a reconnoissance, and remarked: "The material that was in the Revolution is there, Phil, and will conquer."

The men were taking their ease, lying on the ground, some sleeping, others munching crackers, under the shade of their blankets, which they had stretched upon the stocks of their muskets. All was quiet. Mr. D—— had just turned to seek a shelter for us from the heat, when the sound of cannon reached our ears. We paused to listen. Shot followed shot in the direction of the wood. The men sprang to their feet, and I followed Mr. D——, who with others ran to the top of a hill near to look around. I asked no questions, but listened eagerly to what was said, and heard that three regiments under Colonel Richardson had gone in the direction of Bull Run.

Mr. D—— had a glass and used it, but the woods between us and the firing prevented his ascertaining anything; he could only see the smoke. Occasionally the firing would stop, but we could get no information. Two or three hours thus passed. I was burning to go down and run further on, but dared not. Presently an officer who stood with his glass to his eye, said: "There is an orderly coming." All ran down in the direction of the road leading to Manassas, and heard from the man that he was sent for reinforcements.

The Massachusetts men having come upon a rebel battery, it opened fire upon them; advancing with the Michigan and New York regiments, they found themselves raked right and left and had retired to the woods until the reinforcements arrived.

Sherman's brigade was ordered up, and the Sixty-ninth, followed by the Highlanders and the Thirteenth Wisconsin, went rushing on. A wild war shriek ran along the lines as they passed, in answer to the cheers of their comrades.

Mr. D——, with a crowd of others, now took to the road, I with them, and coming to a little eminence, nearer the scene of action, mounted it. As we stood there a cannon ball sped past within a few yards of us, ploughing the ground and scattering the earth for some distance. Mr. D—— turned at the confusion this caused, and ordered me back. I had to obey.

I mounted the first hill again, and stayed there for hours, looking in the direction of the battle. Many men and officers from the regiments below came up to see what could be seen, but, not liking to question them, I gained little information. I saw Ayres's battery return, and heard them say the ammunition had given out. After a time a large party of horsemen passed down the road in the direction of the battle ; they rode fast, but I recognized one of them as Governor Sprague, and heard an officer near say: "There goes General McDowell and his staff."

Soon we saw parties who had gone in the direction of Bull Run, returning, and heard that General McDowell had ordered a retreat.

Very tired and very hungry, I started in search of John, and after a walk of a mile and a quarter reached the place where his regiment had bivouacked ; searched for and found him. I answered the questions put to me as well as I could (for not knowing when they might be called upon, the men had been ordered to keep their places) and then sought rest in the shade of a tree.

A little while after some regiments came back, and the wounded were brought in. To me it was a fearful sight to see those mangled bodies ; it was the first time I had seen the corpse of one who had come to a violent death. There was a poor fellow among the wounded who had his ear shot off close to his head; he appeared to suffer dreadfully.

I turned sick and dizzy at the sight, and for a moment or two did not know where I was; afraid of being thought chicken-hearted I did not go near the wounded again.

The great cry was for water. It seemed as though the men could not get enough; they panted for it under that July sun. The wells at Centerville were said to be exhausted, and they paid any price for a drink.

The camp-fires were lighted, and watching them I fell asleep. John went among the men to hear them talk of the fight, and to learn what prospect there was of a renewal to-morrow. As it grew cooler, the whole force, except the sentinels, appeared to sleep.

So closed with the Army of the Potomac the 18th of July, the day of the skirmish before Bull Run.

CHAPTER XII.

THE BATTLE OF STONE BRIDGE OR BULL RUN.

MR. D.—— was busy the next day, writing his report for the paper, so I staid with John, and did not see him until after dinner. Then he made his appearance in our midst, and joined John and me who were just starting for a walk.

All hoped the attack would be renewed in the morning, but the rumor was that General McDowell had ordered the engineers out for a reconnoissance, and that there might not be any thing done for several days. At this there was much grumbling. The men were anxious to close again with the foe, and were restive under the thought of having been driven back. Besides, the weather was hot, the time long, and they did not know what to do with themselves.

We walked beyond Centerville to the field where part of our division were bivouacked. I gazed about while John and Mr. D—— talked to the men.

In a few minutes John turned and said: "Look there, Phil."

I looked in the direction he pointed, and saw a little boy, who could not have been more than eight or nine years of age, lying in a fence corner, almost covered with tall, coarse grass, his arms embracing and his head resting on a drum, fast asleep.

I walked up to him and taking one of the drumsticks in my hand struck the fence with it in an idle way as I gazed on him.

"Faith, and it's tired he is," said a good-natured Irishman lying near.

"Where does he belong?" I inquired.

"Sure and it's his father I am, and he's one of us."

"Will he go to battle with you?"

"Faith, and he will, we could not do without Mickey and the music; it's a good boy he is. He has just been baptized, and the sign of the blessed cross put on him by the holy father there. May the blessed Virgin have him in her keeping."

He pointed to a spot where the Irish regiments had collected, and where a priest at a distance from the others was hearing confessions and administering the sacrament, as a preparation for the expected battle.

Looking at the boy I turned to John, and said: "He can go."

"It is his duty," he replied. Then addressing Mr. D——: "Phil has a mania to be a drummer boy and I have no peace because I will not gratify his noisy propensity."

The Zouaves looked gay, bright and hot; they flung themselves impatiently about, and grumbled that they had no hand in yesterday's skirmish with the "gray devils."

"How stubbornly patient the Germans are," said John as we moved among them, "they will fight just as they wait. It will be hard to turn them back." And so it was.

Saturday passed in much the same way. The men were irritable, hot, tired. I was awakened about midnight and found orders had been given for a march to battle next day.

When John lay down after that he put his arm close about me, and I fully realized he was going into the fight. I slept only in snatches, and it seemed to me we had but straightened for rest, when the call came to "up and march."

A few indistinct words, a warm embrace, and I was left. The men wheeled past me to join their comrades, who had already fallen in, and were on the march, the bright moonbeams playing among their ranks, and sparkling on their bayonets.

I cut across the fields and joined Mr. D—— at the farm house where he lodged. He was up and ready, and in the twilight of the Sabbath morning, with a heavy heart, I accompanied him to the rear of the central attacking column, which was the First Division, carrying my flag in my hand.

The reserve, who remained behind, called after those who went ahead, and jest and laughter was heard on all sides. "Be sure you bring me a lock of Jeff's hair, Tom." "Ay, ay, you shall have the whole head." "I want the flag on Beauregard's tent for a dress for my girl, Andy." "Remember Hal when you strike," said one, grasping the hand of another, and alluding to a comrade killed a few days before.

So they went to battle.

The moonlight changed into a sort of twilight and day broke. Mr. D—— passed to the front, ordering me to remain in the rear. There were many citizens with us, and the talk was of a battle at Manassas. Crossing a bridge over a little stream, the forces kept on for a considerable distance. When about three miles from our starting point, there was a sudden movement of the troops in front, and the cry came that the enemy was to be seen. The ranks separated, and moved right and left to form for battle, while the great cannon went to the van.

I forgot everything and followed some gentlemen advancing to the scene of action. The boom of our cannon startled us; all sorts of conjectures were made by the group with whom I had placed myself, and men went forward and came back with divers reports. The troops moved slowly on and we kept pace with them. Presently one who had advanced to the front ran back, shouting: "They are in sight; they wave their flags at us." His words were cut short by a tremendous boom of cannon, followed by the loud halloo of our forces, as they prepared to return it.

The leaves and twigs of the trees flew about our heads; I ran back. The balls appeared to be chasing me all the while. Just as I reached shelter, I saw John and some others coming in the same direction—bearing something on their bayonets, which they placed carefully under a tree, and then went back. The lookers-on pressed to the spot. "Poor little fellow!" I heard one say.

I raised on my tip toes and stretched forward, to see the body of the little drummer boy of the 2nd New York, whom I had envied only a few days before, lying mangled and dead, severed by a cannon ball. I do not know what happened for some time after that, but when I came to myself I was alone under a tree, at a distance from the spot where the boy lay. Our forces had moved round, and most of the firing came from a different direction. The air was heavy with smoke, and the whiz of bullets was on all sides.

Filled with fear for John, whom I knew to be in the thickest of the fight, I got up and ran forward, grasping my flag, which all the while had been clasped tightly in my hand. There was a clear space in front, and on each side of it trees covered the ground. Behind the trees, sheltering themselves as best they could, were many lookers-on. I inquired of one what regiments were engaged.

"All, all!" was his impatient reply—without looking at me.

There was great excitement among them; some one

was continually uttering exclamations and telling what he saw. I was moving away, when one caught me and pulled me to the ground, telling me to stay where I was. I heard them speak of the "Run," and the "Bridge," and the charges made, and name the officers engaged, but I could see nothing, and was almost stifled with smoke. As I lay there, the wounded were brought to the rear and given in charge of the surgeons, who had sought a sheltered spot, hung blankets around it, and displayed the yellow flag, or tied their scarfs to the trees.

At first I could not look at these men and moved away; by degrees, however, this feeling wore off, and I went near and gave several of them water, and performed little offices for the surgeons. I was in a strange state. I did not know how the hours passed, but seemed carried along by something within me which worked without my will.

The firing became hotter. Too restless to stay long in one place, having lost sight of Mr. D—— altogether, I started again to see what was going on.

At first, I had feared the balls, every one of which seemed laden with direct death to me. I shuddered at their peculiar whiz, and turned cold as they crashed among the trees, or tore up the earth. Now, as I heard them, I thought they might hurt me, but as they did not, I grew bolder, and approached the scene of strife. I could see the men and recognize some of the officers, but could make nothing of the order of battle. While I stood amid the din, I was seized with a fierce desire for arms, and looked about for something with which I might rush in and strike one blow. With all there was a hot feeling in my blood; a fearlessness in my heart, and a dull heaviness upon me, as I gazed through the smoke looking in vain for John.

I saw a horseman dash across an open space where bullets fell like rain ; I held my breath, and watched him with anxious fear ; but in a few moments he spurred his horse back through the storm unhurt, with one of his legs thrown over the pummel of his saddle. I heard one say he had gone for ammunition.

Colonel Cameron I knew by his broad-brimmed hat, with its black feather ; and our own colonel I distinguished by his horse, a full-blooded black.

I afterwards tried to tell John where I was, and what I had seen, for it seemed to me I had a view of all our division two or three times, but I could not make a connected story. Once or twice our men fell back, and I was carried with them. The dead and dying were all around me.

"For God's sake give me water !"

The words came from a soldier propped against a tree, his right arm hanging loose from his shoulder—his face already white in death. My canteen was empty ; I went back a little distance ; then ran in a diagonal line to the running stream before us, where the fight was thickest and hottest. As I stooped to dip the water up a Zouave bounded beside me, and dashing his face in the stream, lapped it like a dog ; while one of the Sixty-ninth, stripped of every thing but his trowsers, threw himself on his knees and drank from his hands. Another, near, filled his boot and carried it off. We were there but a few minutes, yet the bullets seemed flying in our faces as they dashed the water over us, ploughed the earth, or sunk in the steep bank. I can never forget the look of that man, as I put the canteen to his lips ; he could not speak his thanks.

Blood-stained and ghastly bodies covered the earth ; still the boom of cannon was heard ; the leaden hail rattled among the trees ; the jagged bullets fell around.

Two or three times there was a yell, so shrill that it rang out above the din; one near me said, "It is the Fire Zouaves."

We had retreated to get away from the bullets; but now I went nearer; I knew a fierce conflict raged, but could only see what went on about me; soon I found myself in an entirely different part of the field; I could not tell whether I was surrounded by friends or foes. Among the wounded near was a young lad, some seventeen years of age; his legs were torn away, and he was gasping and trying to undo his shirt; I neared him, and loosed the fastenings. "Where are you from?" "Georgia," he faintly murmured. "A rebel?" He nodded his head. "Are these rebel troops near us?" He again nodded assent.

I was amid the foe; I sat down aghast. In a moment my whole attention was absorbed by the lad beside me. He suffered much; his head sunk on one side, and I thought him dead, when he slowly opened his eyes. "Mother—mother—Jane—Ben," he muttered, "home;" his under-jaw fell; his head settled on his breast.

I seemed as if petrified. I could not look at or touch him, but arose to my feet and stood staring around me. A moment, and there was a rush in that direction, I was carried with it; on we went, rank met rank; there was the sound of musket and the clash of steel. I fell to the ground; was trodden upon; men made a stepping stone of my body as they dashed over me; I got to my feet. The ranks came charging back. A soldier seized me by the arm, as I impeded his way, and pushed me forward, saying, "You are my prisoner." He leaned against a tree for breath before another onset. I unrolled my flag which was wound about the stick.

"The Stars and Stripes," he exclaimed.

"I belong to the ——th."

"Then go behind there," and he thrust me to the rear with a force that sent me reeling.

"Water, water!" Panting and exhausted, the men lay gasping, and some, unable to endure the thirst, made desperate efforts to gain the stream. The day wore on; the firing began to slacken; regiments fell back; there was a lull;—then rejoicing over a victory.

Some threw themselves down for a moment's rest, others looked to the wounded and dying. I set out to find "our company," and see John. The earth at every step was red with blood and covered with mutilated and dying men.

Some little time passed—I cannot tell how long, for I had thrown myself down near the grove used by the surgeons, where the yellow flag was flying—when a number of persons came running rapidly back. The Black Horse had charged upon the Fire Zouaves. The firing recommenced, and in a few minutes the battle raged again. The rebel cavalry came furiously on and were met by the Zouaves, who, shouting "Remember Ellsworth," closed upon them with musket, bayonet and saber.

I stood crouching in the corner of a worm fence, when Union and rebel soldiers came dashing through it, and over the road—red shirts and black horses in rapid confusion; mingling with their tramp were the terrible yells of the combatants, and the heavy strokes of the saber. I got up and staggered back; the yellow flag and the surgeons were gone, and the dead lay in heaps where they had been.

After a time the cry came: "They are retreating!" and two of our regiments, driven by the enemy, went by to the left; others followed and lookers-on joined; there was shouting and urging and thrusting forward. I went with the crowd, who threw each other down in the eagerness to get away from the battle-field, trampling over those who fell. Part of the multitude had re-crossed the little stream we had passed in the morning, when a troop of horsemen came down upon them ; they were met by a detachment of our troops—crash—a dash—a roar—the belching of cannon, and then soldiers—teamsters—cattle —wagons—ambulances—mingled in deadly confusion— fled onward in pitiful panic. I was carried a short distance by the rush, then left where I dropped, utterly unable to move. Several officers with drawn swords tried to bring the men back, but the terrified horde kept on unheeding, fancying the victorious rebels at their heels.

Crawling on one side, I saw a rifle and picked it up ; the touch gave me strength and spirit. I determined to have one shot at the rebels, and so, standing up, tried to steady it, but my knees trembled and I sunk again. With a renewed effort I dragged myself nearer the scene of action; I fired once—twice—but I know not if the balls told ; I only hoped they did. Then, with a tight clutch on my flag, I fell back, fierce joy raging in my heart. Several horsemen passed near but did not see me. I believed John was dead ; there was no one now to look or care for me ; with a sort of desperate feeling I longed to flout my flag in the face of the foe, and believe I could have done it had they come near. I smoothed it out ; the scene swam before my eyes ; I was dying, I knew it,—the din grew less,—the outline of the scene fainter—I clasped the flag tighter. They should find me with my country's colors on my heart.

A rough hand shook me back to life.

It was Mr. D——. I tried to get up but could not. I was not hurt, but I could not stand. It was almost evening, and I had eaten nothing since the night before. Mr. D——

took a flask from his pocket, held it to my lips and bade me drink. "More, more," he said sharply, as I paused for breath. The fiery draught revived me. I asked for John. He hoped he was safe, believed he was, but if I wanted to see him I must exert all my strength to get ahead. I already felt better; we rushed on with the rest, only turning aside to get our horses, which we had left at the farm house, but they had been seized by other fugitives. We got some bread; then, with hundreds of others, keeping to the fields, made for Washington.

On—on—on—the high road was jammed with a moving throng and strewed with abandoned knapsacks and arms. Wounded and almost exhausted men struggled with the occupants of vehicles for possession, and were knocked down, to be trodden on and left to die in the dust. The roadside and fields were thickly dotted with those who had given out, and sunk to sleep or death.

We met members of the regiment and fell in with several of "our company;" they told me John was alive and on the way. After a while I gave out also, as did others. We must rest and sleep. Mr. D—— stood perplexed, for his duty called him to the city. I begged him to go; the men promised to keep me with them, so he reluctantly departed.

Crossing to the far side of a corn-field, we lay down, reduced to such a state of weariness we scarcely cared what became of us. After a couple of hours' sleep we again joined the train of fugitives. A drenching rain fell, which penetrated to our skins. Hungry, sleepy, dirty, sore-footed and sore-hearted, worn and miserable, we reached Long Bridge, and passing crowds as wretched as ourselves, entered the city, which was thronged with people, who eagerly stopped and questioned each fresh group that arrived. Soldiers stood in clusters on the pavements or leaned against the houses, or lay on the steps of public buildings and private dwellings. The rain poured upon them, while ladies, negroes, Dutch and Irish men and women thrust provisions in their hands or put wine to their lips. We came to two ladies, standing on the curbstone before their dwelling, their white faces haggard with anxiety. They held cups to the lips of the weary men tottering by. I eagerly swallowed a draught of the liquor.

"Poor boy! he shakes like a leaf," said one of them. "Go lie yonder,"—she pointed to a carpenter's shop near. I obeyed, and sinking on the shavings, disgrace, disaster and defeat were forgotten in sleep.

CHAPTER XIII.

GOING HOME.

IT was some hours ere I awoke; my first thought was of John, and I went in search of him.

O, that day! that dull, wretched, miserable day! The rain sullenly falling, the depressed soldiers, the terrified and helpless citizens starting at each unusual sound—the half concealed joy of the secesh—I cannot bear to remember, but can never forget! The streets were still thronged; groups of despairing men stood upon the sidewalks and talked, while women, regardless of the rain, mutely listened; worn out soldiers, shelterless, wandered about having no place to go, telling to eager listeners the tale of our disaster. Going about among them speaking words of cheer, rendering assistance, and ministering to their comfort, were many prominent men, among whom I recognized Senator Wilson and others I had seen in Washington.

The Zouaves were reported to have been cut to pieces. I saw several surrounded by eager listening crowds.

I could hear nothing of John.—At length I met a man who told me he was wounded and had come in in an ambulance. After some time I found him.

He saw me coming and opened his arms to me. His first words were thanks for my escape.

"You are hurt—wounded," I cried, seeing him wince.

"It is nothing, a blow from a spent ball—but you?"

"Bruised from being trodden on; that is all."

"Yesterday, my boy, yesterday, to think of it! I would willingly have been left there;" he pointed in the direction of Bull Run, "if my poor life could have helped to prevent this disgrace."

"Why, Captain Phil!" Caton slapped me on the back. "I never expected to see you again after what I heard."

"What?" said John.

"He was in the thickest of the fight."

"I did not mean to break my word, John." I told him candidly how I felt and what I had done.

"And you had no arms?"

"Yes, he had," interrupted Caton, "and he blazed away at them, too. Watson, who was wounded in the wrist and had his rifle struck from his hand, lay in some bushes, where he had crawled to get out of the way of the Black Horse. He saw Captain Phil crack away at them; he called to him but could not make him hear. Afterwards some of the boys picked up Watson, and seeing Mr. D—— he put him on Captain Phil's track."

I showed John the rifle I had kept as a trophy, and which I hereafter intended to use. It was a handsome one and had a curious figure cut on the stock.

John could not walk. The ball had struck him above the ankle, early in the action, throwing him down and sending his rifle to some distance. As he could not stand and was unarmed he was carried to an ambulance, and knew nothing of the panic, until he saw the crowd of soldiers and vehicles cumbering the road. The driver of his vehicle started with the rest, deaf to all his remonstrances and entreaties to stop or turn aside for a moment, so he was among the first to reach the city.

I went up to Mrs. Leavit's; the little woman wrung my hand and kissed me, while the tears ran down her cheeks. She immediately got a carriage, and we went for John.

She took him to her house, and attended to him herself; she saw that he wanted for nothing. His leg was painful, but he uttered no complaint; it made my heart heavy to see him, he was so depressed.

Anxious about his comrades, he sent me out to gather all the information I could get.

One of our men had come in driving a prisoner before him all the way, and delivering him up to the Provost Marshal. Another had been seen to kill two of the foe, and take a third a prisoner, the latter, however, he had stripped of his arms and given the chance of a run for his life, but he saw him shot by another party. A third distinguished himself by his daring in storming the batteries, getting ahead of his company, and returning very reluctantly when called off. Numberless were the incidents of individual bravery which went from mouth to mouth. Several spoke of John's calm intrepidity.

The soldiers were still in the streets shelterless, many of them unable to find their officers, or the rest of the command. Our men were mostly together; they had lost but few of their number. All spoke with rage and shame of the panic.

Caton triumphantly told of one of his exploits. "I was about a hundred yards off, when they came down on the hospital and killed McCook. I determined to fire one shot to avenge Charlie anyhow; so selected my man and dropped behind a shelter conveniently near, from which I aimed at him, and I saw him fall from his horse; played their own game on them, you see, and took him Indian fashion."

One of the drummer boys of our regiment, only thirteen years of age, was killed by a cannon ball.

As I sat talking to John things would come to me that I had seen in the field, which at the time had made no impression. I remembered faces; expressions of the wounded,—that of one man was very vivid. He asked me to unbuckle his belt, and I recalled the fear I had that I would not be able to do it, and relieve him, but I did succeed.

I also recollected the vivandières, going about among the wounded. I saw one of them, while the bullets rattled over her head, raise a man in her arms, and give him water.

Vividly before me was the appearance of several of the wounded who loaded their rifles and fired. One man, disabled in the leg, had tied his pocket handkerchief tightly above the place, and was on his other knee sighting his rifle to fire, when I observed him.

Our regiment was now to return home to be paid off and disbanded, our time having expired. John, although not able to walk, determined to accompany it. His friends would care for him on the way.

Most sad were those days spent in Washington. Fears for the Capitol were, however, soon allayed. The enemy had not followed up the advantage; things began to come to order. Soldiers disappeared from the streets, turning again into camp, and, the first shock over, were no whit despairing, but already began to talk of another attack, when victory should wipe from their standards the shame of defeat.

The killed and wounded were found to be less in number than was at first reported. The dead buried and the wounded cared for, new measures were taken. General McClellan was summoned to the command; hope revived and all took heart again.

We started for home, and after many delays on the way, reached there. We heard we were to have a reception and we *did* have one. When we came in sight of the city, I unrolled my flag (which John says I must keep as a trophy for my children), smoothed, and made it ready. John's wreath was at hand, withered and dry, but precious to him.

It was a bright hot morning, and such a crowd! and such a welcome! It would have made patriots and soldiers of the most lukewarm. Men, women and children thronged the depôt, jammed the streets, house tops and balconies. The military closed to escort us to the breakfast provided for us, fathers, mothers, sisters, brothers and sweethearts and wives plunged through to shake hands with the returned braves.

All were dressed in holiday costume, flags were in the air, banners across the streets, shouts, laughter, and tears greeted the bronzed, soiled, and weather-beaten men, some of whom their nearest relatives could not recognize.

Each man felt himself a hero, and trod like one. I strutted along, shouldering my rifle, my flag held to its utmost height, a target for the bouquets which covered us. I felt like shouting: "It has been to Bull Run." The women seemed almost crazy in their anxiety to do honor to the soldiers; they cheered and waved, and showered flowers and blessings all along the line, at some points actually loading us with these favors.

At length we reached the park, where the breakfast had been provided, and were welcomed with warm words, in a set speech. To this the chaplain replied on behalf of the men. Then we were bidden to the tables, where every luxury money could purchase was provided in the greatest abundance.

"They think we have had a famine down there in Egypt," said Caton, as he viewed the good things piled before him. "I intend to do justice to this fare, Phil."

THE RETURN.

And we all did justice to it, and the people looked on and enjoyed our appetites.

When it was over, every man was surrounded by a group eager to hear his story. I told mine over and over again. The women particularly gathered about me and put to me many questions, and with the most exciting interest examined my flag, which had a few spots of blood on it. They pitied me for being so young, and having been in so much danger.

"Why," said Caton, "Captain Phil would not have missed it for a thousand dollars. I wish I had been in his place with the flag."

"I," said a gentleman near, "would give ten thousand to have been through it and standing where he is now."

"Now is your time then, stranger," said Caton, "you can go in for three years."

It then occurred to me how conspicuous I must have been with that flag on the battle field.

"There Charley," and I passed the flag to Thornley, who was pressing towards me. "I did all I could, and tried to have a good account to give."

Charley seized and looked at it, as though he thought it could speak and tell the story of that day, while the other boys crowded eagerly round. I drew myself up and stood proudly among them, for I had been in battle for my country.

As soon as I could get off I followed John, who had been in the procession in a carriage, but was obliged from the pain of his wound to go home. "Phil," he said as we talked it over, "I am going in for three years when I get well."

"So am I," was my rejoinder, at which he smiled, as I proceeded to place my little Stars and Stripes *above* his withered wreath on the mantel shelf. "Our country first,

John. If I was only a little taller I would try to get a position as color-bearer in one of the regiments under General Benham's command!" John raised himself on his elbow and smiled at me in that peculiarly affectionate way of his.

CHAPTER XIV.

WESTERN VIRGINIA.

JOHN was rapidly improving. He went out every day. Meantime August passed and the first of September found me again in school. I never liked the confinement, and would have demurred about going, but John had such a matter of course way about such things, it left me no room to object. I never enjoyed it so much before as now, however, for at recess the boys surrounded me and were never tired of asking questions about our camp life and Bull Run. I had need to be mindful of John's caution: "Be careful, Phil, you have great temptation to exaggerate." The Southern sympathizers often called "Bull Run" after me, but several of them got pretty severely thrashed, so on the whole they kept tolerably quiet.

Early in October John threw away his crutch. The first day that he did so he came home early in the evening. I was working out my problems; they were difficult and he helped me. When I had done and was about putting up my book, he said:

"Are you through, Phil?"

"Yes, for to-night."

"Put the lamp on the mantel and come here; I want to talk with you."

I did as he told me, and sat down beside him.

After a moment he laid his hand on my shoulder, and looked fixedly in my eyes, while he said:

"I am going in for three years, Phil."

"O, I am so glad!" and I jumped to my feet.

"I did not say you were going with me."

"But I know I am though—you would not leave me for so long a time with the chance of not seeing me again—and—and I, all you have, and you, all I have——" My fears overcame me. I could get no further, but broke down.

He put his arm out and drew me to him.

"You cannot appreciate the anxiety and thought this has cost me, Phil. What becomes of your education if you go with me? I may be disabled—killed. To give you a good education may be all I shall be able to do for you in life."

"You know," I interrupted, "Mr. James said that with you I was securing an education few boys could receive."

"True in some respects; but it is not the kind of education that will enable you to become a good book-keeper or accountant. You are a little over fourteen now, consequently will be between seventeen and eighteen three years hence. My object is to give you a collegiate course, although you have no great desire, I know, to go through college. Do you think, if I take you along with me and both of us live through the three years, you will be willing to go to school when my time is out, and work faithfully to attain the object I have in view?"

"Yes, I am sure I will if you continue to wish it. But I hope you will let me enter the army when I am seventeen. Dick Chase is just seventeen and he has joined a cavalry regiment." John shook his head. "I am running a great risk, Phil, in permitting you to have this army education; but I know your character, have thought it all over, and believe it will be to your advantage.

Should circumstances prove that I have made a mistake, then you must leave me and return to your school. I want you to think it over; in a day or two I will speak to you again. My mind is so fixed upon your going to college that I have made provision for your so doing in case I am killed, a not unlikely thing to happen. When you have thought it all over and decided, I shall consider the compact binding, and should I fall leave it as a sacred legacy to you to fulfill."

"But, John, you never had a college education, and I do not care to be any wiser or better than you are."

"I hope you will be both; and it is just because I have not such an education and *feel* the want of it, that I am determined you shall not."

He then told me his friends had applied for a commission for him, but added: "I shall go as I did before if I should not get it."

Never slow to act when his mind was once made up, in a few days he had settled everything.

I, of course, decided, as he knew I would, to go. The last days of October found us busy with our preparations. As I took down my little flag and shook it out, I said, pointing to his withered wreath which hung below it:

"Does that go too?"

"Yes," he said, quietly, but the color came into his cheek. "We will take them as trophies, they were with us in a dark hour."

When we were putting our things in our knapsacks, I observed an addition to his watchguard, a bright new locket.

"What is that, John?"

"Something to turn the bullets aside," he replied.

The middle of October found us on a boat, going up the Ohio river, on our way to join the army in Western Virginia commanded by Brigadier-General William Rosecrans, John bearing a commission as second lieutenant in his pocket. Going by way of the Kanawha and Charleston, Virginia, we reached, after a tedious journey, the neighborhood of the Gauley river, where it empties into the Kanawha, and joined General Benham's Brigade at Camp Huddlestone. We had heard that General Rosecrans had his headquarters at Hawk's Nest, on the plantation of Colonel Tompkins, a rebel officer absent in that service.

Some two or three days after our arrival, three or four of our men were caught in a chaparral, and were at the mercy of the enemy's guns. Soon it was reported they were all either killed or wounded. An officer with a squad was ordered to bring them in. The enterprise was a hazardous one, as no movement could be made without the knowledge of the foe. The officer made the attempt, and, returning, pronounced it impossible without a sacrifice of his men. Another tried it, with like success. John then volunteered to perform the duty. The colonel, who was a personal friend of his, said to him:

"I advise you not, Wharton; I tell you frankly, I would not volunteer it for my commission. Of course, if it was in my regular line of duty, I should not shirk it; although it is just one of those cases where a man is almost certain to lose life or limb and gains nothing by it. If you insist, it will be my duty to accept, for every effort must be made to relieve the men."

John did insist, and went, returning in a far shorter time than any hoped, bringing all the wounded men and the body of one who had fallen, his little band unhurt, although the foe had kept up a constant firing on them.

About a week after we joined, orders came to cross the Gauley, which we did, and camped upon Loup Creek. There we stayed several days; then started in pursuit of

Floyd, over Cotton Hill or Mountain, which is situated on the Kanawha, opposite the mouth of the Gauley.

Although early in the season, the cold was severe. Tramp, tramp, we went through snow, sleet, mud, and rain, with no shelter at night, and only the cold mud or its frozen crust for a bed. It was a dreadful march.

We came up to them at Union School House, and at Dickenson's Farm. At McCoy's Mills we had an engagement; Colonel Craghan was killed, and the rebels ran in great disorder. We pursued them fourteen miles beyond Fayetteville, the road all the way being encumbered with knapsacks, clothing, and camp utensils, which they had abandoned in their flight. The men bore their hardships bravely, and only grumbled when, after a forced rest of a few hours to recruit their utterly exhausted strength, they were ordered back. General Benham, though very much chagrined with the order, for he felt certain of his prey, nevertheless promptly obeyed, and with what grace he could abandoned the pursuit.

We had marched up the hill, and now we marched down it again. The vim with which the men had gone forward deserted them going back. The weather was inclement, and they were insufficiently clothed, and without the excitement to keep them up. I was utterly done out, and sunk down in a fence corner, where I believe I should have died had not General Benham seen me and ordered a horse to be given me.

> "There was a man of Accomac,
>   And his name was Bully Wise,
> He jumped into Kanawha's bush,
>   And scratched out both his eyes;
> And when he saw he'd lost his eyes,
>   With all his might and main,
> From Kanawha he quickly flies
>   To brag and — run again."

This poetic description of General Wise's campaign I cut from a newspaper.

It was a rough country, inhabited by rough people. Most of the young men were in the rebel army, and the old ones, as the negroes said, "fought on boaf sides," according to what troops were occupying the neighborhood.

The rebel women were inhospitable, savage and sour, and looked daggers at our soldiers, as they crouched over the fire and smoked. There were few negroes, and they were of the rougher kind, and either openly or secretly aided the Federals.

While there I went to the Ohio river (for John and several other officers), to attend to some stores and accoutrements, which were among the missing.

I was leaning over the guards of a steamer at the wharf, listening to some young men giving an account of outrages that had been committed near their homes by guerrillas, when a touch on my shoulder caused me to start and turn around.

"Good evening, Captain Phil."

I took off my cap and bowed. The tones of the voice were familiar, but I could not recognize the person, who was a fashionably dressed lady, with a black lace veil over her face. Confused, and at fault, I stood silent.

With a hearty laugh, and "you do not know me?" she threw back her veil and bent her face close to mine.

"Joseph!"

Yet it was not Joseph either, but a merrier, brighter face, wreathed with smiles, and surrounded with artificial flowers.

"Josephine, if you please. I changed my name with my dress. I am so glad to see you, Captain Phil. I have often thought of you and the good times we had when I went soldiering. I knew you the moment I saw you."

I could not realize that the dashing woman beside me was the quiet lad with whom I had messed, and at whose side I had slept for so many weeks. She enjoyed my astonishment a moment; then stepping to the door of the cabin, beckoned to some one within.

A good-looking officer obeyed her summons.

"Captain S——," she said, as he reached us, "this is Captain Phil, of whom you have heard me speak."

The captain held out his hand and shook mine cordially.

"Did you not suspect that she was a woman?"

"Never had the slightest suspicion."

"I suppose I shall be obliged to shoulder that part of her experience of life," he said, with a satisfied smile. "She thought I intended to join your regiment; she had quarreled with me, so, to spite me and ruin herself, she enlisted before me. You almost cut me out, though."

I did not know what to reply; I did not fancy him much. Turning to her I said:

"Are you married?"

"Yes, two weeks since. He has gone in for three years, and is captain. I thought I had better take him. We are going to Cincinnati on this boat, where he joins his regiment."

"She was afraid I would give her the slip," he said, stroking his beard.

"How is your brother, Captain Phil?"

She anxiously inquired what the men said of her after she left, and blushed with pleasure when I told her they all bore testimony to her propriety of behavior.

"It is some consolation to know that, Captain Phil, and perhaps if I had had a mother, father, or home, I should never have been a soldier. I was desperate that time in Cincinnati."

The boat had been puffing steam for some time, and I

saw they were preparing to take the plank in, so I shook hands and said "Good-by." The captain was very cordial and hoped we might meet again.

I had something to think of now by way of passing the two hours before I could get away from the town. I had a feeling of sorrow for her, although I do not know that I had cause, excepting that her husband appeared careless and indifferent. She seemed bright and happy enough.

On returning, I found a report in camp that several regiments were to be transferred to Kentucky. I hoped John's would be among the number. My only regret was the probability of another commander. General Benham, by his kindness and consideration, had made himself very popular among the troops, while his indomitable energy and his soldierly bearing inspired confidence. We knew it was not his fault Floyd escaped.

CHAPTER XV.

FROM LOUISVILLE TO NASHVILLE.—AFTER BUCKNER.

MUCH to my satisfaction, ours was one of the regiments ordered to Louisville. We found the city crowded with troops; regiment after regiment hourly arriving and departing. We encamped on the opposite side of the river, back of Jeffersonville. The next day I had permission to go over to Louisville. I wandered about all day. I saw General Buell's body-guard passing through the streets—a grand-looking set of men, almost all of them six feet high. The general's quarters were in a handsome three-story house on Fourth street, made conspicuous by the Stars and Stripes floating from the roof, and the sentinel pacing before the door.

Two women passed as I paused there; they scowled at the sentinel. One of them said: "Don't pass under that rag," and they turned out into the street. The other, as she stepped on the curbstone of the next pavement, and paused to scrape the mud off her shoes, muttered between her teeth: "I would like to wipe my feet on it."

As I stood in a crowd looking at some troops passing, I saw faces dark with passion, and heard many a scoff and threat. A showily dressed woman pushing herself along, using her elbows, nearly threw me down, then exclaimed in a hard, loud voice: "Get out of the way, you little viper."

"You mistake, madam," I replied, catching my balance, and bowing, "I am not a copperhead."

"Bully for you," exclaimed a great broad-chested man dressed in jeans, giving me a slap on the back which nearly upset me again. "I see by your traps you belong to Uncle Sam. Keep on; you will be a general some day."

We moved back from the river and were many weeks on the dark and bloody ground. The weather was terribly cold, wet and rainy, and so dull and uncomfortable, with the mud ankle deep, that we could not drill. Picket duty was severe, but the men preferred it to guarding fords or to the tedium of camp life.

I could not help giving vent to my joy by turning a somersault and hurrahing at the top of my lungs when we broke lines and started for Green River, where a large part of our army was. Here we remained some time. The railroad bridge over the river had been destroyed by order of General Buckner. It ran not only over the river but across the valley, was built of iron, and was about a thousand feet long. I heard men say that with one exception, that of Montreal, it was the longest on the Continent. I enjoyed every moment of the time we were at Green River, except the last few days. The weather was pleasant and the camp was all astir. Soldiers were in the woods cutting down trees, teamsters were hauling logs, and the bridge was alive with men working on it above, while the pontooners were busy beneath.

General Buell had a large army to provide for, and he was obliged to keep up his communications. The railroad had to be put in order, bridges rebuilt, and everything got in proper train, ere we could follow the enemy. We could not live upon the country in our march, for there was nothing to live on.

There was skirmishing while we were at Green river, but no real battles. Our entrenchments on the enemy's

POSSUM.

side were strong. At one time the Texan rangers attacked General Willich's German regiment and there was a severe engagement, but I did not see it. Part of our army under Generals Thomas and Schoepff was attacked at Somerset, or Mill Spring, in the mountain region. They defeated the enemy, and General Zollicoffer, the rebel commander, was killed. His army fled across the Cumberland, pursued by our forces.

Our army was on both sides of Green River waiting orders. I spent the days going from one division to another. Many of the men were restive and anxious to be on the road, particularly after they heard of General Thomas's victory at Somerset.

One bright cold morning I had crossed the river and gone up some distance with Jim, the captain's servant.

He suddenly stopped and pointed to something lying at the foot of a tree.

"Dar's a 'possum!"

That said, I looking at it curiously, for I had never seen one before. "It is dead." I tried to turn it over with my foot.

"Yah, yah, we'll see dat."

Jim went back some distance and whistled to his dog. Meantime I stooped down and handled it,—the creature was dead.

In a moment Dandy's yelp was heard, and, to my astonishment, the 'possum sprang up, agile as a cat, and darted up a tree. While I looked blank, fully understanding now the meaning of the term *'possuming*, Jim rolled on the ground and laughed.

We stopped to see General Mitchel's division cross the river. Several of General Johnston's staff were near, looking on.

"Do you see that man?" said one soldier to another, pointing to a gentleman in citizen's dress, who was with the officers. "He is an Englishman. He makes books. I wonder if he is going to make a book about us."

"What is his name?"

"I heard them call him Trollope."

"Why, his mother used to live in Cincinnati; she built the Bazar there. I used to go to dancing school in it; they are a smart family," was the rejoinder.

Caton had re-enlisted and was in "our company." While we were in Kentucky, he and John Stuart had an adventure of which they were not a little proud. We were encamped for a day or two in a litter secesh neighborhood. One night, just after supper, a burly, curly-wooled black came into camp, his bundle under his arm. "The boys" began to laugh at him, telling him horrible stories of the cruelty of the Union soldiers, and in various ways tried to get fun out of him.

Sambo was not to be repressed. He sat by the fire and toasted his shins, at the same time eating corn cake and bacon from the bundle he had brought with him, and laughing and showing his teeth at their threats. Rather pleased with his coolness and confidence they let him alone. After a time I saw Caton earnestly talking to him; soon they went apart together.

The negro had informed Caton that his mistress lived no great distance off. She was a widow and had two sons in the rebel cavalry. She was a hard woman on her hands. She had him whipped for some trifling offense, and had threatened to send him to her brother's plantation in Mississippi. Her two sons, with part of the gang to which they belonged, were in the neighborhood, and they were to visit her that night. She had had turkeys and chickens killed, and pies baked, to give them a good supper; as he was afraid she would send him away with them, he had quietly taken leave.

At the mention of the visit of the soldiers, Caton conceived the idea of capturing them. Lem needed no bribe to secure his services as guide, so, with promises for success and threats for failure, he started with Caton and Stuart, who was eager to participate. Stealing from the camp they made their way to the house, a couple of miles distant on a side road, in an out-of-the-way situation. Lem informed them "there was an awful fierce dog;" so they lay down behind a fence while he went forward.

Presently they heard the dog bark. A door opened and a light gleamed out, but it closed in a moment, and Lem came back.

"Now your time, gemmens," he said; "I guv Pomp a bone. He knowd me; Zampy, she opened the kitchen dor, when she hern him bark. She didn't know I was thar. Ther hosses are right across from the kitchen dor, hitched to the garden fence."

To secure these was the first object; but all five of them were removed without giving alarm, and conveniently placed for escape.

Caton crawled to the window to get a look within. The widow, her daughter, and the five men were seated at supper. The men's rifles were leaning against a stand between them and the door, which opened out on a wide covered or roofed passage way, uninclosed at the ends, with the rooms built on each side of it. Stuart and Caton were to creep into this passage, from which they could make a dash through the door and secure the arms, while Lem fired off a revolver outside, to make them believe they were surrounded.

Lem went round the house and returned.

"Wait a bit," said he, "thar 'bout taking in the last batch ob hot griddle cakes. I hern Zampy say that was all. Then the niggers will go to eating thar suppers and the white folks to talking."

In a few minutes Caton announced that the cakes were in. Stuart and he burst through the door, seized the rifles and, ere the party had gained their feet, held them to their heads, and commanded a surrender.

In telling it, Caton said: "Lem kept up such a shouting and screeching outside, I began to fear something was wrong, and that we had fallen into an ambush."

"You never saw such crestfallen men in your life, when we reached the horses and they saw there were but two of us."

"Hitched, by Jupiter! by two Yanks and a nigger!" was the exclamation.

They threatened to burn Lem if they caught him, and made such demonstrations that Caton told them if they moved a finger they were dead men.

When but a little distance from our pickets, a party of horsemen were heard approaching. Taking the negro's advice they drew back in the woods, dismounted, with their bridles on their arms, huddled the prisoners together, and stood over them with cocked pieces, assuring them at the least noise they would fire.

"I was afraid," said Caton, "that the horses would lead to our discovery, for they were not more than forty yards from us. But the night was dark, sleety and cold, and the men were muffled up and galloping at a furious rate. One of our animals gave a slight neigh, but they did not observe it."

To add to Caton's triumph, it was afterwards ascertained that the party consisted of twenty-five of John Morgan's men, out marauding.

The prisoners were put under guard, the horses handed over to the quartermaster, and Lem advised to keep out of the way of his late friends. He was the most vindictive negro I ever saw; he delighted in the capture of his former masters, and ground his teeth when he spoke of their threat of burning him. When they were within hearing he would sing in the most defiant manner:

> "I've got a wife, and I've got a baby,
> Way up Norf in Lower Canady,
> Won't they smile when they see Old Shady?
> Coming, — coming —
> Hail! mighty day!
> Good-by, Massa Jeff — Good-by, Massa Stephen,
> E'cuse dis darkey for taking aleavin',
> Guess by and by you'll see Old Aby
> Coming, — coming —
> Hail! mighty day!"

It began to rain, regular rebel rain I called it. The mud and slush were over ankle deep. Men could not march nor wagons move in it. The railroad bridge was done and had been tested; we waited only for some improvement in the weather. At length the order "forward march" was heard, and we took the road to Bowling Green. John told me our forces expected an attack at either Peut's Knob or Glasgow Junction, both having strong natural fortifications, but we met no enemy. The road was terribly rough and hilly, the country wild, and, to all appearance, uninhabited. It rained, it froze, it rained again; the mud was deep, the wind cold. We were now forty-two miles from Bowling Green, which General Buckner had, several months before, seized and fortified, and which they called the "Western Manassas." Word came that the enemy were about leaving it, and, anxious to meet them there, we hurried on our way. Our course was through the Mammoth Cave country. The men called it the *sieve*, and under pretense of filling their canteens, strayed from the column, peering into all sorts of queer places. In trying to find the bottom of a cavernous looking hole, I came near going under. John told me that originally the country had been dry and barren; all the rain which fell sunk into the earth and went to feed the underground rivers, which are said to abound, but the holes through which the water disappeared had been stopped by the inhabitants, and large numbers of ponds and small lakes had thus been formed, which gave the farmers a supply of water to cultivate their fields. The fear now was that they would open these holes and let the water down and so make it impossible for us to continue our advance. There was not a river near, and neither men nor cattle could exist on such a march without water. The natives, however, satisfied themselves with throwing in all the dead animals they could find.

The boys cast aside most of their luggage and carried only what they needed, with their camp equipage on their backs. About half the distance was made when, at night, General Buell heard that the rebels were already evacuating Bowling Green. He ordered that the army be on the road in the "wee sma' hours" of the next morning.

I was terribly tired; my boots were wet through, and I was shaking with cold when I stretched myself to sleep. Nearly two inches of snow fell on us through the night. When first I opened my eyes in the dim light I was startled to see the men springing up in their whitened blankets, looking like ghosts in their shrouds.

The first five or six miles of the road was the worst I ever saw; it was like climbing up and down steep rocky paths. The ponds were nearly all filled with dead horses and cattle, but we made a handful of snow supply the place of water. On we went; the bad road was soon passed, the obstructions removed, and, following the blue flag of the regiment that had the advance, we moved rapidly forward on a smooth pike leaving the *sieve* in our rear.

We were nearing Barren river, when Loomis's Battery, its gallant leader at the head, went galloping to the front. The men threw their knapsacks into any vehicle they chanced on and marched double quick. The sound of cannon soon gladdened their ears, but they reached the bank of the river only to be disappointed. The bridges were destroyed, and there was no way to cross. Cold and weary, they prepared to pass the night on the ground under their blankets, when the order came to move. Marching through the snow to the ferry, some three miles below the town, some built fires and tried to keep warm while their comrades mended an old boat to cross in. Others waited for the pontoons. At last a part were ferried over, and pushed on, reaching the town at daylight, only to find it deserted. A few Texas rangers hastened out as they hastened in.

Loomis's Battery was stationed on a hill overlooking the place. When the rebels found we were near, they sent a flag of truce to General Buell asking for six hours in which to leave, but he ordered the battery to open on the town. I was looking through a glass, and saw the people scamper as the shell fell in the streets. They had already sent off their artillery and ammunition. Now they fired the city. All the railroad buildings were burned, and immense piles of corn, wheat and bacon were destroyed.

When our boys entered they ransacked every corner and filled their pockets, laying in supplies of tobacco, and surfeiting themselves with sweets. I saw great brawny men with their hands full of candy sucking it like children. I had my share too.

Our whole army was up, in and about the town. The women and children and men not in service had gone off to Nashville months before, and left the place in the hands of rebel soldiers. Some of the houses had been used for officers' quarters and for hospitals, and others had been taken by the cavalry as stables for their horses.

Bowling Green lies in a valley commanded by hills. The hills had been fortified and their sides filled with pits dug to shelter the rebel force. I went with John to visit Mount Airy, from which we had a good view of the country. Then we went to Underwood and Webb Hills. All these had handsome houses upon them which had been occupied by rich people before the war. I could not but think what a bitter thing it must be to them to be obliged to leave such homes and become fugitives, believing, as most of them did, that they were in the right.

The army had orders to pursue and press forward, so our stay at Barren River was short. News had been received that General Buckner, with whom we had been hoping to have a fight, had been ordered from Bowling Green to Fort Donelson, where he was taken prisoner with ten thousand men. John told me that the defeat at Forts Donelson and Henry was the reason they had abandoned their stronghold here; that they were on the road to Nashville, and we must be after them and clear Kentucky.

CHAPTER XVI.

NASHVILLE AND PITTSBURG LANDING.

WE lost no time, but pushed on to Tennessee, and were the first Federal troops that reached its capital. We found the bridges over the Cumberland River destroyed, and, having no means of crossing, could not enter the city. While the Engineer Corps were rebuilding the bridges General Nelson sailed up the river with his fleet and took possession, planting the Stars and Stripes on the capitol building.

This was a great disappointment to General Buell's command. We had marched far and toiled hard for the honor of being the first to deliver the Rock City and unfurl the banner of beauty over it. However, we laughed the disappointment off, right glad to see the flag of the "Cincinnati Ducks" on the spot where we would have been proud to have placed our own.

John heard me grumbling about it.

"Ah! Phil, Phil!" said he, "you must learn there are many things in life so certain apparently that you have only to clasp them, yet you never possess them."

"But we worked hard for this."

"So did others and got it."

I never saw a more dismal-looking place than Nashville was when we entered it. No houses or stores open, only soldiers to be seen in the streets, no markets, nothing that looked alive but the military and the negroes. The white women and children were hidden away somewhere. They would not even look out at us, but the blacks hung on the gates and fences, laughed and joked and bobbed their heads in their happiness, moving off very reluctantly and with slow steps in obedience to voices which issued from the closed shutters of the houses.

"Where are the white people?" said I to an old negro.

"Miss Ann and de young ladies peeping up dar." He pointed to the barred windows of the second story.

General Buell had his headquarters at Edgefield, and the army lay about the city, which had been formally surrendered to him by the mayor.

After a few days, when it was discovered that although we were "Yankees" we neither robbed nor murdered the citizens, stores and houses began to be opened and women appeared in the streets.

How they despised us! The people about the country were secesh of the bitterest kind, and it seemed utterly impossible for them to express their detestation of us. To the women especially, the sight of a Union soldier was gall and wormwood. I was on the street one day, and saw a poor sick fellow in the Federal blue tottering along in the sunshine, supporting himself with a stick, when a handsomely dressed woman passed. She flirted her garments as she neared him and made such a breadth of skirt, that, endeavoring to get out of the way, he set his cane on her flounce. She felt the strain ere he could remove it, and, turning like a tigress, snatched her garment from his reach with,

"Don't make a door-mat of my dress, you hungry-looking caitiff, you."

The poor fellow trembled and said not a word, but I laughed aloud derisively.

Lieutenant F—— was passing an elegant mansion one morning; two women were standing at one of the windows, and a servant was sweeping the hall. The younger woman, as she saw him coming, took the dust-pan from the negro girl, and leaned out and emptied it upon him, muttering something about "mud-sills" as she did so. He glanced up, quietly brushed off his coat and walked on. Of course these women were not "Southern ladies." Not so quietly as the lieutenant, however, did a private named Hays take such an insult. A female standing upon the steps of a house in the city spit upon him as he was sauntering along; he dashed up the steps, and, boxing her ears soundly, resumed his walk.

When the men teased him and good-naturedly flouted at his striking a woman, he scratched his head in perplexity and said:

"Well, as a general thing, 'taint becoming for a man to hit a woman, but, you see, my dander was riz, and when I git my ebenezer up for Uncle Sam I generally pitch in. 'Twas his soldier was insulted, not me."

We were six weeks in Nashville. I spent most of the time going about the city, which was a very handsome one, with beautiful gardens and cultivated grounds surrounding the houses. Often when I was sauntering about the children at play in the yards would call to each other, and standing at the gates or leaning on the fences would flaunt the "Stars and Bars" in my face, calling "Yankee, Yankee," after me. They did not fear me because I was a boy.

One morning John awoke me with,

"We have marching orders, Phil."

"Where do we go?"

"To reinforce General Grant."

Ere long we were on our way to Pittsburg Landing, a hundred and fifty miles from Nashville. The boys took to the road with a will, panting for the fight. All know how we reached there that Sunday afternoon. I wish I could tell you of those two days as others can—as John told me. The surprise—the desperate fighting. How the foe occupied our camp the first night. How the gun-boats saved us, and how the next day we drove the enemy on the road to Corinth.

We reached there just in time not to be too late. I can never forget the sight of those panic-stricken men clustering under the river bank. All night long our forces were crossing the river. The drenching rain came and we were without shelter. I wondered if the men felt as I did, a burning, gnawing impatience to do something, as they waited their turn to be transported over the river to the scene of action.

I sat with my back to a stump, under a great tree which threw wide its blasted limbs. Every now and then I would fall asleep, nod and start from my uncomfortable slumber, to shudder as I awoke to the realities which surrounded us.

Early in the morning we heard firing up the Corinth road. The battle had begun again. All day long until three o'clock in the afternoon it continued. Then the cry came that the rebels had given way. General Grant headed a charge of six regiments and drove the foe like sheep through our camp, which they had occupied the night before, the cavalry taking up the pursuit and following them towards Corinth.

Many boys with whom I have talked confused Shiloh, Pittsburg Landing and Corinth. Pittsburg Landing is a landing on the Tennessee river, in Tennessee; a road leads from this landing to Corinth, Mississippi, a distance, I think, of about twenty miles. It was at Corinth, at which is the junction of the Memphis and Charleston and the Mobile and Ohio Railroads, that the rebel army had assembled.

One of General Grant's camps was near Shiloh Church, a small log building in the woods between the Landing and Corinth; another was along the road leading from Pittsburg Landing to Corinth. The enemy attacked and surprised the camp at Shiloh on Sunday morning, April 5, 1862.

"These are terrible Sundays, Phil," John had said to me the night previous; I could but contrast them with our quiet ones at home; I told him so.

"God will bring good out of this dreadful evil," he replied, "hereafter *all* can enjoy just such Sundays, with their solemn bells and holy quiet."

Monday night fell upon our exhausted but victorious men. The din of battle was over. The rebel General Johnston was dead; our General Prentiss a prisoner. We were surrounded by the dead and dying, corpses strewed the country round.

Men with torches had gone out to search for their comrades. One missed a father, one a brother, another a friend. Were they dead, wounded, or taken prisoners? None knew. It was only through inquiry and searching they could find out.

I dreaded the sights I should see, but I could not keep away; so, though feeling feverish and sick, unable to eat, hot one moment and shivering the next, I joined a party which was making its way through the gray mud and slush. It was terrible. I shuddered as the lantern was turned on the faces of the dead, more ghastly in its light, and my head grew dizzy at the thought of the wounded who must spend the night amid such horrors.

We passed a pile of corpses. Looking back, I saw an arm moving feebly—"See! There, John, there!"

We stepped back; the arm swayed faintly. One, two,

three—half a dozen bodies were removed, and a poor fellow was found beneath them, who still breathed, but was wounded in the thigh and arm. The battle raged furiously where he fell, and he, fainting from loss of blood, was unable to move; his comrades, hurled back, had fallen upon him and he was buried beneath them. Our voices had reached his ear, but his parched lips could make no sound. Succeeding in extracting his whole arm he had made the feeble movement of his fingers which had attracted my attention and saved his life.

His first motion was for water, which he eagerly drank; this revived him, and he was carried to shelter, where his wounds, which were not mortal, were dressed.

Suddenly one of the men who had stooped over a body, turning its face to the light, said, "Thank God, 'tis father!" Tears rained down his sunburnt face, as they helped him to raise the old man whose white locks were dabbling in blood. The surgeon bent over him and put his hand on his heart.

"He lives," he said.

His head had rested in a little pool of blood and mud. A handkerchief was wet with whiskey and his face was wiped with it, and some of the liquor forced between his teeth; then he was carried to a stretcher and borne away. The surgeon thought he would recover.

"If I could only find Ned," said a youth of about twenty, who was searching for his brother.

"I will help you to look," John said; "let us go over there."

We heard Caton was missing and spent hours on the field looking for him, meeting party after party engaged also in looking up their friends. We saw nothing of Caton, and hoped he was a prisoner. Exhausted, shivering, my teeth chattering, although the night was warm, I at length went to camp, leaving John with the poor boy still searching for his brother. One of the surgeons, seeming ready to faint from exhaustion, stood drinking hot coffee from a tin cup, and answering the questions of some officers between each draught. I heard him, in a stifled voice and with tears in his eyes, tell the following :

"I was passing over the field," he said, "when a groan and cry came from a body I had stepped over and thought a corpse. I turned; the man was on his back and requested me to put him face up. As I did so I saw he was dying. I stooped to another near by, and while helping him, heard the dying man say : 'This is glory! this is glory!' Thinking it was said in bitterness and regret, I stepped back. 'What is glory?' I asked. He raised his arm feebly and pointed to the sky; ''Tis glory to die with my face upwards,' he whispered, and his breath left him."

I had wrapped my blanket about me and dropped to the earth to sleep, when a man near turned and said: "Captain Phil, Caton is dead; he fought like a tiger, and had a dozen bullets in him. We brought him in yonder." I got him to go with me to the spot. His comrades had washed his face, smoothed his hair and straightened him, intending to bury him on the morrow. His look was calm and sweet. I folded his arms across his breast and put my little flag in his hands; then dragged myself back. I was in a raging fever, and knew nothing that happened for several days; then I spoke to John of Caton. He told me they had buried him, and pointed to my flag, which was fastened above my head in the tent. Caton, he said, had loaded and was sighting to fire when he stepped over a poor rebel boy who begged piteously for water. He stooped and released his canteen to give him some. Just then our men fell back, and Caton stood erect to find himself in the midst of the foe. He was called upon to surrender and his reply was a bullet. The boy he had aided shouted to them " not to shoot him," but it was too late ; he was down. " His last act was a kind one," said John, " and he had determined never to be taken prisoner."

I was in the hospital for some weeks, and as soon as I was better John insisted that I should return home with one of the surgeons who was going. I went, and the change was good for me. In a little time I was as well as ever. I had promised John to enter school again, but it was so near the vacation they would not receive me.

John wrote me of the evacuation of Corinth, and told me of the eagle of the Eighth Wisconsin, which always preceded them to battle, and which the men believed could not be captured. It was there in our fight, side by side with the colors ; every exertion was made to take it by the command of the rebel general, but it screeched at them in derision and flapped its wings in their faces. It was no rebel bird.

John's division had marching orders and spent much time looking after railroads and guarding bridges. They went to Huntsville, Alabama, passing through Jacinta, Tuscumbia, Florence, etc., and camped at Battle Creek, thirty miles south of Chattanooga, on the Tennessee River. He described most of these places to me, and said there were Union men in all. That the old flag would sometimes make its appearance from the inside of feather beds and other hiding places where it had been stored for safety, and gladden their eyes ; but generally the people were either secesh themselves or afraid of their secesh neighbors. He gave me many interesting incidents of the contrabands, hundreds of whom were employed in camp, driving teams, fortifying, etc. He described the sight of them coming in in parties, with their children on their backs and their bundles in their hands, as sad, yet ludicrous. Eager for freedom, they had little idea what it meant—only knew it as no master, and no whipping.

He went into particulars concerning one man who had been a sort of valet and house servant, and had several times accompanied his master to the North. He was quick and intelligent; he came into camp mounted on his master's best riding horse, which he had "*borrowed*" for the trip. John pictured the fume of the owner who followed his "*chattels*" next day to recover them.

They were five weeks at Battle Creek, then started again for Nashville in pursuit of Bragg, who had got in their rear. What a race it was! They marched from Huntsville, Alabama, to Louisville, a distance of three hundred and seventy-eight miles, to find him still before them. Sore-footed, almost ragged, they hurried on, thinking to overtake him before he reached Louisville; but he turned aside and left them in the lurch.

In the meantime we had "a scare" at home.

Kirby Smith suddenly appeared in Kentucky, threatening Cincinnati; he seized Cynthiana, Frankfort and Lexington, having there defeated our troops, mostly raw volunteers. People said he was pushing on for the Ohio; that he had twenty thousand men and artillery; that he would burn Cincinnati and capture all the flour and bacon for the starving Confederacy.

The fall term of our school had just begun when the news came. Martial law was proclaimed by General Lew Wallace, who had done us such good service at Shiloh, and who was put in command of the city. All business was suspended, and citizens were ordered to report for duty. All the men, and the boys who were old enough, joined military companies and drilled every day, or were formed into working corps, to labor on the fortifications over the river, back of Covington. In a day or two the enemy's pickets were known to be within six miles of that city.

When the news first came there were no troops for defense, but everybody turned out. Some of our teachers went, as did several of the older boys, and Charley Thornley and I went with them. I had fastened my flag to the bed post, but I took it down, and Charley and I carried it in turn.

I never saw people so roused; the news spread like wildfire. Every train into the city came crowded with troops—the streets were alive with armed men. When the "squirrel hunters" came by hundreds, each armed with his own peculiar weapon, a sure marksman and certain of his prey, the enthusiasm and excitement was intense. The whole State was up and doing, with Indiana, headed by Governor Morton, to help.

The market houses were turned into eating places. Day and night they were supplied with hot coffee and provisions, which the ladies served to the regiments entering the city. A pontoon bridge was laid over the Ohio, and gun-boats plied the waters.

Charley and I were with the working brigades ordered to the trenches. Turning out by wards, they were organized and marched over the river. Such weeping and wailing! The streets on which we assembled were dense masses of human beings; wives and children had collected to bid farewell to their loved ones, as though they were never to see them again.

The rebel forces were within about a mile of Fort

Mitchell, but their pickets kept very quiet. Once only some skirmishing took place. I believe it was about the seventeenth of the month that they fell back to Florence, on the Lexington turnpike, some ten miles from Covington; here there was a skirmish between one of our scouting parties and about a hundred rebels, in which we killed some five or six of their men and wounded as many others, and put the rest to flight. We had one killed and one wounded. After this they retreated rapidly, destroying the railroad bridges on their route.

We were just one week at Fort Mitchell, which was on a hill commanding the Lexington turnpike; Charley and I enjoyed every hour of it, and were sorry when, the danger over, General Smith having retreated, we were ordered home.

Thus the "great scare" ended. We returned to the city in triumph, and had a welcome that cannot be described. The ladies brought their jewelry from their hiding places, and fished in their cisterns for the silver which had been dropped there, while the bankers called back their gold they had sent on a trip to the lakes, and all settled quietly down again.

Then came another excitement. General Bragg threatened Louisville. General Nelson called upon the citizens to turn out and defend their city, and remove the women and children. But this passed over—Bragg turned aside to the interior of Kentucky.

The next news I heard was that the ——th was at Louisville, and John sent for me to come to him there.

Once more I threw my books aside, put on the blue, and with knapsack and flag, prepared to join "our company."

CHAPTER XVII.

THE CHASE AFTER BRAGG.

THE day after I reached Louisville, the pursuit of Bragg was renewed.

John said: "You go with me, Phil. If you will rush into danger, it had better be where I can have an eye on you."

He alluded to our little service in Kentucky.

"You know you would not have had me do otherwise."

He smiled and shook his head.

"I am afraid I shall be obliged to let you enter the army, Phil, that you may learn how to obey orders. Do you really think you would like being a machine, with no will of your own, controlled entirely by the words of others?"

"If you call a soldier such a machine—I do."

"I have made up my mind, when you are seventeen you may do as you please, provided you let me have peace until that time."

"That is not very long to wait now," I replied. "If the war lasts I shall certainly go in, but only as a volunteer. I have no taste for the regular army; don't want to make a life business of it."

It was the first or second of October, 1862, that we again left Louisville. Bragg was ahead of us, and "the boys" were very anxious to get up to him and have a fight, which they thought would take place at Bardestown. The rebels, however, had a good start, and we did not come upon them until we reached Perryville, where we had a battle.

It was the 8th of October, I think, when we came in sight of the town. The enemy had determined to stand fire, so had posted themselves on the hills about a mile and a half back of the place ; had planted their batteries, and with everything in their favor, waited for us. Generals McCook, Mitchell and Rousseau commanded. The fight commenced in the forenoon, and lasted until night, about five hours. It was called a victory, but the men did not appear to rejoice much over it. Colonel Lytle, of the Tenth Ohio, was wounded, and for a time supposed to be among the dead, but the brave Tenth had still their gallant leader a little longer. He was acting brigadier that day, and John said he could never forget his heroic bearing. John felt very anxious about him until he ascertained his fate. They had been boys together and he was much attached to him.

Our colonel gave me a duty to perform for him which kept me at some distance, so I saw but little of the battle of Perryville.

After seeing to the dead and wounded we again started in pursuit of Bragg, who was again ahead of us, having "made tracks," as the boys said, directly after the defeat. We were nearing Salt River. I had often heard the phrase, " Going up Salt River." When one man wished to be severe on another, he would say, " I will row him up Salt River," or when a man was disappointed in getting an office he was said to be " sent up Salt River." I never knew the thing to be actually done, save by General Buell's army when in pursuit of Bragg.

The bridge over this stream had been destroyed, and the water was low, so it had to be forded, the skirmishers going ahead. As I stood on the river bank, and saw the long line of men winding down the hill-sides and plunging in the water, I thought they fully realized going over "Salt River."

On we went, pursuing the enemy through Kentucky. We passed camp Dick Robinson, which was in Garrard County. It was occupied by Federal troops, and was the home of Union men who had been compelled to go there for safety. Our course was in the direction of Cumberland Gap.

There was constant skirmishing in the advance. The rear of Bragg's army felled all the trees along the road to impede our progress; the pioneer corps were kept busy clearing the way.

The weather was unsettled and cold. One day we would have a rain which would seem to penetrate to the marrow, thoroughly chilling one. On the next would come a snow storm, accompanied by a driving wind, which brought the sleet right in our faces, almost blinding us, while it melted beneath our tread, making a soft, slushy mud through which we had to splash ankle deep. I must confess I wished myself at home during this march.

One evening, at the close of a very uncomfortable day, Smith and Jones saw cows feeding at a distance, across some fields which bordered the road.

"A drink of good warm milk would not be a bad thing, Sam." Jones pointed to the animals.

Smith nodded assent. They watched their opportunity, for orders against straggling were stringent, and, dropping behind, soon gained the field where the cows were. Smith could not milk. Jones sunk on one knee, and having no vessel to hold the fluid, milked into his mouth until he was satisfied, then offered to perform the same service for Smith, who dropped to the earth, and with his knees on the ground, his hands on his knees, and his mouth raised, was intent to catch every drop of the precious fluid which Jones was sending into it. They were both unconscious of the approach of any one, until a kick in the rear sent Smith spinning to some distance, the milk in his mouth nearly strangling him. Looking round they saw the colonel.

While Smith rubbed his hurt part, for the colonel's heel was of iron, Jones turned to that officer:

"Won't you take your turn, sir? It is mighty good."

"Good! you great calf!" Jones dodged the blow aimed at him. "If you are not in your places in the column in five minutes you will march the rest of the way tied to the tail of a wagon."

"We made tracks after that, you can bet on it," said Jones, when telling it. "I saw the colonel was only putting on mad. He was almost choking to keep from laughing at the figure Sam cut, on his knees, his mouth stretched from ear to ear, the milk dropping from the corners as from a puling baby's."

Many of the men were foot-sore, but I heard little complaining, although some were dispirited with their long marches and want of success.

Fording the streams was a most uncomfortable business for the infantry. I know I shuddered when we came to one.

At length we reached Wild Cat Mountains and followed them to the top, then the pursuit was given up, much to the mortification of the troops. Bragg was allowed to escape from Kentucky with all his baggage and almost his entire army.

For nearly a year they had been chasing, first Buckner, then Bragg, and now, discouraged and mortified, after a short halt were ordered to move in the direction of Nashville, which was threatened by the enemy.

It was the 2d of November when we arrived in front of that city, and went into camp, where we remained for nearly two months. Thanksgiving followed not long after we were settled, and we thoroughly enjoyed it.

General Buell was removed, and a new chief, Major-General Rosecrans, was appointed, and now commanded the Fourteenth Army Corps.

Nashville was girdled by our tents, which circled it in front, covering the hills and extending out on the Murfreesboro', Nolensville and Franklin roads, to the distance of eight or nine miles.

I went frequently into the city, which was fortified on all sides. Most of the beautiful houses were shut up or occupied by the Federal officers as quarters. General Rosecrans was located in one of the handsomest of these dwellings. The city looked as though nothing but war had ever been carried on in it; soldiers filled the avenues, banners hung in the air, cavalry galloped through the streets, and cannon rolled over the stones and frowned on you from the fortresses, while barricades stopped your progress. Almost every woman you saw wore mourning, and looked at you as though you had caused her woe.

One day early in December, John went out with a foraging party, over the ground which lay between our camp and the enemy's. They had seized a quantity of corn and were preparing to return with it, when a company of rebel cavalry came in sight and attacked them. They had to fight, and, after a short skirmish, came off victorious, thanks to a detachment of artillery which had accompanied them. These skirmishes took place every day, and the men liked the excitement.

One day I was in Nashville, where I had been sent on an errand to the quartermaster's department, and saw one of the oddest sights imaginable.

A band came through the streets playing the "Rogue's March," and following it were some forty-five or fifty men, their heads ornamented with funny white cotton night-caps, trimmed with red flannel. They were accompanied by a guard.

I was told it was a punishment inflicted by order of General Rosecrans because they had been guilty of the cowardice of surrendering to the rebels without striking a blow. Some of them seemed to feel the disgrace, others looked sullen ; some again as if they did not care at all.

On the 24th of December orders came to march next morning. The men rent the air with their shouts, and joked each other as to the Christmas gifts to be expected, preparing with glee as though for a frolic. Their joy was short-lived, however, for that very evening, when all was in readiness, and the chances of the morrow were under discussion, the order was countermanded.

With murmurs of discontent and mutterings of "another Kentucky campaign," all sought to forget disappointment in sleep, and be ready to spend Christmas in camp.

CHAPTER XVIII.

MURFREESBORO'.

CHRISTMAS, with its thoughts of home, was over. The next morning the army began to move. Lieutenant B—— had captured several horses from the rebels. One of these he purchased from the quartermaster and presented to John; he gave it to me, saying that I could keep and use it, provided my so doing involved little expense, and no trouble to any but myself. The horse was a small black one, with a close cut mane and tail, which gave him a bobbed appearance; but he went like the wind and was hardy and tough. I called him Lightfoot.

Full of my acquisition I forgot John's orders, and several times in my eagerness to display my new friend ventured further in the advance than I should have done. Once I was in the midst of General McCook's Division, which had taken the Nolensville pike, when a smart skirmish took place, in which eight or ten men were killed. The whizzing of the bullets about my head quickened my recollection of John's injunction to keep near him, and I moved in his direction at a rapid rate. Our division had taken the Murfreesboro' road, while General Thomas's was on the Franklin pike.

The men were in excellent spirits, eager for the work, and sure they would route the Graybacks long ere they reached Murfreesboro'. The officers said there was a bitterness in their speech and action very different from the feeling displayed in the beginning at Bull Run.

Christmas had been a soft, mild day, but about an hour after our march began the rain came down on us and continued steadily, penetrating everything.

John's company was in the rear of our brigade. The front was far ahead, and the constant firing heard from that point told of some sharp skirmishing. The men commented on this, and fought the cedars in the way to keep their hands in. One broad-shouldered six-footer from an Illinois prairie was particularly anxious to get along, and restive at the sound. Every now and then he gave his trowsers an impatient hitch and clutched his rifle with a more determined grasp. Evidently all his life he had been on his own hook, and restraint galled him.

"Hear the cusses," he would say, as the sounds reached him. "Leftenant, can't we git ahead?"

At one juncture, when the firing was brisker, he cried out: "I'd like to have a hand in sending their souls a-kiting."

"You had better pray for them; they have wives and children at home," said a middle-aged class-leader from Michigan or Wisconsin, who had fallen back and was trying to regain his place.

"That's the best we know of them; no harm meant, it's my way of talking, only let's git shut of them." Then eyeing his rebuker from head to foot with a keen side glance—"May be you're the chaplain, stranger? If so, you've a mighty big contract on hand, praying for their souls while we punish their bodies; but you look as if you might be a fighting parson."

The road was bad, through forest and cedar brakes, and our progress slow. I wished to gallop on, but John would not permit it. Poor Frank Hanson was brought to the rear, killed, and several others also who were wounded. The men looked soberly after them as they were borne past, and struck up " Jordan is a Hard Road to Travel."

Our corporal hurt his thigh so that he could not walk. John offered him my horse, which he thankfully accepted, and I bade adieu to Lightfoot, and took my place again in the ranks beside John, who was not mounted.

"You'll find Jordan indeed a hard road to travel, Captain Phil," said Jones, slapping me on the shoulder as I fell in step before him.

"To tell the truth, I am not sorry you had to resign your four-footed friend, Phil; he was likely to take you into trouble. I have been thinking for the last hour that permitting you to have him was not the most judicious thing I ever did," was John's remark.

I sang loudly for a few moments to drown my disappointment, then in the excitement of the march forgot it. Very tired that night, I slept soundly.

We were late next day taking to the road. In the evening we reached Stewart's Creek just in time to save the bridge, which had been set on fire. Here we bivouacked, and stayed till Monday morning; thanks to General Crittenden who, I was told, opposed the Sunday march. He said he thought it best to be on the right side of the Master above, as we were soon to go into battle and perhaps to appear before Him. All enjoyed the Sunday rest. I saw our Methodist and Illinois friend sitting on a log in close confab; I drew John's attention to them. He said the prairie man's name was Job Smith; he belonged to his company, and was a character. The other he did not know. John and I had a good talk on Sunday. I saw he was trying to prepare me for the worst; he took my Bible and wrote these verses in it :

> " Lowly and solemn be
> Thy children's cry to Thee,
> Father Divine :
> A hymn of suppliant breath,
> Owning that life and death
> Alike are thine.
>
> Tremblers beside the grave,
> We call on Thee to save,
> Father Divine :
> Hear, hear our suppliant breath:
> Keep us in life and death
> Thine, only thine."

The next day we crossed the creek and continued on the pike. There was sharp fighting on the front. In expectation of a general engagement, John ordered me to keep with the teams, so I fell to the rear. We were close on to Murfreesboro' ; in sight of the enemy's intrenchments ; could hear them plainly at night. Things looked serious ; the men were earnest and expectant ; so we proceeded until the 31st.

The pioneers were engaged cutting roads through the cedars for the teams ; all was bustle and preparation, putting things in position for battle. I did not see John all day Tuesday ; slept at night on one of the wagons ; and was roused in the morning long before it was light with preparations for an attack.

Anxious, restless, excited, my only thought was of John ; he might be wounded—killed ; I had not seen him for so many hours. It was necessary constantly to remind myself of his command, and my promise to stay in the rear, to keep from the advance. It was hard, very hard, when I saw boys but little older than myself exultant in the thought of the conflict. I began to feel my brother had required too much of me.

The roar of battle began. Word reached us that

McCook's Division had given way. Ere long, crashing through the cedar brakes, dashing forward, came fugitives from that corps ; two or three at first, followed by numbers, filled with consternation and alarm. The rebels were at their heels. The teamsters looked eagerly into each other's faces ; hangers-on mounted their horses ; the guard adjusted their arms and waited expectantly, while the routed men passed on.

A little while and a staff-officer made his appearance with an order ; I edged close to him to listen to what he said. He was in a state of wild enthusiasm. General Rosecrans had stationed his forces between the track and the pike ; masked his batteries ; the ranks had received the fugitives as they came ; opened, let them through, and closed like veterans. The pursuing rebels, supposing they had the road clear to Nashville, were shooting them down like squirrels. Our masked batteries opened upon them; they were struck with astonishment; paused; made an ineffectual resistance; wheeled—the tables were turned.

While we rejoiced over this, told in hurried sentences, a shower of bullets suddenly whizzed about our ears. The old indescribable feeling came over me ; I dodged. I felt that the next shot must certainly carry off an arm or leg ; then came the desperate conclusion that, boy as I was, I must stand up to it any how ; I was covered with shame at the idea of feeling like a coward. A dashing, a clashing, another volley ; demands to surrender ; and we were captured. A party had come upon our rear—we were prisoners. With blank, astonished faces, the men recognized the fact. The rebels rummaged the wagons ; jeered us, and claimed a complete victory over all our forces. Time passed slowly by. Another sudden discharge of musketry, confusion and strife—the teams were recaptured by our men—we were free.

News from the front told of disaster and a fearful loss of officers. Divisions had to fall back for want of ammunition. While we waited the turn of events, the men speculating on the result, straining eyes and ears for information, or joking and telling little incidents of their recent capture, I tried to learn something concerning John; I questioned all who would answer me. One said he was in the reserve; another thought him a prisoner; while a third knew his regiment was engaged—one statement contradicted the other. In a state of wearing uncertainty, feeling really ill from anxiety, I went aside and seated myself against a tree.

I had been there but a very little while when I saw a squad of rebel cavalry dashing across some fields. They fired as they came, and in a few minutes were on us. Resistance was useless; they outnumbered the guard two to one. An officer with a bright red head of hair commanded them. Riding up to a quartermaster, who shone in a new suit of clothes, he held a pistol to his head with,

"Your cap?" The cap was resigned.

"Your coat!" Slowly it was drawn off.

"Your watch!" This demand produced a remonstrance, which was cut short by the rejoinder,

"Another word and I will blow your brains out!" The watch followed the coat.

"Your pantaloons!" Reluctantly and with an indescribable look the inexpressibles came off amid shouts of laughter from the Graybacks.

"Your boots!" The chivalric Southerner held one in his grasp his hand outstretched for the other, when a yell from a group of teamsters, and a whiz of balls from a little distance caused him to turn in his saddle—our friends were at the rescue.

The quartermaster understood the state of things in

a moment, and danced around in his drawers, vest and stockings in a most ludicrous manner, brandishing his boot and shrieking frantically: "Shoot that red-headed scoundrel; shoot him, I say; down with the thief!" Attracted by his mad gestures, a stout trooper spurred to the rebel's side, seized his horse's rein, thrust a pistol in his face, and bade him surrender himself a prisoner. With one glance around, the officer yielded his arms.

Springing forward like a tiger cat, the quartermaster seized a revolver from one near, and, holding it to the breast of the rebel, jerked out with spasmodic contortions: "My cap, my coat, my watch, my pantaloons, my boots," making him deliver them one by one, and jumping frantically at each piece as it was presented. The spectators were convulsed with laughter; the quartermaster shouldered his wardrobe and sought a more convenient space to dress in, muttering not very amiably the while, and the rebel officer was put under guard with the other prisoners.

This game of capturing and recapturing was played so often during the day, that in the evening one of the teamsters, in mortal terror, with downcast eyes, trembling limbs, and slow steps, dragging his "snake" after him, sought a sergeant and inquired which side he belonged to. When told he was still in the Federal service he made his "snake" ring again as he cracked it around his head and went off rejoicing.

Various and contradictory were the reports of the conflict which reached us. Prisoners were sent back, ambulances arrived with the wounded. At one time they told us our artillery was all captured; at another, that we were driving all before us. Night, however, came at last, and with it the certainty that our forces had not been driven back; but there was mention of fearful loss in officers and men. If not a defeat, it was no victory.

"A pretty figure we'll cut in an official report," said one of McCook's men.

"The truth is," said another, talking to a group, "we were whipped; but General Rosecrans did not know he was whipped, and he would not stay whipped."

I could hear nothing of John; it was the first time since the beginning of the war that we had been separated for so long a time. In a state of utter exhaustion I lay down and slept soundly.

An order came the next morning for the train to advance, which it did. I heard of John; he was ahead. Towards evening I reached him. He hugged me close when we met, saying: "Thank God, Phil, we are safe after such a terrible day."

John was on duty near the river, and sent me to a less exposed position. There was some fighting, but it did not amount to much. John had a horse killed under him.

The next day there was a terrible conflict. General Crittenden's corps was engaged. The firing was deafening; the dead lay in heaps; the enemy was driven back almost to Murfreesboro'. Part of the forces crossed the river in the rain, mud, and darkness, and occupied the heights. Amid all this blood and slaughter I was thankful and happy as I lay that night beside John in our bed of mud, with no shelter from the rain, which fell steadily, for my *all* was unharmed and near me. John was almost exhausted, but he talked to me before we slept—told me something of the battle.

"If I did not know it was for God and the right, Phil, I could not stand it," he said in conclusion. I was wakeful and restless, and lay for a long time watching the camp fires gleaming in the darkness; the forms that moved athwart them appeared like demons in the lurid light. It brought to mind Dante's Hell, which I had read to John the winter before. I thought over everything—our father, our mother; I could feel their presence almost. How their spirits must rejoice over John! Lieutenant G—'s words came to me in speaking of him: "A Christian soldier, doing his duty for God and his country."

Not far from us lay an officer with his feet to the fire. He arose in the night to kick the brands together; a voice from the mud, at a little distance, hailed him as he stood in the light——

"Halloo, Joe, is that you?"

"Why yes, Jim; were you in the fight?"

"No; the rascals captured my ammunition train; my horse's legs saved me. Heard from home lately?"

"About a fortnight since, all were well."

"It's a little damp."

"Slightly."

They sought the earth again. They were brothers, and it was the first time that they had met for more than eighteen months.

On Saturday it was dark, gloomy, and rainy—a dreadful day. The men appeared serious and depressed, notwithstanding their victory. There was a sharp contest up the Murfreesboro' road. The rain and the state of the earth made it almost impossible to move. The pickets were firing all day; two of John's company were wounded while on that duty.

Our men had an antipathy to being handled by the rebels after death. "Don't let them put me under ground," you would hear them say, speaking of the chances of their being killed. Passing a spot where the carnage had been greatest, we saw a man near some bushes stooping over another and trying to raise him. We drew near, and found it was Job Smith; the person he was trying to aid was the one they called the "class-leader," and he was dead. Job turned as he heard us.

"He's gone where *they* daren't show their faces. You'll just help me to put the earth over him, won't you? He had a mighty soul." He raised himself and wiped his face with his sleeve. I saw his right arm was in a sling and bandaged.

"You see I got hurt. I had kind of taken a liking to him there. He told me his history—how he was wild in his youth, but he got converted at a big meeting, when the Lord made His presence known amid the prayers and the psalms—how he married and had five children. Then the war came, and he thought he must come and fight these ——. I speak hard," he lowered his voice and checked himself, "but I mean no harm."

"Well, the wife and children tugged at his heart-strings; he did not know what to do, so he prayed on it—and he came. He warn't dead when I found him; he pinted to his mouth; was parched for water. He had lain here since Wednesday, with all the rain on him; just dragged himself to this clump. It's wonderful how wounded men will try to get to any stump or stick near, as though there was shelter in it." Job wiped his face again. "'I've tried to do my duty. It's a righteous cause. Be true to it, friend; fight on, and trust in God's mercy.' These were his last words."

Job paused a moment. "I ain't of much account in this fix"—he touched his arm—"but I'll give any man a month's pay who'll help me put him decent under ground."

They dug his grave where he lay. Job took his watch,

memorandum book, and some other things from his pocket for his wife.

"I promised to see she got these, and to tell her to trust in God. If the Graybacks let my soul loose before I git a chance, why some comrade who writes a better fist than I do will let her know about it," he said, as, stooping over the dead man, he sawed a lock of his iron-gray hair from his head with his pocket-knife, and laid it reverently between the leaves of the book.

The dead lay in all conceivable positions; most of them had quiet, serene faces, as though they had died with their heads upon their mothers' breasts. We saw in one place the gray locks of a man of sixty dabbling in the same pool with the fair curls of a boy of eighteen, and both wore a smile. Yet there were many who had died hard; whose faces were yet distorted and drawn, even in the peace of death. I had seen enough. Fatigue, excitement, and fasting—for I had been unable to eat any breakfast within the sight of so much blood and the horrors of that battlefield—overcame me—I fainted.

I was lying by the camp fire when our corporal came up.

"Much obliged for your horse, Captain Phil, but I do not think I shall want to borrow him again; he liked to have been the death of me."

"How?"

"I had crossed some fields, and coming to a house which stood in an out-of-the-way locality stopped for a drink. In answer to my 'halloo,' a couple of little niggers made their appearance. One of them exclaimed, as soon as he caught sight of me: 'Golly, Jake, here's one of Linkin's soldiers on massa's bob-tailed black.' Almost at the same moment the door of the house opened and two rebel soldiers presented themselves. Both fired, but by good luck neither of them hit me. I put spurs to bobtail, and they mounted horses, which must have been hidden in the rear of the house, and after me. We had a hard ride, but I had the advantage. Reaching a clump of trees, I kept their shelter while I gave them a volley. One of them was hit in the shoulder and stopped; the other came on, sending a bullet through my hat, and showering patches of mud on me; but his horse stumbled on the ploughed ground and nearly threw him, and when I reached the road and looked behind he had turned back."

A private who lay near and heard this, laughed and said: "Not long ago we were out after horses, and came to that very house. We seized that black, and I was leading him away when a very pretty girl made her appearance, and going up to the animal threw her arms around its neck, caressed and patted it as though it had been human, cried, and begged the officer in command not to take 'her horse—her own riding horse, given her by her father. No one had ever mounted him but herself. She had had him so long it would distress her dreadfully to part with him.'

"The lieutenant was not tear-proof; he could not stand it; ordered me to let the horse go. She seized its bridle, bowed, smiled, and was profuse in her thanks, but there was a wicked gleam in her eye as we rode off. The very next day, in a skirmish, Lieutenant B—— captured that horse and its rider, as ugly a customer, in the way of a rebel, as you would wish to see."

The enemy had evacuated Murfreesboro'; our cavalry were in pursuit. The infantry did not move. We had lost such a number of horses that it crippled us; the artillery could not be forwarded; heaps of carcasses cumbered the battle-ground. The business of the hour was caring for the wounded and burying the dead.

Thus ended our week of battles.

CHAPTER XIX.

AFTER THE BATTLE.

THE first opportunity I had I returned to the battle-field. With all its horrors it had a fascination I could not resist. I might be of some service; might give help or water to some poor mangled fellow dying alone. When I thought of the wounded exposed to yesterday's dreadful weather I shuddered.

A squad detailed to look after such were talking of a soldier they had buried, who proved to be a woman. They then spoke of the young scout, Frank Martin, who was badly shot in the chest, and who, they said, was a woman. She belonged to the Second East Tennessee Cavalry, had entered Nashville with the regiment, having joined it some time previously. No one suspected she was not a boy until she was wounded and her shirt was opened by the surgeon. They lauded her bravery in the highest terms.

I had seen Frank once. She had been out scouting, and was on horseback before the general's tent awaiting orders, when I stopped to look at her. She was slight, and looked young; had reddish hair and blue eyes, and made a pretty-looking boy. She had borne all the hardships of this campaign without a murmur, although it had tried veterans; had waded Stone River with the troops, and had been the bravest among braves.

This brought Joseph to my mind, and I told them her story.

"Just like a woman," said one. "Cross her and she is the devil. You might as well try to turn that river up stream as to try to stop a woman when she is in love."

"Frank is under guard, to be sent home," said another; "though it's no use; they might as well let her alone; she is bound to have her way, and she'll enlist in some other regiment."

"There are more women in this army than we know," continued the first speaker. "There's that one from Michigan. I kept guard with her many times. I'd as soon have thought my mother a man as she a woman. She did not flinch at anything. She stood the rain and cold, and kept picket guard as well as the best of us; smoked, chewed, swore, and drank whiskey, for all the world like a man, and a fast one too. Here the other day her husband was killed in the ranks right before her face, and she kept ahead, stepped over his dead body, and charged the rebs."

"She's a tough one. I don't care for that sort. Her being a woman is only a mistake. It's the Frank Martins who make me wonder and think there's something wrong."

"Take care, don't tread on that chap, he is alive."

They raised him; he was gasping his last. In a moment or two they laid him down; he was dead.

Beside him was a Graycoat, with whom he had evidently been in conflict. The man in charge stooped over him.

"Here, comrades, this poor fellow is in a bad fix; but there's life left: for how long God only knows. Bring the stretcher this way; we will let the surgeon see him as soon as may be; and, Dan, you give him some water. Fulfill Scripture, and do good to your enemy for once."

On we went, hour after hour. Near noon we saw, close

to the swamp, among many still forms clad in blue and gray, an old man evidently dying. He had half raised himself from his bed of mud and gore, and, leaning on his elbow, was propped by the dead body of a comrade, his head bowed upon his breast. There was a deep wound in the head, another in the chest.

One gave him some brandy. After a few moments he revived and muttered indistinctly.

"What is that he says; it is a name," and the man kneeled down to listen.

"Do you know Harry L——s?"

"No."

"Some more." He pointed to the brandy flask.

They raised his head and poured a little in his mouth. After several efforts he swallowed it. Seeing he was dying, the men began to prepare to leave him to attend others who needed their services more. He observed the movement, and, clutching with his hand, whispered: "Don't."

"Will you stay with him, Captain Phil? It will only be for a little while; but he may have something to say. He is an old man and must have a family."

I assented, and they left me.

He muttered to himself. Occasionally I could catch words. "Harry,"—"not fire at his old father,"—"Lucy—forgive him—Yankees." Then he opened his eyes; they seemed quick and bright. He glanced round in a startled way, rested them a moment on me, and closed them again. I gazed at the signs of the battle around me and waited the end.

A sort of breast-work had been made of the limbs and tops of trees, torn by shell and ball from the neighboring forest, and behind this a squad of rebels had fought. Before me a shell had exploded, killing several horses and scattering the earth in all directions. One man had lost his head by it, and his body lay straight in death, his right arm thrown up as if to protect his face. Several had sought the shelter of these branches to die. One had printed his name in the mud beside him; another had his red cotton handkerchief over his face. While I gazed two officers appeared a little way off. I recognized them as John and Lieutenant Thomas Murdock, and gladly hailed them.

John opened the old man's shirt, while Lieutenant Murdock wet his handkerchief and bathed his face. The brandy he had swallowed had taken effect; he raised his head and sat upright. After one or two gasps he made a motion to his breast. John drew forth his watch; he nodded assent, and tried to reach a pocket in his shirt. John aided him, and produced a small memorandum or pocket-book, between the leaves of which were several letters addressed to Henry L——s. The pocket-book had the same name in it, added to which was: "Georgie, send them." He fell back, closed his eyes, and murmured several indistinct words. Presently we made out "Home," — "My God," — "My heaven," — "My all." His mind wandered.

"Sing,

'When I can read my title clear,'

Phil," said John, who had been stooping over him, "he is trying to repeat it."

I began it. He opened his eyes and worked his hands feebly together until he got them clasped.

"Kneel beside him," said John, "he hears you; but he is going fast."

His eyes followed me as I dropped and sang close to his ear. He tried to raise himself. Lieutenant Murdoch lifted him in his arms. He gasped—a hollow sound came from his throat. I stopped.

"Sing on louder, Phil."

I continued. Gradually his eyes became fixed. As I gave the last line,

"Across my peaceful breast,"

there was a sigh; his head fell on one side; he was dead.

John stooped, as Lieutenant Murdoch laid him down, and cut a lock of his gray hair from his head, placing it in one of the letters. As he raised himself he said: "He is old enough to be our father, Phil, and we will bury him as tenderly as though he was."

We left him and moved on over the field, rendering what assistance we could. We chanced upon an Irishman belonging to Company K, who was desperately wounded. He was begging for a priest. We knew not where to find one just then. He piteously bemoaned that he had not been baptized, and implored that it might be done for him. John told him he believed, in his Church, in case of emergency any one might baptize a dying man, and offered to perform the rite for him. He gladly assented.

Taking from his watch chain a little jet cross he had worn for years, he put it in the wounded man's hands. We took off our caps, standing uncovered, while John, making the sign of the cross, first upon the man's breast then upon his forehead, went through the usual formula.

He was evidently much relieved; but he did not die. In a very short time he was again in the ranks doing good service. When he restored the little jet cross to John on regaining the regiment, he said: "May the holy Mary keep you, leftenant, and if the devil ever cheats me into going into battle again without the blessed sacrament, he'll be a smart devil, that's all."

I picked up the photograph of an old lady, whose son must have worn it on his person. One of the men had quite a collection of letters procured in the same way—a lock of long light curly hair was in the envelope of one of them. He also had a pocket handkerchief with "Mary" embroidered on it.

We approached one place where the battle had raged terribly—a heap of dead told of the nature of the strife; a soldier who stood near us stooped and turned the face of a corpse at his feet, upwards.

"It is one of the color guard of the T—th, poor fellows! the whole eight were killed gallantly fighting in defense of the flag; they determined it should not fall into the hands of the enemy. Emory carried it through, although he was desperately wounded."

On our way to the pike, crossing the cotton-field we encountered dead men, mules and horses, fragments of artillery, carriages, caissons and accoutrements lying in heaps together, their disposition showing the fierceness of the fight. We met two men carrying in a wounded rebel, who had dragged himself to the shelter of a cedar thicket where he had lain since Friday. They paused for a moment to rest and I stepped up to look at him. His face was strangely familiar, but I could not place it. As they lifted him again he opened his eyes. He was Morris, Carrie's brother, who had taken me prisoner in Virginia. I told John of my discovery. He followed the men who had him in charge to the hospital tent where the surgeons were operating, saw he was made as comfortable as possible until his turn came to be examined, after which he meant that all attention should be paid him.

John and Lieutenant Murdoch were talking of Mike, the Irishman whom John had baptized, when the lieutenant said: "My brother James, who is ordnance officer in General Johnson's division, told me of a singular thing he saw a few days since."

"He was riding with some others in the direction of Murfreesboro', when they came upon a dead rebel lying close to the road. One of the party alighted and went forward to examine him; in a moment he called the others to come near; they did so, and saw tattooed upon the dead rebel's breast, from which the shirt had been removed, a perfect representation of the crucifixion, the cross, the Saviour, the women and the crowd, their faces distinct, and right through the center of the cross, piercing the breast of the Saviour, had gone a minie ball, clean—leaving no jagged edges. It was so remarkable that the body was ordered to be taken in for others to see it, but when those charged with the office went for it, it was no longer there."

They spoke of the week which had passed, and Lieutenant Murdoch, who had acted as aid to General Van Cleve, described the fortunes of those days in the most enthusiastic manner.

"I thought all was lost and I hoped a shot would kill me, as in desperate, sullen silence we awaited orders—powerless, watching what we believed to be the entire rout of the army—not a word was spoken.

"The batteries were massed, the life or death of the army hung on the issue. Our eyes were fixed upon the woods, where the enemy must come out; they were making a *détour* to reach us—would they come within range of our batteries? Suddenly with wild yells they swarmed forth. There was a cloud of lurid flame—smoke—the swoop of shot and grape, the whistling of balls, the whirring shriek of shells, the crash of shivering trees, groans, cries, then an instant's silence.

"Had we gained an advantage? A shrill shout told of triumph; another, then there was a charge, and heaps of mangled forms cumbered the ground, and shrieking fugitives, flying from the hurtling fire, proclaimed the tide had turned.

"We scarcely breathed as this passed before us, but when we saw the scattered host we turned our faces in congratulation to each other, and were not ashamed that they were wet with tears; they were our Thanksgiving."

I was not sorry to hear that our trains were up, as we had been rather short of provision the last twenty-four hours, and the men were anxious for their rations. I took my meal with Lieutenant Murdoch and John. Several times the recollection of what I had seen made me faint and sick, and I found I had not yet become inured to the sights of a battlefield.

Just before sunset I saw Private D—— walking towards the place where his company had their quarters with something in his arms, which he was carrying tenderly. Curious to know if he had found a baby, I made my way to him. It was a dog having hair of a beautiful shiny black. The private had come across him on the battlefield whining beside his dead master. The dog's leg had been broken by a shot, and his tail carried away. D—— had splintered and bound up his leg, and avowed his intention to take care of him, having already named him Rosy.

I saw John coming from the hospital. He had been to inquire for Morris. The surgeon told him fever had set in and there was little hope for him. He did everything for him that could be done, but he never recognized me, and died in a few days, delirious. John took charge of his few things, and wrote a long letter to his mother, after seeing him decently buried and putting a head board at the grave.

While we were talking Colonel Kennett passed. "There is a gallant Cincinnatian," said John, "none did better service during our week of battles. Philip, did you know General Garfield had been appointed Chief of Staff in place of the gallant Garaché. Ohio may indeed be proud of her sons; they are as brave in battle as they are wise in council."

CHAPTER XX.

CONTRABANDS IN CAMP.

"WONDER what de ginrel's arter now; no good 'ill come on it," growled a voice in the midst of the joyful clamor which greeted the announcement that we were to move at daylight on Christmas morning.

"What are you grumbling for, you piece of polished ebony? think your skin in danger, do you? I tell you what it is, if the rebels catch you they will broil you alive before your time comes; move along; see that the fire is kept up, and put some elbow grease on my musket. There will be precious little sleep in the Fourteenth Army Corps to-night, I can tell you."

"Some on us 'ill sleep our last, I reckon. Plenty more days in de year to mobe b'sides dat on which our bressed Lord was born. Christmas good as Sunday anyhow, I guess. The ginrel's mighty pertickler to do nuffin on the Sabbef day, but de very best day ob all he makes dis whole army shuffle. No good 'ill come on it, see ef it do —dis nigger knows."

Then as the echo of the cheers with which the news had been received reached him from the distant ridges, "De men holler as ef dey was agwine to a dance. Yah, some ob dem dance t' nudder tune 'fore long."

Ned dragged himself off, and was soon seen polishing his master's musket, mumbling to himself as he rubbed, and evidently ill at ease.

"What do de leftenant tink ob dis move, Captin Phil?" he inquired of me a few minutes later.

"He likes it—is anxious to get ahead."

"'Twont do; de debil's got a hand in it; de Lord will smite us like de Philistines. I know'd somethin' was a gwine wrong"—an ominous shake of the head—"I dreampt ob crabs last night—sure sign ob ill luck."

"Were they going backward?" I laughed, and he gave no answer. "What is your objection to to-morrow, Uncle Ned?"

"'Jection! I'd like to know ef all the Christians don't keep Christmas? even niggers has a holiday den; but de ginrel's a Catholic."

"Catholics think as much of Christmas as any of us, but the general believes the movement necessary."

"We'll see, we'll see," and still shaking his head he left me.

A few hours later his face was radiant. The order to march had been countermanded. He rubbed his hands and laughed heartily at the disappointed men, who, irritated at his rejoicing, kicked at his shins in passing.

"Bress de Lord, you'se got dem dar feet to kick wid, and don't hab to tramp on dem to you're deaf t'-morrow! I tought the ginrel hab more good sense and 'ligion, too; 'new Father Trecy hab anyhow."

"I tell you what 'tis, Captin Phil"—he joined me as I left the tent—"I'se gwine to improve de 'casion. I'll gib de niggers sumthin' to think on t'-morrow; dey'll show de whites ob dar eyes."

"Are you to preach, Ned?"

"Yes, Captin Phil; I's 'vited to gib a sermon in de woods; de 'ristocracy 'mong de Union cullud pussons is comin' from de city."

" 'That is the reason you were so anxious we should not move to-morrow ? "

"No, sar. I didn't think you'd 'pune my motifs." He spoke with considerable dignity. "De Ole Massa ob us all ub dar "—he took off his old ragged cap and pointed upward—" will hab His days kept. Dis army could 'spect no victory ef it move on de day he was born ; He Prince of Peace. Ef de niggers don't sing de Star ob Beflehem with loud hallayluyas dis Christmas den dey know nuffin. Yah, dey know de day ob jubilee hab come."

With his thumb to his nose Ned walked off.

While at Bowling Green the officers wanted a cook, and, recommended by one of the teamsters, Ned had offered, and was accepted by the mess. He accompanied us to Nashville, and while there requested that they would take his son as his substitute, as he wished to enter the service of an officer who needed a servant.

He was about forty years of age, and had all the negro characteristics ; was shrewd, quick, cunning, very religious and superstitious. He had been a slave, and hated his former condition with an intensity I never saw any other negro display. A Methodist minister, he had great influence among his people, was eloquent after his manner. Some of our men had heard him and pronounced him a " great preacher." It was suspected that he wished to be near the officers to pick up all the information possible ; for he generally knew all that was going on.

"Dandy Jim," also a servant, was envious of the notice taken of Ned, and in answer to John's question one day, as to whether the blacks did not think a great deal of him, said : "Yes, sir, the Southern niggers seem to set some value on him ; they can understand him. For my part I am not used to their kind of talk. I was brought up among Northern whites, and slave language is new to me; I cannot say I am much edified by Brother Watson's preaching."

John laughed and said, when Jim got out of hearing: "Human nature is a queer thing, Phil. That is a well-educated, well-behaved, well-spoken mulatto, yet I do not believe there is a man in the company who has not more confidence in Ned; perhaps it is that we feel the one is real, the other an imitation."

Ned justified the liking all had for him. His son was murdered by the rebels, and it was touching to see him when he found the body. One moment he would cry over the cold form, and the next—"Bress the Lord! he hab died in a good cause—'twas all he had, and de good Massa was—was—welcome to him."

"He died free, Ned," said one of the boys.

"Yes, massa, and in de battle for de free." This thought seemed to console him. He had great admiration for Colonel Moody, and often wished he was in his regiment. He called him "de Lord's Captin." I saw him on the battle-field helping the wounded, and one of the privates reported that he saw him raise a dying man in his arms and sing Canaan for him, the tears running down his cheeks the while.

Ben was another of the "institution" who afforded me amusement. His face was round, polished as ebony and quite as black; his body crowned with an immense head, covered with mixed black and white wool; his eyes were quick and bright, his mouth like a cannon, filled with perfect rows of ivory teeth; his nose flat and broad; his figure short, stout and humped. He had long lean arms finished with hands like claws, while his bandy legs started from the center of his thin splay feet and rocked in their sockets, giving his body a rollicking motion which made you instinctively make a move out of his way when you met him. He was often around doing "chores," but I never knew where he belonged, who hired him, or aught about him.

> "Ole massa tell us Linkin's folks
> Are only poor white trash,
> Hate de nigger like de debil,
> And sell dem all for cash;
> But Sambo knows the proclamashun —
> Dis nigger's cute, you see;
> It turn him almost white with joy
> To think he's gwine to be free.
> Git along, git along, git along, Josey."

"What do you want to be free for?" said Kiler, taking his pipe from his mouth and lounging against a tree. "You don't know when you are well off. Your master was good to you; you had plenty to eat, drink and wear; free people have to work as hard as any niggers, and look out for themselves when they are sick, too."

"Yes, massa"—Ben thrust his tongue out and lolled his head from side to side—"ole massa was right good to us; but we had to work if we wanted tu or no, come and go, agin it or not. Like your dog Pomp thar, you make him fetch and carry, lay down and git up, as you wants him tu, and you kick him, pull his years, and then you throw him bones, and pat him, jist as you likes; but Pomp's afeard of you." Ben chuckled and shook his head.

"Ef he's lying in the sun when you comes by he gits up and wags his tail, afeard you'll kick him. Pomp don't feel free; he knows he's got a marster, and so does the niggers."

"Free! Nobody's free; I am not free. I have to lie down and get up, tramp and halt, at the word of command, like any nigger; and if I don't I am shot or hung, and you are only whipped."

"Yes, massa, but you chuse to be a soldger; nigger don't chuse tu be slave. You mind little while, nigger mind all his life."

Kiler laughed.

"How did you find out about the proclamation, Ben?"

"You see, massa,"—Ben was in his element, for he had quite an audience by this time—"when a body's own skin don't belong tu hisself, he's p'ticler about de chances ob getting it hurt; niggers larn dis arly, and dey get wary and cute—always sleep wid one eye on de massa, and look stupid and act stupid when dey wide awake and har bristling." He paused to shake his head. "De massa will talk, and de niggers keep dar eyes shut and dar ears open. De women cuter dan de men, and dey hear all de talk in the house, and dey tell it in de cabin, and de niggers on one plantation tell it t' tudder, and it git all about, and we hab our sines and our s'ieties, and de niggers find out enuf; dey no fools. De Lord bress you, when we hab de big meetin' and thare's anything tu tell, the preacher he gibs de nod and de wink, and de nigger understands."

"Suppose you are found out?"

"Golly, massa, makes me creep all ober tu think ob it! But we ar'n't often found out; dose dat are de hottest tu git away, talk most agin Linkin; and ob nights, when we know dat de feet dat makes no noise are round de cabin, dough we don't see 'em, we laughs at de cussed Yankees, and calls dem 'poor white trash.' Yah!" Ben's head went like a pendulum.

"It's a good thing to be free. Anybody hit dis ole carcass, Ben can hit back; nobody got any right to hurt his skin but hisself. It's a mighty nice feelin'. I licked two niggers and a white boy when I know'd I was free, just tu feel I could."

"You are a scoundrel, Ben."

"May be, massa, but white folks make me so."

"Why don't you fight for the Union?"

"Gwoine to, massa, when I can git a chance; worked on the fortications at Nashville; hear dar dat some ob de niggers in regiments fight like bars; niggers no cowards ef dey are slaves. A nigger would hab sabed Hartsville, but de white captin tought him a fool, and wouldn't listen. He hear his marster on Saturday night tell his missus they gwoine to 'tack it next day. He had permission to go tu nudder plantation tu see his wife, but 'stead of gwoine he swum de river on a mighty cold night, when he like tu froze, and gave 'formation to our side, Morgan was a comin'; but dey laffed at him; 'twas all he got for his trouble—guess dey laffed t'udder side 'fore mornin."

"Some say you are a rebel spy, Ben."

"Dey do? What for spy for folks dat break my back and make me work all de same when I hab de mis'ry? Wait till dis nigger gives dem 'formation, dey'll hear Gabriel blow his trumpet fust."

"You told us a little while ago your master was good to you."

"Some white folks don't know nuffin. Spy! Ha, ha, ha! I wants tu speak to de kernel;" and Ben rolled himself off.

One of the boys following the camp had a banjo, with which he sometimes enlivened a weary hour; at the sound of it the negroes shuffled their feet and bobbed their heads intuitively; the bodies of the black teamsters would wriggle instinctively in their seats in time to the tune.

I had expected to find the slaves swarming like bees, and was astonished that so few of them were with the army. When I spoke of it, they said: "Dey hab been sent furder Souf to keep dem out of tro'ble."

Those with us were always laughing and joking, full of mimicry and odd sayings, and appeared to have no thought of to-morrow.

I had often heard of a negro turning pale, and supposed it a figure of speech. While the battle was raging I had proof they could and did turn pale. When the right wing gave way, and the mob dashed among the cedars, several blacks near me stood their ground. One was almost of Egyptian darkness; his hands trembled; I saw his knees knock together; while gradually his face became of the color of ashes. Another started to run, but afraid the guard would shoot him slipped between the animals drawing the wagon; stooping low he was unobserved. When the cavalry of the enemy made one of its pounces on us his visage was streaked and of a leaden hue.

"Golly, massa," he said afterwards, with a long heavy breath, "dis chile tought his time hab come when he saw old missus' son on dat big gray. You'se could hab heard dese ole jints crack as dey gib way and let me on my knees; my teef strike t'gedder so I could not pray, I could only whisper, 'Lord! Lord!' Use see, it's one ting to be shot and killed like a white man, nat'ral like, and anudder to be murdered like a nigger."

Here he caught sight of Jake, who had jammed himself in among a cluster of thick cedars, and, white with scratches and red with blood, was scrambling out.

"Thar's that nigger now. He like Zacree; he climb de tree, but not for tu see him Lord. Why, Jack, yuse better take car dat dar underbrush; de sesh been a pepperin' dem bushes. Yuse all blood—ha, ha!"

There was a good looking man of about thirty who kept near the teams and seemed but little concerned with the fortunes of the day. The crashing of the balls among the trees, and the sulphurous air half stifling them, drove the rabbits, of which the woods were full, out into the road, and made them so tame they were easily caught. He employed himself collecting numbers of these, which he killed and strung together, expecting to sell them to the officers and thus turn a penny after the battle was fought. Hiding them in a thick, dark spot of undergrowth, where he felt sure they were out of harm's way, he straggled off in search of more.

Hardly was he out of sight when one of the guard who had watched his movements appropriated the whole, and invited his comrades to a "game supper" when the day should be over. After a time the darkey returned with a turkey, some chickens and a half score more rabbits on his back. He was grinning in delight. No sooner did he make his appearance than those who had seized his former haul attacked him with entreaties for a share.

"No, massas, no," dodging first this way, then that, to keep out of their reach. "I must see de color of your money fust; dis chile b'lieves de officers will be hungry and hab a good ap'tite for de hot stew for supper when dis day's work is ober."

He soon discovered that his "plunder" was gone, but was wise enough to say nothing about it, although he looked very downcast. I think his second lot must have shared a like fate, for later in the day I saw one of the rebel cavalry galloping off with a string of small animals thrown over his saddle, wonderfully like that I had seen in Sambo's possession.

They would have done him little good, however, for he was killed next day, without having derived any benefit from his acquisitions.

Ben remarked, as he touched the body with his foot: "He tought hisself a mighty smart nigger, but he warn't smart enuf to git away from de bullits."

"We gwoine to be free," seemed to be the one thought of all the slaves I saw, both at Nashville and elsewhere. I had never been among them for any time before, and their drollery, queer talk, and singing had such a charm for me that when I met one I generally had something to say. They asked many questions, knew all about the "proclamashun," and had the most extravagant ideas of the benefit they were to derive from it.

I saw but two of them who appeared at all doubtful— one a broken down, desponding woman with two children, who wished she was "wid ole missus ag'in on de plantation," and an old man who shook his head and "didn't know."

Jim, the boy who was killed at Murfreesboro', had a beautiful voice. He sang "Ginger Blue" with great expression, and would have been a star among the minstrels.

> " De moon gwoine down, pitch dark de night,
>   Cold, cold the dew am falling,
> I fear dis darkey see a sight
>   Dat set him wool a-crawling.
> Who dar ! who dar ! a goblum cuss't ?
> 'Peak ! or dis minstrum's banjo bust !
> 'Peak ! and dy se'f unrabb'l ;
> 'Peak, goblum, 'peak ! but whe'r'r or no,
> Dis minstrum drap his ole banjo
>   And try a little trabb'l.
>   Tro' de woods — cut along —
>   Furder back, you boog a boo !
>   Tro' de woods — drap de song —
>   Nimble chile ob Ginger Blue."

Suiting the action to the word he ran off, and it was the last I saw of him.

"The fierce passion and fever of the battle," as John called it, over, the unhurt men, almost as exhausted as the wounded, were trying to get a little rest, when a negro man came to the spot where John, just off duty, had thrown himself after many hours' hard work, and with tears streaming down his face, said : " Come, massa, do come and see a poor boy all de way from Jarsey who's had bofe his hands took off."

We went. Insensible from loss of blood, there, in the mud and rain, lay a lad of about sixteen or seventeen, with no hands, the same shell had taken them both ; one at the shoulder with the arm, the other at the wrist. His mother was far away, watching, waiting, blessing him, and he lying on the wet earth dying, with only a poor negro to weep over him.

"Sights like that, Phil," said John, after we had done all we could for him, " rouse all the bad in the soldier, and cursing the authors of the rebellion for the time, they want to take the vengeance which belongs to the Lord."

The boy lived to be sent home, and I heard died there in the hospital.

I was talking to Ben one day, and expressed my surprise at not seeing more runaway slaves.

"Most ob dem sent Souf, massa ; and many niggers afeard ob being sent back ef dey git away afore Janevery. Den dar's de dogs ; white folks no idee ob de difficulties ; niggers know all 'bout it, and dey watched close as de skin, and de least 'spission and dey most skinned alibe."

"How do they manage to get away from the dogs ?"

"Dey take to de water ; dogs afeard ob de alligators."

" But alligators eat men as well as dogs."

"Yes, sar ; but when dar's a fire b'hind and a fire b'fore, de nigger looks tu see which is de biggest ; he more afeard ob de dogs dan ob de alligators. Den ef he's easy in de joints he can git a tall cane and gib big jumps like a toad and fool de dogs, and put dem off de scent, so git time; while dog snuffin' 'round for de hole his heel make in de ground, he way off. Niggers l'arn a hard way, but dey know suffin'."

"What is fetish, Ben, you are all so secret about?"

Ben looked carefully around before he spoke, lowering his voice almost to a whisper:

"I hab no fetish, Massa Phil; no b'lieve in dat thar kind ob worship, nebber du no good. Dar's Cato, his fetish am a black snake; he put him in his bed and git whipped 'cause he steal de milk he feed him wid." He suddenly stopped, and his voice sunk to the lowest whisper. "Here come Race; he Congo nigger, and dey du say he make his fetish du drefful things tu niggers he hab a spite ag'in. I'd ruther talk tu you 'bout it some udder time, Massa Phil." Ben rolled himself off before Race got within hearing.

CHAPTER XXI.

IN CAMP AT MURFREESBORO'.

THE army was settled in and around Murfreesboro', and the different commanders were engaged in putting things to rights again after the battle, which takes more time than people who stay at home know of. The dead must not only be buried, and the wounded sent into hospitals, or shipped off, but order and discipline must be restored ; companies and regiments looked after ; cannon, arms and accoutrements put in order ; measures taken to prevent any surprise, and fortifications built to strengthen the situation and prevent the possibility of a defeat, should there be an attack. In so crippled a state does a great battle always leave an army, even though it has been victorious.

There was plenty to do and force enough to do it, so the days and weeks passed quickly. Bragg, badly whipped, had fallen back to Tullahoma, a little town on a small creek, about thirty-five miles from Murfreesboro', and directly on the railroad between Nashville and Chattanooga. Our lines stretched to some five or seven miles beyond Murfreesboro', which was a pretty town, with wide streets and handsome houses, four or five churches, a college and a public square ; but it was peopled by soldiers, not a citizen, woman or child was to be seen. All had run before, or after, Bragg.

There were a few handsome houses in the country around. In one of these, about three miles from the town, on the Shelbyville turnpike, Generals McDowell and McCook had taken up their quarters, the owner having decamped, taking all his live stock with him. General Rosecrans was well housed in a mansion belonging to a rebel judge, also an absentee; but there were neither so many nor such elegant residences in this region as I had expected to see.

There was much work, some fun, and considerable restlessness, among the men; during the winter they could hardly bide their time to move. While here, I got in the only serious trouble I had been into as yet. Some of "our company" were vexed that they had been caught foraging on their own account, and appropriating sheep not intended for them, which sheep had been seized and served upon the officers' tables. They determined upon revenge. There was about the camp one of the ugliest, dirtiest looking curs I ever saw—everybody threw at it, and everybody kicked it—it was always in the way. Two or three of them entrapped this dog; took it to a thicket, killed, skinned, quartered and dressed it; then managed to be caught by General ———, while conveying it to their quarters. Of course the mutton was confiscated, and it was eaten at General ———'s table.

The fate of Mungo was whispered around, and whenever General ——— or any of his staff appeared in sight there would be a whistling and barking, and the officers began to have an uncomfortable suspicion that the *mutton* on which they had dined might prove something else. One day John was quite sick, and was sleeping in the tent. I was sitting at the opening, and General ——— passed; almost involuntarily I whistled, then barked. He stopped, turned and fiercely demanded what I meant. I was so confused I could hardly answer, "I was only imitating a dog, sir." The general turned purple in the face, muttered something, and walked on. In a few minutes a corporal appeared, who awoke John with the information that he was under arrest. John inquired "what for?" He did not know, but thought it was for permitting his men to be disrespectful to his superior officers. John was marched off to the general's quarters. He knew nothing of the matter, and stated that he did not. It was suggested that the officers had been sold; the men would have their fun, and it was best to join in the laugh, so the matter was dropped. John reprimanded me for my share in the offense, but I could see he was not very angry.

I often went out and spent the day with the pickets. One cold day I was out on the railroad with H—— and C——; we had built a fire, and stretched a blanket on two tall sticks to keep off the wind. C—— was giving me his experience in soldiering, when H——, who was pacing back and forth on the track, his rifle on his shoulder, said: "There comes some one well mounted." We moved from our shelter to see who it was. A man on a splendid brown mare was speeding from below rapidly in our direction. When within speaking distance, H—— halted him, and demanded his business. He wished to see General ——, and requested to be allowed to pass in. He wore a cap pulled low over his brow, and tightly over his ears, from under which locks of gray hair hung out. A woolen muffler was around his neck, and he had a large cloak well wrapped about him. While H—— hesitated, and his horse was curvetting and snorting in the frosty air, he turned it suddenly; a gust of wind tore our blanket from the poles, and sent it in the animal's face. Affrighted, it reared and plunged; the man's cap was blown from his head, and with it the gray wig he wore, disclosing a head of brown, curly hair. His endeavors to keep the cap in place tore the cloak away, and discovered around his body a belt well filled with pistols and a knife. With an exclamation H—— fired at him, but missed ; C—— followed suit ; but finding his cap gone, the rebel put spurs to his horse, throwing himself flat on his neck, and was soon out of sight. C—— declared he hit him, but we did not think so. I captured the blanket which had blown some distance, and C—— had a chase after the cap and wig ; the latter at last lodged on the end of a rail. We speculated as to who and what the man was, probably a spy ; he meant mischief at any rate ; we were unanimous as to his riding well. H——, to console himself for not hitting him, insisted he did not keep his horse in a straight line for two leaps, but curved him in and out in scollops.

I often went to the blacksmith's shop to see them shoe the cavalry horses, and hear the men talk ; I liked to hear of their dashes. General Rosecrans was increasing this force, and there were some quite young boys among them. The forge was set up under the trees ; and one day while I was there several officers sauntered up, and remarking upon the youthful looks of two new recruits, one of them said :

"Our boys are the true heroes of this war. I have seen more proofs of courage, coolness, endurance, forbearance and determination among them, than ever fell to my lot to witness among the same number of men under the same circumstances.

"'There was Ben, the little drummer-boy of the T——th ; his round apple head, rosy cheeks and curly hair, gained him the sobriquet Baby, and as 'Baby Ben' the men knew him. No braver heart beat in man's bosom ; only twelve years of age, and not a great deal higher than his drum, he stepped forth like a general, with flashing eyes, quick breath, and eager hands; his whole soul in the music. The very sight of him inspired us; the most craven coward would have refused to fly in view of that gallant boy. He was with us at Pittsburg Landing; rat, tat, tat, through the long and bloody hours, went his sticks; he never faltered; where the men were fighting hardest there he was beating "Hail Columbia" with all his strength. "God bless that boy!" I heard a hard pressed private say, a man who had slain his foe and drawn back to catch breath and wipe his face with his sleeve.

"'What are you doing here? Put yourself out of danger,' said one coming on him as the enemy opened fire, and thrusting him back.

"'It's my business to do the drumming and yours to do the fighting, and I am going to attend to mine,' was the sturdy little fellow's reply, as he took a bite of the cracker he had suspended by a string about his neck; then stepped forward rattling away.

"But 'Baby Ben' saw a bloodier field next day. When the wounded were searched for, he was found drenched to the skin, beside the remnants of his drum, it shattered by shot, with a wound in his side and two of his fingers gone.

"Insensible from loss of blood, he was carried to the surgeon. He revived under the pain of probing, but not a word escaped him after the first groan. When it was over, his hand dressed, and he laid on his bed, he turned to me, who stood near, and faintly whispered:

"'Didn't we beat them?'

"'Yes, my boy.'

"'Can't I never drum any more?'

"When assured he might yet do so, he buried his head in the bed clothes and softly cried."

"The day I got this" (the officer held up his arm in a sling) "a pale, slim lad, just from the hospital, staggered before me out of the ranks with 'I am hit,' placing his hand on his side. I gave him one glance. Shot fell thick and fast, and we had no time to look after the wounded; but the lad's face haunted me even in the din of battle, and then I was struck myself and fell with a ball through my thigh and my arm was broken.

"The tide of battle swept by and left me; the ball through my side had only made a flesh wound and I managed with my right hand to wrap my handkerchief about it. I thought of that poor boy. I knew his mother. I dragged myself in the direction I had seen him fall. He lay a little aside from the path of the fight, his head on his arm. I called out, 'William, William;' he was not dead, had only fainted, and was reviving. I felt in my pocket for a small metal flask of brandy. It was there, and about half full. I wet his lips and forced some of it down his throat; he sat up and spoke:

"'It is all over with me, captain; are you hurt?'

"'Only a broken arm and a flesh wound in my thigh. Come, you must not give up; let us get back under cover of the bushes; if the scoundrels should win the day they will bayonet us.'

"With much difficulty, assisted by what little aid I could render, he at length managed to gain a clump some distance off. The effort made my thigh bleed dreadfully, but I succeeded in clearing a space with my sword, and we lay down.

"So exhausted were we that it was some time ere either of us spoke; but at length with great effort he said:

"'Do you think you will ever get home, captain?'

"'I hope so.'

"'Will you see my mother and tell her I tried to do my

duty. I am young to die, and I did hope I should get safe through and go home and see them all; but it's God's will. The ball is here;' he laid his hand upon his breast. 'It's killing me!'

"His voice was very faint. I did all I could to reassure him, and promised, if spared, to see his loved ones at home, trying to cheer him, although I saw he was going fast.

"'Take a lock of my hair to mother, and give Mary my Bible;' he tried to take it from his breast; I assisted him. 'Jacob must have all my pay for his law studies—and—and—' he paused, 'I should like them to give Bessie Watts my white rabbits.'

"The sun set, night was coming on; he dozed, then roused and said in stronger tones :

"'I can hear their groans. Did you see that poor fellow by the road, who had lost both his legs, captain? How I wish they would come and help you; they can do me no good. Our boys are victorious, I know; I saw them when I slept. They will be along presently, but it will be too late for me.'

"So, not suffering much apparently, at intervals he talked and dozed.

"Some hours passed thus, then a mortal agony seized him; his frame was convulsed with it. It began to rain. I could only press his hand in the dark and starless night and try to whisper peace and comfort. He murmured of his mother, Bessie, Mary; was silent for a little, then spoke again :

"'How good the rain feels—if I only had a drink from the spring under the beeches where they all came to bid me good-by. I am afraid I trouble you, captain. Be sure to tell them I tried to be a good soldier. It hurts me to speak, will you say the Lord's prayer for me?'

"Resting on my well arm, with my mouth close to his ear, I repeated the blessed words, the pattering rain seeming as an accompaniment. He dozed again. I knew from the convulsive movements of his limbs that he suffered, but he spoke no more; his hand grew cold within my clasp, and as the first faint streaks of day appeared he ceased to breathe.

"I slept from exhaustion. My men found me with the body of the boy stiff at my side, the rain silently falling on the living and the dead. Did any man ever die," asked the narrator, "a braver death than that?"

For a minute no one spoke; then this officer patted me on the shoulder, as he rose from the wagon wheel where he had been sitting, and said:

"Could you meet death like that, my lad?"

"I don't know, I could try."

I went out several times with expeditions to seize horses. The rebels tried every way to keep them from us, but we generally managed to get a respectable number. Once we found a beautiful horse up-stairs in a house, where it had been led when the alarm of our arrival in the neighborhood reached its mistress's ears. Hearing the neighing and pawing of our horses, it whinnied and showed its head at the window, despite the efforts of the little negro who had been shut up with it to keep it quiet, but whose curiosity to see "Linkum's men" had made him for a moment disregard his charge. I did not wonder at the owner's anxiety to keep it, for it was a beautiful animal, high-spirited, yet gentle.

There were several skirmishes with the enemy during this season, and some prisoners were brought in. Bragg was said to be now here, now there; the last report was that he was at Horseshoe Mountain, strongly fortified. Early in June John, who had been made a captain for good conduct at Stone River, told me that preparations were going forward for a move of the whole army. Orders might be published any day. The roads were good, and our artillery and ammunition wagons could travel. All was business and bustle; great piles of army rations—bread, sugar, coffee, and flour—were being shifted to the different corps for which they were intended, while hay and corn accumulated for the present use of the horses.

CHAPTER XXII.

MARCHING ON.

AT last the welcome orders were published, and "forward! bully!" was the cry of the boys as, on the 24th of January, they left Murfreesboro' behind them, and started on the Manchester and Shelbyville pikes further into Tennessee.

General Wilder's command took the Manchester road, and were soon heard from, driving the enemy like cattle through a hollow which runs for several miles between the hills, and is called Hoover's Gap. They were completely scattered and whipped. There are several of these gaps or openings in the hills along this route, and the rebels generally posted themselves in them and disputed the passage with our men.

While the infantry plodded their weary way, the cavalry continued ahead and tore up railroad tracks and chased the enemy through the mountains. General Wilder's command were out over a week, and did not return until driven to do so by hunger, although it rained all the time. I never saw a more wild, wan, miserable-looking set of men than they were when they came into camp, and dropped down anywhere to sleep. They looked more like brigands than troops, for their clothes were torn and dirty, their eyes heavy, and their hair matted. They had had little if anything to eat, for the mountains over which they had passed were uninhabited, rocky and bare, and they had failed to supply themselves with rations, while their only sleep had been taken in the saddle.

So we kept on skirmishing every day. General McCook had a sharp encounter with the rebels, for I saw many wounded men going to the rear. The foe was entrenched at Shelbyville, which our cavalry took after a brisk fight, much to the satisfaction of the citizens, who were almost all Union people.

Advancing upon Tullahoma, we came to the "barrens" upon which it is situated, a soft, spongy soil, then soaked by the rain, in which we sunk at every step. There was joking and laughing as we proceeded, and some one called out the lines of a play I had often taken part in at home with the girls:

> "We are marching forward to Quebec;
> The drums are loudly beating;"

Only the drums did not beat. What is the next line? The last is:

> "The British are retreating."

"The rebs are following the example of their friends," said one coming up; "the general has just heard they have *skedaddled* from Tullahoma."

"They will have to frog it," called out another, "and jump from dry spot to dry spot."

"Hurrah for the Fourth of July in Tullahoma!" went up in a shout. We did occupy Tullahoma, and Bragg kept on his way to the Tennessee River. We followed him, when the general got ready, literally with our tents on our backs, over mountains and through gorges such as an army never passed through before. Starving and destitute people daily came into camp with horrible tales of the sufferings of Unionists in East Tennessee. They warned the officers of the impassability of the road for an army.

"Doctor, what is the matter with Hatch?" said John, one morning, as he moved from an ambulance where he had placed one of his men, whom he had found staggering in the road unable to keep up.

"Home-sickness, captain, nothing more or less; he is good for nothing and I have given him a certificate which will send him to hospital in the rear."

"But, doctor, he has fever, look at his eyes; he eats very little, and is so weak he can scarcely stand."

"Precisely, he can't stand, but it is home-sickness and naught else, a disease which the department will not believe in, but a disease nevertheless, and one which will give Hatch his ticket of leave in a month, if he is not treated accordingly. He scarcely speaks—never smiles—and only eats enough to sustain life, sits always with his head hanging on his breast, and his arms listlessly at his sides."

"He is a strange fellow." John answered. "At Stone River he was punished with extra duty almost every other day for reading when he should have been attending to other things, and kept himself so dirty that Lieutenant F—— had him taken to the river, his hair cut and combed, and his body scrubbed with sand—it was not gently done, yet it did not improve him."

"Just so,—he is no coward, but he wants what the common people call 'ambition,' and what we know as energy. He is of peculiar temperament; let him go home for a short time and I warrant he comes out all right."

Hatch was sent to Cincinnati to hospital, where he came near dying. At length he got a furlough to go home, and in a couple of months after joined us as well and bright as any one.

He had a confused and foolish look when he first returned, and the " boys " greeted him with : " How's mammy, Hatch ?" " Did you get enough pap, darling ?" " Hush a by baby." After a while this chaff was dropped.

The hot days of the last of July found the whole army congregated in and about Winchester and Tullahoma. General Rosecrans had his quarters at Winchester, in Mary Sharp's college. I had a day's ride with John over to Decherd, where General Thomas's Corps was; then up to Tullahoma to see General Johnston's division ; over to Manchester and Hillsboro, then back to Winchester, where General Jeff. C. Davis had command. At and between these points, and much higher up, the army lay. The men were in excellent spirits, joking at Bragg's run ; reports said most of his army had scattered about the country, that he was at Chattanooga fortifying, etc. In crossing the Tennessee he had burned the bridge at Bridgeport, which was said to be the finest in the country. But this would not delay us much, for when ready the boys said they should pontoon or walk the water.

We were passing a field in which two negroes were at work ; they stood looking at us. One of them leaned his arms on the top of the hoe, and as two officers rode near began to sing :

> " God made man, and man made de money,
> God made de bees, and de bees made de honey,
> God made de debil, and de debil made sin,
> God made de big hole and put de debil in."

The negro's manner was peculiar. I heard one of the officers say : " He means something by that song," and spur up to him. A few moments after the officer rode ahead in a furious gallop and the men said he had information for the general.

At length we were over the Tennessee, having crossed

at four different places with little molestation, and taken several noted guerrillas in the skirmishes we had. We camped on the Georgia side, in the neighborhood of Trenton, where General Rosecrans had his headquarters.

It was now the month of August, and Chattanooga, the rebel stronghold, was our destination. It was supposed that Bragg would make a resistance there, as he was well fortified.

On the 20th General Wilder's cavalry reached the hills on the opposite side of the river from Chattanooga, and shelled it, burning some boats in the river, and doing other damage. The whole army was now moving rapidly up and soon the work began. It was reported that General Bragg had been removed, and that General Joe Johnston was now in command of the rebel force.

There was some trouble one day about a misconception of orders in one of the regiments, and an officer in the regular service rode up, and, angry and excited, swore at the men, and made threatening gestures with his sword. This the independent volunteers would not stand, and they audibly muttered their discontent. "The Hessian," came through one man's closed teeth, "he's like a nigger driver." "He fights for the pay, it is his trade," said another; while a third spoke out: "We will duck him the first chance, like we did that regular who struck Jim Lane with his sword." They laughed at the recollection, and their good humor was restored. I noticed the difference between the appearance of the white people all along our route, and that of the same poor class I had seen at home. The Southern "poor whites" had clayey complexions, and mostly light hair, which hung uncombed about their faces. The men were generally tall, thin and stoop shouldered, looked as if they did not often laugh, and as if every movement was a trouble. I thought their stoop must come from bending over the fire, often necessary in that mountain country, or from their always sitting with their heads down watching their feet, as they shifted and worked them in the sand, which appeared to be their chief employment. The women looked ignorant of the use of water, their hair hung in knotted strands, and their complexion and teeth were of the same hue as their gowns, which were of dingy yellow homespun.

They were almost always obliged to take the "dip" from their mouths before they could answer a question, and many whom I saw here and elsewhere not only dipped but smoked and chewed. They raised a stalk of tobacco, if they could not raise anything else. I really think they considered it the "staff of life." They never hesitated to ask for it, and if they could get none would beg the soldier for a few whiffs from his pipe, and put it wet from his lips into their own. These women swore, too, like troopers. Kiler said he thought there was swearing enough in the army, but he believed the Southern people had made a contract to do the swearing of all creation. And they were so ignorant. Out of a party of twenty-five refugees, who came in one day while I was at Gen. ——'s headquarters, all of whom were people over twenty, and one a man over seventy years old, but one of them, and that one a woman, could read and write.

The negroes knew much more than they did. They were constantly inquiring the uses of the most common utensils. Some of them had never seen a coffee mill; they pounded the berry when they had it; yet they were, John told me, much above the average class of the inhabitants. The women and children had left their homes at night on foot, leaving horses, wagons and household goods behind them to divert suspicion; and were joined by their husbands, who had been hiding in the mountains.

Traveling by day and hiding by night, nearly starving, they had tried to reach us and at last did.

Early in September we took Chattanooga, having been manœuvering around it for some time. It was done without a battle; as the front of our army marched in, the rear of the rebel army galloped out. The day after it was taken Archbishop Purcell, who was on a visit to General Rosecrans, celebrated high mass there.

CHAPTER XXIII.

CHICKAMAUGA.

"CAPTAIN," said Kiler, addressing John one morning as I was getting ready to go out to the signal station with S——, "Phil knows and sees everything that is going on. I don't believe a bit of adventure could take place in this corps without his having some knowledge of it. He is everywhere."

"I think he makes the most of his opportunities," said John, laughing, "and it is well he does, for he will have very little recreation when this war is over. If he lives to get through, he has years of hard study before him."

"He can live upon what he has seen, and will have more to tell than any man among us. There is one thing I can say for you, Phil. You are obliging and brave, and that is why the men are always willing to have you along."

My coffee was very hot, and almost scalded me. When I stopped coughing, I said :

"Yes, but I shall be seventeen shortly, then I am in for it."

"If that is the case," returned Kiler, "you had best take your pleasure while you can. You won't like being in harness You have had too much liberty. Nothing but the good of the country could make me come and go at the bidding of others."

To tell the truth I was beginning to feel this myself. When we first joined the army John had the idea of my studying some every day. He had given this up, and no longer kept so strict a watch over me. Although I knew all the time that I was under his eye, it did not trouble me, for I was always freer when with him than when he was not by. I read a good deal of any books I could get, and we talked much of what was in the papers we chanced to see. I always told him what I had seen and done through the day, and he explained our situation and movements to me.

He let no opportunity slip of reminding me of my promise of study, and I retaliated by jogging his memory concerning his promise to let me join the army. But as the time drew near I began to have less desire to enter the ranks. I was now fully accoutred as a soldier, but went and came as I chose, or as John permitted, sheltered by his rank of captain. Should this privilege be cut off by orders I was prepared to enroll my name, but in the meantime was content to let things take their course. John, I knew, would never burden government with my expenses, be they great or small.

I liked to go out to the signal stations with the corps when on duty. The highest point accessible was generally selected for observation and for signaling to the different wings of the army. If there was a tree on it so much the better. The tree was climbed, and, seated in its crotch, or on a secure limb, glass in hand, the officer in charge swept the horizon and scanned well all within his view. By means of the signal flags, which were Greek to all but those in the secret, others transmitted messages or orders, and others again took down observations or replies. Sometimes they were discovered by the enemy, and became a mark for the sharpshooters, which was not so pleasant. At night signals were made with torches or rockets.

While in this region I had an adventure of which I was not a little proud. The general of our division wished information concerning a certain point. I heard some of the officers speak of it, and I told John I knew I could get the information wanted, begging him to let me try. He refused. The danger of being discovered was great, and if caught I would be killed outright. I insisted, and was backed by Kiler, who said John was trying to make a girl of me. As a last argument I told him I thought it mean to let me have all the advantage of being with the army, and when I could, not let me render a service. This touched him, as I knew it would. He listened to my plan, saw it was practicable, reluctantly consented, and took me to the general. The general approved, and gave me his orders. The next morning I was to start.

That night I parted my hair, which had grown rather long, down the middle, and put it up in curl papers all round. I had been dreadfully sunburned, but my skin had blistered and peeled off, and was now white and clear. John and Kiler presided at my toilet in the morning. Kiler had undertaken to procure the necessary garments, having written a list of what I needed. So a very short time saw me dressed as a girl, with hat and veil on. The character was not new to me, as my readers know; for besides my representation in Virginia I had always personated the female in the plays of our Thespian Society at home. When my dressing was completed by hooking round my waist a homespun riding-skirt of butternut color, John smiled for the first time, and said, as he glanced at my face surrounded by curls under the veil:

"I think you will pass, Phil, for on examination I should hardly know you."

"Yes, he looks like a girl of about fifteen," said Kiler; "but mind, Phil, don't forget your r—r's when talking—no Yankeeisms—cry if needful, and do not stay a moment longer than is necessary."

"Whar's the capting?" I drawled in reply.

"That will do; go."

With a last injunction from John to be cautious, I departed, a little tremulous at the danger I was to brave.

In due time I reached the enemy's pickets and requested to be taken to an officer. The men put several questions and one of them was disposed to joke me. I insisted that I had business with an officer; and after a short parley they proposed taking me to the nearest one. We were on our way, when riding towards us came a general, attended by his staff. He questioned the guard. I approached him and while he closely regarded me, and I felt the color come in my face and my voice tremble, I told my story. My father and only brother were in the army; my mother was ill—supposed to be dying; our "niggers" had run off, save one old woman now with my mother. I had heard that my father's regiment was here, and had come to see him.

"What regiment is he in?"

"The ——th Georgia; Colonel B."

"The company?"

"I don't know; it is over a year since we heard from him, and there has been a change."

The staff were all attentively regarding me; I began to feel dreadfully nervous. One of them came a little nearer and questioned as to the locality where I lived; this was getting in too deep water for me. The general, who had turned to speak to another officer, interrupted, and in an impatient tone said:

"The ——th is not here, my girl."

I knew that well, for I had heard it from a prisoner I had questioned ; I began to sob and cry violently.

"The house is in the hollow ; (sob) the Yanks took our last cow ; (sob) mother is sick ; (sob) I want to see father." (Sob, sob, sob.)

From nervousness and excitement real tears came, and I took care they should see them.

"There, don't cry ; we will see what we can do for you ; your father's regiment may come up."

I whimpered : " I must return to my mother and would come back to-morrow."

"Yes, do ; " evidently wanting to get rid of me.

"Can't one of the officers go with me—the men crack jokes at me. I am afeard." I caught my breath at every word. There was a laugh, but the general said :

"Captain, this is in your line, I believe ;" speaking to a young officer, looking very little older than myself. He sprung to his horse. I uttered my thanks behind my handkerchief and we rode off.

My escort was very kind; he begged me to dry my tears, and assured me my father's regiment would be up with the reinforcements expected to-morrow. I began to be anxious for the success of my mission as I had accomplished little so far, so I brightened up at this, rode slowly, and asked *innocent* questions.

"Is this all the camp ; I never had seen a camp before ?"

"Oh, no ; would you like to go round ? If you do not care for a mile or two, I will take you."

"I am afeard mother will need me ; but then, I think I might go a little way." In my ignorance, I asked questions which amused him greatly : What those men were at that place for? Where those soldiers were going ? If this was all the army, etc. ?

Proud of his superior knowledge, he enlightened me, dilating and giving me items I never dreamed of getting. At last, when about to part, he said: "Miss Fanny, I shall look out for you to-morrow." Fanny was the name I had given him as mine.

"But," I replied, "you told me you were going away; I am so sorry."

"Yes; I over-heard the general say our division would swing round to-night, under cover of the darkness, but I shall manage to be here when you come to-morrow; I am on General S——'s staff."

We bade each other a very tender good-by; I had all I wanted. I looked back once or twice after we parted, and he kissed his hand to me in the distance. He was a gallant, and, no doubt, a brave youth, who thought it no harm to talk a little tenderly to a green girl.

Tired with the effort I had made to keep up my character, and to remember all I saw, I nevertheless rode hard until I reached the camp. The general was well pleased with what I had to tell him and thanked me cordially.

While we were in and about Chattanooga, I paid visits to the springs around, several of which have stories or traditions connected with them; for this was once the headquarters of the Cherokee Nation, who had possession of Georgia. I remember reading an account of John Wesley and his brother Charles, in their young days, coming to this country and preaching to the Indians at Savannah. I was in hopes I might find some relic of these people, but there was nothing to be had that I could get.

The village itself is like a nest dropped among the mountains; hence its name, Chattanooga, which means Hawk's Nest. Rossville, a little south of it, is named from the great chief, John Ross, who lived there, and

THE PARTING.

whose house was used by General Rosecrans for a hospital. Chattanooga is a pretty place, built on a point made by a sweep of the Tennessee River; it has some nice gabled and flat-roofed houses, several bridges, churches, etc. The Southerners used to go there in great numbers, before the rebellion, to spend the Summer months. The air is cool; the scenery magnificent, and springs gush from the earth in all directions. Lookout Mountain, from the top of which there is a grand view of the country round as far as the eye can reach, is some two or three miles from the village. No wonder the rebels considered Chattanooga their stronghold; it appeared to be almost a second Gibraltar; they must have spent much time fortifying, for they had good works. Very few of the former inhabitants were left when it was occupied by our army; they had done as we often did at home in our plays, "followed their leader" and run. I often thought it would be a great pleasure to be once more in a place where there were plenty of women and children.

The grave-yard at Chattanooga was crowded with rebel dead—each grave numbered; cattle or sheep might have lain below for aught the numbers told to the contrary. It was from the hills opposite the town that General Wilder shelled it, paying his compliments to General Bragg in a manner so marked that the rebel leader, who did not want any "more grape" at that time, took French leave, and established himself across our path in the mountains. I never could understand why this manner of going was called "French leave," for I have always heard the French were the most polite people in the world. I suppose the rebels thought

"He who fights and runs away,
Will live to fight another day."

At any rate they left. John always checks me when I say anything like this before him. He says there never were better fighters in the world than the Southerners; that he is proud of them as Americans. They had a bad cause, and their education was worse. Imagine ourselves brought up under slavery, etc.

Parts of the army had been coming up, divisions changing places, and other movements going on. John told me there would likely be a battle, for the enemy held all the gaps in Pigeon Mountain, and we must have them to go on our way.

John had been so occupied I had not much talk with him. I was, myself, all the time back and forth between the village and the camps, which lay around and below it, on the Rossville and Lafayette roads. The enemy was close to us; so close that in places the pickets could talk together.

On the night of the 18th of September I was quite sick and restless. Generally I slept like a log—but that night I was conscious of a subdued movement in the camp, which half roused me in my wakeful moments. John was on duty, and was not with me all night. There had been heavy skirmishing that day.

When morning dawned and I became wide awake, I thought some magician had been at work during the darkness in the night. The whole army had shifted. I did not know any of the men about me, and it was after some time, and only after I had made many inquiries, that I ascertained where our corps was. The men were too busy to attend to me; they laughed at me; "they did not know;" they turned from me with, "here's a little chap lost." One asked me if I did not want a bell on my neck? another said "ba-ba." They thrust me back out of the way.

While I was yet in a maze and could scarcely understand the change that had been made, only knew that our part of the army was not there and another was, there came a terrible firing, and word passed that the enemy had opened on General Negley's division. In a fever now to find John, I went from point to point; it was late in the evening when I came across the regiment. It had been in action, many were killed, but John was safe. How that day passed I cannot tell; the battle raged and surged back and forth; there were rumors that the enemy was beaten, —that we were beaten—that this regiment and that had been cut to pieces; that prominent officers were killed, and still the fighting went on. In the midst of all the sun set—the night came—and the moon cold, pale and beautiful, lighted up the ghastly battle field of Dead Man's River, which is the meaning of the Indian word Chickamauga.

"How is it, John?" I said, as shivering I ate my cracker, for I had had nothing all day.

"God only knows the end," was the reply, "it is not near over yet; they will keep us out of Chattanooga if they possibly can, but," he said, after a pause, "they cannot. Try and sleep, Phil, your teeth are chattering."

The night was frosty, and I was cold and worn with fatigue and excitement. The earth was damp; we had no fires and nothing warm; I could not sleep. I lay with some poor fellow's knapsack under my head for a pillow, and an overcoat I had picked up over me, thinking and picturing what was going on. Muffled sounds were in the air, which was still sulphurous. I could hear the groans of the wounded lying near; "water, water," would come from parched and dying lips, but we had no water. At length sleep overcame me, and I awoke with the sun shining in my face. It was Sunday; again on that day were we surrounded with blood and carnage.

My first thought was, General Rosecrans does not fight on Sunday, if he can help it. He could not help it, and we did fight.

The enemy attacked us. Who can tell of the blood—the horror—the fright of that day? Our regiments were mowed like grain; as the ranks of one were thinned, another sprung to its place, and so the day went on. The rebels were fighting for Chattanooga, the hope of the would-be Confederacy. If they lost it they lost all.

They fought like demons, rushing to the onslaught with a wild, unearthly yell, which made me put my fingers in my ears when I heard it. Almost double our number, they felt they must succeed. First a horseman came with the news that General Davis was routed; followed by another, who told of disasters to Generals Van Cleve and Crittenden; McCook's red battle-flag had gone down; the right wing was beaten and had fallen back; General Rosecrans was a prisoner. Those who went to see came back with tales of disorganization; the enemy was in Rossville; the road was crowded with soldiers, cannon and wagons; Generals McCook and Crittenden had lost their commands, but had escaped and fled to Chattanooga, etc.

Later in the afternoon, report said that General Thomas had fallen back to Mission Ridge; then came word of the fearful strife between his division and the rebels; of the blood that flowed like water around and about his blue battle-flag; of General Granger's aid. All felt the end had come. It did come. Night closed in, and we were *not* defeated; we held Chattanooga.

I slept well that night, although my bed was the sidewalk of a public street in that town; but I had good company there. General Thomas's victory had been the last word brought us in the evening; but we knew not what the morning had in store for us. Should we cross the Tennessee? would they attack us again? I heard the probabilities discussed as I went about with John, who was looking up the missing of his command. Men seemed in a maze; one insisted General Rosecrans was a prisoner, when we knew he was at Chattanooga, issuing orders. I heard an officer say, he did not dream of disaster; that his division had driven the enemy back on their front after hard fighting, and he thought the whole army had done the same, when the cry came of a stampede to Chattanooga.

As the hours wore on we found there was to be no retreat. General Thomas had saved the army. General Garfield had volunteered to carry to him news of the rout, which he did at great risk. This was the first intimation Thomas had of the disaster. John told me that, late in the afternoon, when General Thomas's host were the sorest pressed, though not yielding an inch, he gazed at the sun and thought of Joshua, and wished he had the power—not to make it stand still, but to make it go down. They were looking for reinforcements, and, like "Sister Ann," watched for the "dust arising" that would tell help was near. Suddenly he saw at a distance the red, white and blue crescent shaped battle-flag of General Gordon Granger; and, "Phil," said he, "I did as you sometimes do—I cried like a child, as I galloped over the ground with the news." I sprung into his arms and hugged him—my noble brother!

We had fallen back; the enemy had possession of the battle ground, and some of our hospitals, with our dead, wounded and dying, were in their hands; but we had

Chattanooga, for the occupation of which they had shed so much blood.

General Rosecrans had published his orders to fortify and stand by Chattanooga to the last, and great works sprung up, like mushrooms, in a night. In a couple of days we were impregnable. The fortifications, which the rebels had built with long months of toil, we had increased and strengthened, until they were a wall upon which they could dash themselves only to destruction.

What wonderful tales men told of the fray! I heard one say that his brigade had to yield their ground; the hospital, with their wounded, was under fire; the men took the poor sufferers upon their backs and carried them four miles out of reach of the shells. Others told how the colors of regiments had been saved by individual valor, when almost within the hands of the enemy. Books could be filled with accounts of acts of heroism and hair-breadth escapes made in those two days. I saw a man showing his watch, with an indentation in it made by a bullet, which, but for the watch, would have reached his heart; another held up his foot, with the toe of his boot, sole and all, cut neatly and squarely off; its being about half an inch too long saved him; an Irishman, a good Catholic, took from the breast of his blouse a yellow and worn paper, with some faint writing on it—a prayer for deliverance from violent death, which his father had worn for thirty years, and which he truly believed had saved his life from the ball that went through his sleeve.

Near noon, John came up to me and said:

"Phil, Tom Murdoch was wounded, some say killed outright, on Saturday. I can find out nothing about him. I wish you would hunt up Captain James Murdoch, and see if he knows anything of his brother. Lytle was killed yesterday ; they never shot a braver or more gallant gentleman."

This was said in a husky tone, and he turned quickly away. Without a word I went in search of Captain James Murdoch, whom I knew to be tenderly attached to his brother. I did not find him, but was told he had heard of his brother's being wounded, and was looking for him.

Captain Thomas Murdoch was a close friend of John ; we both loved him as a brother. He entered the army at the first call for men, and was at Bull Run ; afterwards was with General Benham in Western Virginia, as second lieutenant in the Thirteenth Ohio, and was in all the long marches with General Buell. He became first lieutenant, then was promoted to a captaincy for bravery at Stone River, where his horse was shot under him while acting as aid to General Van Cleve. He was my beau ideal of a soldier ; modest, brave, enthusiastic and chivalric. I heard one of the officers when speaking of him say he was a true soldier. All that we could hear of him was, that he was wounded on Saturday at the head of General Van Cleve's line of battle ; he had risen in his stirrups, and shouting to the men, " Come on, boys ! try them once more ! " was shot while waving his cap. He was conveyed to our hospital at Crawfish Springs, and this hospital had fallen into the hands of the enemy ; afterwards we had the particulars of his death from one of our surgeons in charge of the wounded. He died, as he had lived, "one of the many full of hope and promise, who gave their lives that the country might live."

Our loss was heavy. I knew of the fall of Colonel Jones, Captain Russell, Captain Paschell, and scores of other brave officers and privates ; but the rebel loss was greater than ours. The army of the West had whipped

Longstreet's famous corps, who had come from Virginia to teach Bragg's men how to fight. Western men had set them a hard lesson and compelled them to learn it. I had heard of "little Johnny Clem" at Murfreesboro', but first saw him at Chickamauga; he was in the midst of a group of officers who were making much of him. He had entered the army as drummer boy to the Twenty-second Michigan, when he was only ten years old; he afterwards became marker to the regiment; he was a little bit of a fellow, and a great pet among them; had been with them about two years; they said he never seemed to think of danger; he had distinguished himself in Sunday's battle by killing a rebel colonel, who, seeing him using his gun, had called to him:

"Stop, you little Yankee devil, or I will put a bullet through you."

Johnny said nothing, but took deliberate aim and fired away; the bullet went through the rebel's heart, and he tumbled from his horse dead. I should have liked to talk to him; but 1 did not have an opportunity. After I saw him, General Rosecrans made him a sergeant for his bravery, and the ladies presented him with military accoutrements. He was from Newark, Ohio, and was the youngest soldier in the army.

Another Michigan regiment also lost a drummer boy, or rather girl, in this battle. She was from New York, was eighteen or nineteen years of age, had joined at Detroit, and was with it in all that long and dreadful march made through Kentucky. She was also wounded in Sunday's battle.

When told she must die she sent a despatch to her mother, and died calmly shortly afterwards.

The rebels were in a valley, and occupied both Lookout Mountain and Mission Ridge. They had thrown up breastworks and had a battery on a ledge about half way up Lookout. The pickets of the two armies were so close they often talked to each other. From the top of Lookout six or seven States are visible, and one of the grandest sights to be seen anywhere lies spread before you.

We had been fighting to keep Chattanooga, which is in the State of Tennessee, but the battle was fought in Georgia on West Chickamauga Creek, and on the ground lying between Rossville, Gordon's Mills and Crawfish Springs, extending almost to Pea-vine Creek. Rossville is but a half mile from the state line of Tennessee, and Crawfish Springs is eight miles from it. Our wounded were taken to Stephenson, Alabama, some thirty miles from Chattanooga. So the army was operating in three States at once, as John explained to me.

When we were falling back, Private Flinn was told by some one to make tracks out of the State of Georgia. He stood still a moment, and shaking his finger in the direction of Tunnel Hill said : "By Gorra ! just as sure as I can stand in one of your States, and have my feet in three of them at the same time, just as sure you will feel our grip again."

Many boys of my age, and some older ones with whom I have talked, supposed that a line of battle means that the enemy's men and ours are drawn up in lines opposite each other, where they stand still, take aim and fire until one or the other gives way.

This is not so ; the armies, of course, are opposing each other, but they usually take advantage of any slopes, hills or trees in their path ; they throw up breastworks of stones, earth or logs, posting themselves so as to be as little exposed as possible. Often, from the nature of the ground, and for better security, they lie down on their stomachs, and fire in that way ; when in ranks the front rank fires and falls to its knees, the second firing over their heads, and so on.

Certain divisions also have particular points to hold, which they do as best they can. Then again the whole army is not always engaged at one time. Divisions are placed quite a distance apart, but near enough to come to the help of the others when ordered so to do, and there is a reserve corps to be relied on in extremity.

Nothing is allowed to interfere with the range of the guns; houses are burned, trees cut down and the whole country laid waste; every obstacle must be removed that in the least obstructs the view. It was so about Chattanooga. The destruction of property was terrible. After a few hours' work, I have seen families who had been living in handsome houses with gardens and orchards, deprived of them and have nowhere to lay their heads. Scores of dwellings, many of them with ornamented grounds and handsome outbuildings, were thus cleared away, and the inmates had to seek for shelter where they could. Everything except what was needed for defense was swept from between us and the enemy.

The harvest moon shone in the heavens, but I shuddered at it, for it brought to mind the cold, stiff forms that lay but a short distance from us, many of whose still white faces were upturned in its rays; beloved forms that were bleached in the sun and whitened by the frost. Thoughts of them would come to me when I awoke in the night, and I would shiver, but not with the cold. The enemy would not let us bury our dead.

CHAPTER XXIV.

CHATTANOOGA.

WE were strongly intrenched. Our fortifications on the enemy's side were three deep. Their guns commanded the town. Now and then they took a shot at us but did little damage. There was occasional skirmishing between parties, and attacks were made upon our wagon-trains, in one of which the rebels killed the teamsters and burned about two hundred wagons. They would also pounce upon ambulances containing our wounded, but with these exceptions all was quiet.

Squads of deserters would come in; loyal men from East and Middle Tennessee, armed with old muskets or shot guns, kept in their homes to destroy wild game, gaunt and ragged, but resolute-looking, burning and eager for revenge, and longing for action. So the days went on, and towards the South, at least, we might consider ourselves in a state of siege. We bided our time, although rations began to be cut down.

There were many, many missing! How many lay in the Golgotha just outside us? how many wounded and dying languished in rebel hospitals and prisons we did not know. Our surgeons and nurses, contrary to all the usages of war, had been kept as prisoners; none had returned to tell the tale.

Kiler had been shot in the leg. One day as I helped him to an easier position than the one he occupied, he said: "I am afraid, Dick, Neff has gone, too—Jones says he saw him fall from his horse when he was shot, but he could not help him. I hope the ball killed him; he would not bear being a prisoner. If he could not hit them with his arm he would with his tongue, and they would kill him. Poor fellow! he was as generous as he was brave."

As he was an officer, I was in hopes we should hear something of him; but we did not. His body was afterwards found on the battle-field, recognized by the thoughtful care of his devoted mother in working his name on his stockings. It was conveyed to Cincinnati and buried among his friends.

Chattanooga was a great hospital. The wounded were everywhere, and daily friends arrived to look up their loved ones, dead, wounded or missing.

Among those who came on this errrand was Mr. James E. Murdoch, who hoped to get the body of his son, Capt. Thomas Murdoch, but he could not. The battle-ground was in possession of the enemy. While he was with the Army of the Cumberland, under the shadow of Lookout, with the whistling of balls for an acompaniment, he read and recited patriotic poems to thousands of the soldiers gathered to hear him. He excited their enthusiasm until they became almost wild. One day there was an unusually large assemblage. He had but begun his reading when the guns from the mountain opened, but he continued without interruption, for the balls whistled harmlessly over our heads, replied to by the huzzas and waving of caps that greeted the close of the poem.

He was one of the many who, not firing a shot, did yeoman service for the cause, without which it would have failed. Surrendering himself to the work, he held himself ready, without money and without price, to give entertainment at the call of any Aid Society needing funds.

MURDOCH RECITING TO THE SOLDIERS.

We realized we were in a state of siege; rations were short; men got thin on small allowance; and hundreds of mules and horses died daily.

It was wonderful the love the loyal people had for the flag; and what they endured to keep it. Women often begged me for my little one. A starving party came in one day and a woman drew a tattered bunting from under her clothes with the exclamation: "I swore they should never put their dirty hands on it." Col. J.——, attracted by the cheers of the men who had witnessed the act, told the following incident:

When marching to Chattanooga, the corps had reached a little wooded valley between the mountains. He, with others, rode ahead, and striking into a by-path, suddenly came upon a secluded little cabin surrounded by a patch of cultivated ground. At the door an old woman, eighty years of age, was supporting herself on a crutch. As they rode up she asked if they were "Yankees," and upon their replying that they were, she said:

"Have you got the Stars and Stripes with you? My father fought the Tories in the Revolution, and my old eyes ache for a sight of the true flag before I die."

To gratify her the colonel sent to have the colors brought that way. When they were unfurled and planted before her door, she passed her trembling hands over them and held them close to her eyes that she might view the stars once more. When the band gave her "Yankee Doodle," and the "Star Spangled Banner," she sobbed like a child, as did her daughter, a woman of fifty, while her three little children gazed in wonder.

They were Eastern people, who had gone to New Orleans to try to improve their condition. Not being successful they had moved from place to place to better themselves, until finally they settled on this spot, the husband having taken several acres of land here for a debt. Then the war burst upon them; the man fled to the mountains to avoid the conscription, and they knew not if he was dead or alive. They had managed to support life, but were so retired they saw very few people. The younger woman expressed some fears that the rebels would discover this demonstration and kill them, when the elder replied: "Let them: we can go up to God as surely from the valley as they from the mountain tops."

Leaving them part of their rations the men passed on.

It was about the 18th or 19th of October that General Rosecrans left the Army of the Cumberland. The Departments of Ohio, Cumberland and Tennessee, had been made into one under the name of the "Military Division of the Mississippi," and General Grant was appointed commander of the division. General Thomas became commander of the Army of the Cumberland, under General Grant, and vowed he would hold Chattanooga if we starved.

One of our signal stations was at Cameron's Hill. The point from which observations were taken was a crotch in a tall tree, reached by a ladder. I was sent there one day with a message to an officer, and he kindly allowed me to take a trip up the ladder and have a look through his glass. It was a clear day, and nothing could be more beautiful than the view. The town of Chattanooga was before me, its streets filled with our soldiers, their white tents dotting all the open spaces; army wagons, and people on horseback and on foot were hurrying across the various bridges, companies were exercising or parading on the commons, tents covered the suburbs, looking like villages of canvas interspersed with trees, and having here and there a house. These stretched away to the deep dark woods, behind which the rebel camp was plainly visible. The smoke of its fires hung like a thin cloud against the range of somber mountains in the background, while all around were lofty, rocky peaks, and about the whole the Spoon River (the Tennessee), wound in and out, in and out, like the coiling of a great silver serpent.

Going back we met a party of deserters from Bragg's army, under guard. One of them called out :

"Lookee, you powder monkey, you came near spoiling my mug the other day. I am glad you missed me, for I should have hated mightily to have had to come down to such a morsel."

I made no reply, but the corporal said :

"So, you spotted him, did you, Captain Phil? I heard you had been doing a little fighting in the battle on your own account; there was enough of him to hit."

I was mortified, for the man was six feet tall and very broad-shouldered.

The latter part of October, General Hazen's brigade with some hard fighting opened the river from Bridgeport to Brown's Landing, making a way for our supplies to come by water. The rebels were taken by surprise and ran. The river was cleared, a bridge and steamboat built, and the rations, which had been hauled overland by wagons, were now delivered by water to within two miles of the town, and all once more had enough. The first boat was built by Michigan men, and called the Chattanooga, a set-off to the locomotive built by Massachusetts men in the early part of the war.

General Hooker had a sharp fight about this time for Lookout Valley, but the mules did him nearly as good service as any of his regiments, and such as mules never did before. The armies were sleeping after the day's strife, when suddenly, from some cause or other, the mules became alarmed. The alarm spread, and they dashed forward like frightened sheep right in the face of the enemy's pickets, who, mistaking them for a cavalry force, fired and ran back to a brigade not far from them, screeching, "Hooker's cavalry is on us." Awakened from their sleep by the sound of musketry and galloping hoofs, the rebels supposed they were surprised and surrounded, and took to their heels, leaving everything behind them.

Our men, recovering from the confusion of the accident, demanded to know what was the matter; they were informed by the astonished teamsters, with the addition that they believed the mules were possessed of devils. They set off in pursuit, and not only returned with their own property, but had them loaded with knapsacks, blankets, and rifles, abandoned by the enemy. The rifles proved to be Enfield, and were nearly one thousand in number. Another accident occurred here, which also caused much merriment. The boys were fighting their way up a ridge. At the foot of a steep hill a regiment stood in file ready to fall in when ordered. A negro, who was above, became exceedingly terrified at the firing, and in trying to dodge a cannon ball, lost his balance, and doubling up rolled down the steep declivity, separating the ranks, and knocking a man out of each in his passage. The men saw him coming, and in the uncertain light thought he was a shell. When Sambo reached a level spot he stopped, and jumping up shook himself, felt first his shins, then his head, and much to the chagrin of those he had hurt, and the amusement of those he had not, said, in great perplexity:

"Golly, massa, dis nigger tought him was killed."

There was soon to be another battle. This was evident from the movements going on. I questioned John, and he told me he thought there would be an attempt to wrest Lookout Mountain from the enemy when Sherman, who was on his way to Chattanooga with all his force, should come up. Troops were changing position, and wagons were hauling great loads of timber up the river, in which direction none but soldiers were allowed to go, but no one knew anything. If you asked what was going on, the answer was sure to be, "I don't know."

On the 19th of November, some of General Sherman's command came in " the boys" said, and going up the valley camped at the foot of Walden's Ridge. That night orders were published that each man should supply himself with two days' provisions, and one hundred rounds of cartridges. "'Unconditional' was going to take a pop at them, that was certain," said the men. There was joy in the prospect, which was changed to some grumbling on Saturday morning, when it was found these orders had been countermanded in the night. The rumor that there was going to be a battle had got abroad among the people, however, for when the mists arose from the hills around the city, they were seen to be dotted all over with persons who had come out to see the show. It reminded me of Bull Run.

John told me privately that the postponement was on account of General Sherman not having arrived ; that there was to be a general battle, in which he would take an important part ; that the bulk of his army was then on the road between us and Bridgeport. The commanders were doing everything to mask their movements from the foe, as they wished to take them by surprise.

The grumbling and wondering went on, helped by the weather, for on Saturday morning when we got up we found it raining. It rained all day until evening. Then the spirits of the men rose, we would be sure to be up and at them on the morrow; somehow our best fighting had always been done on Sunday.

Sunday passed and there was no battle, and no sermon from the "devil's pulpit," as the men called a heap of rocks up Lookout, from near which they were sometimes shelled. Kiler, who had caught the rumor of the expected engagement, and was as cross as man could be, worrying on his mattress, asked me to tell John to come and see him. John had put him, in a manner, in' my charge, and did various little things for him.

"So, captain, we are to have a fight," he said to John, as we stepped in to see him, Sunday evening.

"The boys seem to think so," was John's reply.

"Humph! and here I am, tied like a dog to a stake; I would not care if it was a great wound, or if I was in great pain, but to be kept here for such a trifle as this."

"A bullet through your leg is not considered a very small thing," said John, and he tried to reason with him; Kiler would not listen.

"Come," he said, impatiently, "stop preaching and sing for me; if ever a man was cut out for a parson you are."

John sang several hymns. When he arose to go, and stood by Kiler shaking hands, Kiler drew him towards him, as though he had something to say, and kissed him. It sent a pang sharp as a knife through me, for I knew he was thinking of the morrow, and the probabilities of seeing John again. He only said:

"Give them Hail Columbia, captain."

He was a queer fellow. His brother had entered the army, was made prisoner, escaped, was chased by bloodhounds, retaken, and died in prison. They were the only children of rich parents. After his brother's death, he joined the regiment as a private, to avenge him, he said. He had been wounded in the last battle, and was nearly well, but had caught cold, and his wound had become inflamed. When in action he fought like a hero. He refused to be sent home, preferring to stay near the army to being where he could have every comfort and luxury. He spent his time writting letters to his mother, ofttimes in rhyme, and almost always illustrated with the funniest and most grotesque drawings imaginable.

Monday the 23d was bright and clear ; the enemy's guns and ours exchanged the compliments of the day, no unusual thing ; indeed Moccasin Point and Lookout were constant in such little attentions to each other, keeping up a cross-fire over the Tennessee.

That something was about to take place was evident, when, near twelve o'clock, brigades with drums playing, and banners flying, arms brightened until they shone like silver, and every man in his best array, marched out and took possession of the open ground between the river and the railroad right below Fort Wood. Again it reminded me of the display at Bull Run. The heights around were crowded with people, as they had been the day before.

It was a reconnoissance, they said, and they watched the movements of the brigades as they fell into line of battle, or turned off into the woods, with intense interest. The enemy watched also, not expecting an attack, thinking we were having a review ; but when night came, and the reconnoissance was over for the day, they found this review had cost them their first line of entrenchments. Our men, exultant in their success, had thrown themselves down to rest, ready to be up and doing at the first tap of the drum. John told me, that night, that it would be a great struggle, and explained somewhat how he thought the different points would be attacked.

It was late when I awoke on Tuesday morning, November 24th. All was bustle and expectation; the army was in motion and, I was told, had been since two o'clock. Sherman's men had arrived. Rebel pickets had already been driven from the bank of the river by a force that had come down it, and we were now entrenched on ground but a little while since held by the foe. I could not tell where all the men had come from; they were crossing the river, swarming in the boats; lining the shore. There was no longer silence or secrecy; cannon bristled all along the banks of the Tennessee, drums beat, and flags flapped in the morning breeze.

Our forces were between Lookout and Mission Ridge, and General Hooker was storming the mountain. Never was there such a scene; the men fought right up the steep sides, ridge by ridge, oftimes holding to crag and bush, with the fire from the enemy directly in their faces; they never flinched nor wavered; General Geary on one side, and General Hooker on the other, meeting on the top. The dead fell in their paths; they rushed over the bodies, following the colors, which kept ahead. The roar of musketry and cannon, reverberating from the mountains round, was almost deafening, and with it could be heard the yells of the rebels and the shouts of our men. One moment the smoke hung low and hid them in a pall; the next it melted away and you saw them struggling, as though it were in mid-air, fighting upon points and ledges, or hurling each other into space.

It began to rain, and night came on; breathless the army and the people watched Lookout. It grew dark, darker—the mountain loomed like a great giant black in the night; the flash of musketry, the explosion of shells, the lightning of the cannon revealed the forces fighting amid the clouds and the darkness. I could but think of Paradise Lost and the battle with Satan, the description of which we used to parse in school. It might have been his expulsion from Heaven.

We marked General Hooker's course by the fires kindled by our men, as they gained the ridges. We in the valley shouted and cheered, as fire after fire told they were reaching upward. Unmindful of weather or darkness they kept on, climbing, as they fought, great heaps of rocks, that jutted in their path at almost every step, and at length they gained the summit.

It was past midnight when they lay down, conquerors of Lookout, with our army stretching almost to the foot of Mission Ridge.

I was weary enough that night, and slept heavily and late, forgetting all about Kiler, whom I had promised to see, and to tell of the progress of the battle. In the morning I was awakened by the most terrific shouting and hallooing.

"What is it?" I said, rubbing my eyes sleepily.

"Look there! Look there!" said one, seizing my arm with the grip of a vice, and swinging me round with a jerk that sent me spinning, at the same time pointing to the mountain.

From that huge fan-shaped group of rocks that crested Lookout, the Stars and Stripes, borne on the wind, stood straight out, flaunting in the face of General Bragg, as he gazed at it from his headquarters on Mission Ridge.

It had been placed there by the officers of the Eighth Kentucky. A moment before I had shivered with the cold, but I was hot and strong at that sight; and, darting for my little flag, I seized and waved it, hallooing and shouting as loud as the best.

The roar of battle from the direction of Tunnel Hill told that General Sherman had begun to fight for possession of Mission Ridge; hour by hour it continued.

The crest of Mission Ridge was crowded with rebel soldiers, a living mass; presently they rushed upon our force, and the cry came that our boys were running.

A breathing spell, then there came a movement near our center; the troops there were seen to rush forward into the woods, behind which were the enemy's lines of rifle pits protecting the ascent of the mountains. These pits our men were ordered to take. Like a torrent, bearing everything before it, they swept on; then there was a dash, a crash,—the rebels were seen to run; the rifle-pits were ours; cheers and shouts, caps in the air, and frantic exclamations told the tale.

A few minutes more, and up the Ridge, from which blazed the enemy's guns, sending showers of balls in their faces, with shouts of defiance for the foe, and cheers of encouragement for each other, the men rushed.—Breathlessly they were watched; up, up, and on they toiled, Sheridan in their ranks. One moment they were hidden in smoke, belching forth in the midst of which came the roar and flash of the cannon, as though the mountains had rent and opened upon them. Still they kept on, till hot and breathless they reached the top, charging the amazed foe, who turned and fled by hundreds, throwing down their arms.

General Baird's division still fought on the left, seeing which, the boys turned the captured cannon on the rebels and gave it to them with their own guns. The day was ours. From Fort Hindman, where the rebel flag had floated a little while before, the Stars and Stripes were now seen. Our troops had been ordered to take the rifle-pits, and they had taken the Ridge.

The Graybacks were in full retreat. "Chickamauga, Chickamauga!" had rung like a trumpet call along the lines. One little fellow, but a boy, belonging to the Sixth

Ohio, made it tell. He captured a rebel captain, who very naturally refused to go to the rear at the bidding of so small a soldier, whereupon the little patriot thrust him up to the breastworks, and, giving him a kick behind which sent him head-long down the hill, shouted, "Chickamauga, hang you."

As night came on and one portion of the army learned what the other had done, shouts filled the air. The attack had been made in six different places. Of course, I can but feebly describe the one I saw and watched. There were so many prisoners, we scarce knew what to do with them, officers and men; and for trophies, besides flags we had arms and artillery in abundance.

Thursday morning showed the foe had fled from Tunnel Hill, which was all of the mountain ridge the last night's fight had left him, and was in full retreat, a line of smoke marking his course, and telling the means taken to retard pursuit.

The army rejoiced over what it had done. Men praised each other's deeds, but all praised the gallant color bearers of the storming regiments, who had mounted the ridges ahead of their comrades, challenging them to follow, while they planted the banner in the midst of the foe.

John told me he heard a gentleman belonging to the Christian Commission tell our general that while the troops were shouting at the sight of their standard on Mission Ridge, he met some soldiers carrying another in a blanket, and asked who they had there?

They replied: "Our color-sergeant."

He requested them to stop a moment, and stooped down and said:

"Sergeant, where did they shoot you?"

"Most up the ridge, sir," was the reply.

"I mean where did the ball strike you?"

"Within twenty yards of the top—almost up," he answered.

His thoughts were all on his flag, he had no word for himself or his suffering.

"I mean in what part of your body are you wounded?"

The gentleman removed the blanket and saw his arm torn away, the bone of his shoulder in fragments, and the flesh hanging in shreds.

The poor fellow gave one look towards it.

"That's what did it. I was hugging the standard close, was almost up at the top, when the shell knocked me over; two minutes more, and I would have planted the colors on the top.—If they had only let me alone a little while longer—I was almost up, almost up;" and with failing breath he repeated, "almost up; almost up;" until his eye was glazed and his voice gone.

CHAPTER XXV.

AT CHATTANOOGA—IN WINTER QUARTERS.

WE were in winter quarters, "accumulating supplies" those who knew said, for a great campaign farther south in the spring. Things were dreadfully dull ; a little skirmishing now and then was the only break in the monotony of camp life. The enemy, now commanded by Hardee, had fallen back to Dalton. We were fortified and considered impregnable in our nest.

Christmas was again passed in camp. There was some fun going on ; many received boxes and other tokens from home, and were cheered by letters and presents. To others it was a sad season.

I had never seen General Grant. One cold morning I saw an officer standing near some of the fortifications in conversation with several others ; he was a short and not a stout person, with "pepper and salt" hair, little sharp bright eyes, and a closely cut beard. He wore a slouched hat, crushed down on his forehead, and a coat somewhat the worse for wear. I had often seen him going back and forth, generally in the company of other officers, and had particularly noticed his little sharp eyes, and that he was always smoking a cigar. I twice passed the group and had stopped near it once for several minutes when I saw him take a glass from one of the officers, and heard him addressed as general. John approaching me said : "Phil, that is General Grant."

"Where?" I turned, looking right and left and all around me.

"There, immediately before you. Why," seeing I was still staring around, "you were just looking at him." There were many officers near and as yet I did not distinguish him.

"See," John turned me by the shoulder, "the middle one in that group; he is now knocking the ashes off his cigar against the tree."

It could not be possible that the plain looking officer, with slouchy air, who was always smoking, and who, some how, I had set down as a poor officer with a large family at home of whom he was always thinking, was General Grant. I said so to John.

He laughed. "Why, Phil, I thought you had been long enough in the army not to judge a man by his dress, and surroundings. Clean collars are not found on trees, and service like ours is likely to take the gloss from a uniform."

"That is not it, John," I said testily, provoked at my want of discernment. "The general looks well enough but "—

"Yes, well enough for a working general, but you expected more fuss and feathers."

"Well, I did," I said laughing, "but I should have known better. I forgot the descriptions we have had of him at Vicksburg."

I kept in the neighborhood of the general after this, but at a respectful distance. I wanted to watch him. John told Kiler, who was about now, of my stupidity, and my remark, and he, saying he owed me one for forgetting him during the last battle, told it to several others. I was much annoyed at their calling out after me, whenever the general came in sight: "Hurry, Captain Phil, hurry, here comes the poor officer with the large family."

"Faix, and it's he has a large family, Captain Phil, and I hope he'll be after looking after them better than the auld soul who lived in a shoe ; by jabers she only gave them a blistering and sint them to bed. Arrah and the army's his family to be sure," said Patrick.

Returning from Bridgeport in the cars one mild day with John, we chanced upon a party aboard, most of whom John knew, who were going to stop at Shellmound in order to visit Nick-O-Jack cave, which is situated at the foot of Raccoon Mountain, some fifteen miles from Chattanooga. I begged John to let me accompany them, and, as the gentlemen had no objection, he consented.

We stopped at Shellmound station, and piloted by one of the party who had been there before, after a walk of nearly a mile reached the entrance. This was a broad chasm extending half way up the straight face of a cliff some seventy or eighty feet high, with shrubs and saplings growing from the crevices and large trees on top. The opening or mouth was nearly one hundred feet across. A little river, about thirty feet wide, issued from one side of this aperture and directly under the opening widened into a basin ; a small boat, upside down and bottomless, lay half out of the water on the bank. Formerly the only way of getting in and out of this cave was in a boat on this river. I stooped down, and scooping up some of the water in my hand tasted it ; it was anything but pleasant and was of a green color. I must confess I had some tremors about going in ; it looked like trespassing on the dominions of the prince of darkness. The gentlemen had beguiled the way since we left Shellmound talking of the cave, and had told wonderful stories of its having been a hiding place for robbers. The question arose might it not now hide rebels ? The mouth of the cave was in our possession in Alabama, but its extent was in Georgia. It had been explored some six or seven miles, and there might be an outlet in that direction which the traitors knew and used; however I said nothing, but followed the lead.

We entered by the road made on the left by the saltpetre makers, the river being on the right. The front part of the cave was cumbered with old timbers, hollow logs, and iron kettles. I stumbled over rocks and dirt, up and down, following the line of tubs, which were fixed along the wall, one above the other, two and three high, to catch the drippings from which the saltpetre was procured. It was not all one space, but there were apartments, some large, others small, with beautiful smooth sides and roofs; the farther we went in, the more wonderful it was. There were shining crystals like icicles hanging from regular arches over our heads; and beside and around us the dark sullen-looking river kept on its way in the channel it had wrought for itself, telling no tales.

We spent several hours within it, poking into the leach tubs, examining the logs and other articles used by the rebels in their saltpetre making, after we had satisfied our curiosity concerning the cave itself.

I sat down on a rock, or on the edge of a tub. While waiting I threw the clay out with a stick, or tried to break off stalactites, or cast stones into the river to sound its depth, and threw the light from my pine-knot down into it; I listened to the gentlemen talking, mostly of the war, each telling some experience he had gone through. Then they made an estimate of the value of the cave, its future uses, what might be made from it—at least while the war lasted, and pointed out the great loss it was to the foe, etc.

Once more we were out in the daylight, and glad was I that I had said nothing of my fears. We looked around us for a few minutes; then were ready for something to eat, and, after that, being desirous to take the first train for Chattanooga, we hastened back to Shellmound.

I never ceased wondering at the "common people" of the South, "the poor white trash;" they appeared to have no idea of putting their wits to work to better their condition, their only thought was to "make shift" for the time being. I have seen a man take twenty minutes day after day to bolster up a gate to keep cattle from his yard, when with a hammer and nails I could in ten minutes have made it secure. If a wagon broke down, they would tie it up, if it could be tied; and so keep it tied until it broke down again. If their harness gave way, they out with a pen-knife, cut two holes, and tied it together, and it remained tied month by month. They never dreamed of mending it. "What's the use? That holds;" they would say. The unsightliness never troubled them in the least; they had no eye for it, and this was not only true of the common people but of well-to-do planters.

Their houses were in the most worn-out condition; everything was going to ruin. They never had much, were not able to get more during the war, and had not taken care of what they had. The common candlestick of the country was a potato, sometimes a bottle. Of plates and dishes there was the greatest scarcity. I have seen whole families eating their meals from broken pieces of crockery with their fingers. One very decent family had no forks or spoons; Private Webb, who had quite a talent in that way, got some hard wood and carved out of it a pretty set of spoons and three-pronged forks. He polished them, and they were very neat. Any housekeeper would have prized them. These he presented to a woman, who appeared very grateful. The next time he went that way there were but two left! "The children tuk 'em ter dig and shuvel with, they did." One-third of these people were barefoot and the remainder wore shoes made of cloth with woolen soles. Their clothes were homespun; as for household linen, towels, etc., they had none.

"Where did you get that parrot, Charley?" said Kiler, as we came suddenly on a man who had an ugly, ravenous-looking bird fastened by a short chain to a stump, he holding a tempting morsel, at which the bird was snapping.

"I bought her from a woman on the tramp here for a piece of tobacco. Hang Jeff Davis,"—this was said to the bird, who again snapped at the cake—"she did not like to part with the thing, but could not resist the weed. She loved the parrot much, but bacca more. The confounded beast is secesh and she won't say 'Hang Jeff Davis.' She has got to, though, or starve; she said 'Damn the Yankees' fast enough when I first saw her. I have thrashed that out of her, though. She can talk glib as any one when she pleases to call for crackers or—" "Polly wants a cracker," interrupted the parrot, catching at the word.

He took a cracker from his pocket and held it up before her; she dived at it.

"You want it, do you? You have to say 'Hang Jeff Davis' first."

He put the cracker back and held the cake before her, repeating the sentence; she only screeched the louder, "Polly wants a cracker."

"Let me try," said Kiler, holding it towards her; she made a vicious plunge at him, and buried her beak deep in the fleshy part of his hand, drawing blood.

"Ha! ha! ha! she knows better than to try that game with me," laughed Charley.

Once more he held the cake, and, to his great joy, the

parrot screeched again and again, "Hang Jeff Davis," "Hang Jeff Davis," "Hang Jeff Davis."

Delighted, he caught her up, stroked her feathers and stuffed her with cake as she sat upon his shoulder, every now and then poking her bill into his beard. "She cost one reb his life," he said, fastening the little chain which held her to his button-hole. "'Twas in our last battle. I thought I had left the thing safe in camp, when just as we expected the summons 'fall in,' she came whirring along and perched on my shoulder—her place when we travel—screeching 'Polly wants her breakfast.' I had forgotten to give her anything when I left. One of the boys threw her a cracker, and I fastened her in a tree at a little distance; she kept quiet as long as she had the hard tack to file her bill on.

"Presently our turn came, and the bullets crashed all around us, making the splinters dance. She became uneasy, and flying the length of her chain from limb to limb, shrieked her whole vocabulary over and over. We were sent back a little, and while we were waiting orders the rebs came nearer the tree where she was making such a fuss. I watched them, for I did not want to lose her. One stepped forward and raised his piece, when suddenly she began to shriek 'Damn the Yankees, Damn the Yankees.' She must have caught the word from them, for I had stopped her at it. A loud laugh ran along their line and the chap lowered his rifle and made straight for the tree, determined to capture her. I wanted to wring her neck, but I was not going to let them have her to make fun for them, so I drew a bead on him and popped away; he fell, hit in the head. I ran from my place, seized her chain, and dragged her off, the bullets whistling round me. I half throttled her when I got her back, and she has never said 'Damn the Yankees' since." "Hang Jeff

Davis," "Hang Jeff Davis," vociferated the parrot as he finished.

"I would not take fifty dollars for her," he said proudly.

I enjoyed getting near the camp fires at night, and listening to the men's talk, for they had all sorts of strange adventures to tell. They thought of the dangers gone through only to exult in their escapes, light-hearted and merry. To hear them you might suppose there was no bloodshed or war in the world.

Private P—— was a capital horseman and had belonged to the courier line; he was one of the best riders at a time when it was important to keep up a constant communication with the distant parts of the army. Furnished with a fleet horse, a courier started, galloping a certain number of miles to a station, where another, already mounted and waiting, received the despatch; this man without a moment's delay set off over the ground he was to travel to the next point, which was often a designated place in the woods, where some five or six men bivouacked, and kept guard.

About the time of the siege of Knoxville very important despatches were entrusted to the couriers, and the rides were dangerous. P——'s turn came. His course was over the most difficult part of the road.

"It was nightfall," said he, "and the chap before me had been due fifteen minutes. I sat on my horse wondering at the delay. It was going to be a hard ride, though but five miles, for it had turned cold and sleety, with the wind from the North, and it was getting dark as a pocket. The road I had to travel was only a track through the woods, and to make it pleasanter we had information that bushwhackers were abroad in the neighborhood. I was talking over the danger with Smith and Jones, at the same time decorating Wild Fire's bridle and girths with boughs of cedar, for the want of something else to do, when the other fellow hove in sight, riding at a tremendous rate. I stopped to ask no questions, but got the papers, and was off in a twinkling, he calling after me that the rebs were on our track.

"You remember Wild Fire. He had more sense than most men, horse though he was; fleet as the wind, he knew exactly when to snort and when to be still; he knew the road, and though it was so dark I could not see his head, I trusted to him. We had done almost half the travel, when, getting to the top of a steep hill, the road being nothing but a narrow gorge cut by the water running down in wet seasons, I paused a minute, to let him get breath, and to pull my collar closer about my face, for the wind was driving right into us, and bringing with it little frozen particles, that stung like points of steel—were those voices I heard amid the storm as it swept by?

"I lowered my head and listened intently, and as I did so I touched Wild Fire's ears, and found he was pricking them up. The wind dashed in my face, bringing the same sound, human voices sure enough. In a minute I was on the ground. I happened to know the spot, for I had once stopped not ten yards off to examine a hollow tree, thinking coons might be in it. My eyes had become somewhat accustomed to the darkness, so that it was not quite so inky as at first. I led Wild Fire some four or five yards off, and fastened him to a clump of cedars, told him to be quiet, and went in search of the hollow tree. I had some little difficulty in finding it, as it was closer to the path than I thought; however, I stumbled on it, and very comfortable quarters it was. Hardly was I fixed when three men came along single file, and paused a few feet from me. After some curses on the weather, they proposed stopping where they were, and I found by their conversation I was their object.

"'He'll be likely to rest a spell when he gets up here, or go slower,' one remarked. They dismounted and fastened their horses; as they did so, one said: 'I thought I saw something moving yonder?'

"'So you did, the wind in the cedars; don't you git skeart, Bill!' Bill declared he was not skeart, using some hard words at the same time, and they seated themselves against a tree with their backs to the wind, a few feet from my hiding place, and began to talk, having first taken a drink from a flask, which with jokes they passed from one to the other. They were rather annoyed at my not making my appearance; they wanted my despatches and had some other work on hand for that night, for which they feared they would be too late. They told of two poor fellows they had hung that day. My blood was all in a boil, but I sat still figuring out what I was going to do.

"In a few minutes I crawled out from the tree. They neither saw nor heard me. I made my way to where Wild Fire was tied, and, slipping his bridle over my arm, cautiously crept to where their horses were fastened; fortunately for me, a few feet in their rear. Wild Fire knew what I was about, and walked like a cat. It was but a minute's work to loosen their animals; then, springing on Wild Fire's back, in a blast of the wind that came crackling through the trees, I rode close to them and fired.

"One of them, with an 'Oh!' fell forward on his face. The others sprung to their feet and turned towards me; then, with a strange sort of cry, and without firing a shot, ran for their horses, which were now tearing through the woods like things possessed.

"Safe in my saddle, I gave them a couple more shots

at random ; then, putting spurs to Wild Fire, went like mad. We had traveled a half mile when I heard shot after shot from the spot we had left. When I reached the post, a wild sort of cry was uttered by the guard, and they halted and questioned me before they would let me advance.

"I soon discovered the cause of their alarm. The cedars with which I had fixed up Wild Fire's ears stuck out like great horns, and those I had put in his bridle and girths made him look more like a harnessed devil than a human in the darkness. I laughed heartily. About three weeks after that some half a dozen of us passed that way again, and lying right where I had shot him was the body of the rebel ; it had been gnawed and torn by some wild animal. The leaves and earth around were clotted with dryed blood, a trail of it showing that another had been badly wounded. The boys helped me ; we dug a hole and put the body in it, cutting a stick to mark the spot. I can kill a man in battle without a tremor, am glad that he is down ; but somehow I don't like to think of that man there. I often wish I had not seen him."

"It would not trouble me a bit," said one. "They were after your life. Even the law allows you to kill a man in self-defense. I suppose the chaplain would say your putting the cedars there was a special providence. Queer, warn't it ?"

"How was it you and Captain Phil got away from them t'other day, Bill ? The colonel was hard on Captain Phil about that."

"He disobeyed orders, I reckon."

"I had no orders," I answered sharply.

"You came near having no need for any more. It don't do for small chaps like you to stray so far from camp ; however, it was as much mine and Dan's fault as yourn."

This was an adventure about which the colonel had reprimanded me severely, and John, who was very angry, and knew my proclivity to tell such things, had forbidden me to speak.

"Why, you see," Bill began—"you know Dan, the colonel's nigger? He's as smart as any white man I ever saw. We went out for a hunt, and met Captain Phil a little way from camp, who joined us, and we strayed off further than we thought. We were in the mountains, some six or seven miles off, and were on a sort of a low ridge after a coon, when suddenly Dan said, 'Golly, massa, thar's the rebels.' I looked, and saw on a ridge opposite us twenty horsemen; they saw us as we saw them, and, firing a volley, put spurs to their animals. I thought we had gone up. But Dan, seizing Phil by the arm, said: 'Come on, massa, come on.'

"We ran some two hundred feet across the smooth plat where we had been standing to the other side of the ridge, and went tumbling down its rocky face, urged on by the shouts of the rebels, who were after us in the valley. It was very cold. A creek ran at the foot of the ridge, which was frozen, except where it tossed over the rocks. You know what queer places there are all about these mountains, and how springs spout out everywhere? About half way down the side we were going there were several frozen to their source, as was shown by the large pieces, like curtains of ice, and heavy icicles, hanging from the earth and rocks.

"In one place we had observed that the water had frozen as it fell in a broad sheet eight or ten feet in length, which hung down the straight face of the cliff. It was to this place Dan made his way, clinging to rocks and shrubs, Captain Phil and I following. 'Hurry, massa, hurry!' he said, in a whisper, as we reached it. 'I har dem comin' tu de top on t'other side.' Scrambling over the projections of earth and rocks, covered with shrubs and trees, he let himself straight down beside this ice curtain, holding to a root, and then dropping off. Captain Phil and I did the same, and found, when we stood beside him, that there was plenty of space between the ice and the earth for a man to creep. He motioned, and we went in. Gathering some leaves and sticks, he quickly came after us, and stuffed them in the hole; leaving a small opening for a lookout. The action of the water had cleared out a spot sufficient for three or four men to lie in, having the rock overhead for a roof. Leaves had drifted into this hollow, making a soft bed, which was warm and dry, and the place was secure, too; for, unless you were beside it, you could not tell there was an excavation there, the ice curtain so completely screened it, except the hole at the side we had crept in at, and made it uniform with the face of the cliff. It was just like standing on the rocks behind the waterfall at Niagara, with the whole fall between you and the light."

"On a small scale, Bill."

"Of course. Well, we had hardly drawn breath after our run, when we heard them above us. They beat the bushes, poked among the rocks, and scoured the ridge over and over. At length they stood on the smooth plat above our heads. We could hear every word they said. They swore awful oaths that they would have us; we must be hidden somewhere; it was impossible for us to have escaped. The infernal nigger—they would tan his hide for saddles if they caught him. Then they stamped their feet, saying it was confounded cold; and, to amuse themselves, they threw bits of rocks down and broke off pieces of our ice curtain. Dan looked a little anxious at this, but he kept still. They soon tired of it, and concluded to make a fire and wait for the others.

"Accordingly, they grouped themselves, and prepared for a stay. We found from their conversation that they were a marauding party, doing a little private business on their own hook, and were now on their return from burning the house of a Union man and turning his family out into the woods. 'Poor white trash!' whispered Dan between his teeth; 'dey meaner dan skunks.' I had discovered this by their talk, their use and abuse of the r's.

"I was very tired, and after a time fell asleep and awoke in the night with the cramp, to find Dan also asleep and snoring. Awaking him we concluded to take turns until daylight, as it was no use to try and escape now, for we did not know how the enemy had distributed himself, and it was too dark to make discoveries. Captain Phil slept on.

"In the gray of the morning Dan cautiously moved the leaves and went out to reconnoitre. He was gone some time, and returned as noiselessly as he went.

"The party above consisted of twenty-five men; they had bivouacked on the open plat at the top of the ridge, from whence they were able to see the country for miles around; six of their number were posted as a guard, two of them occupied the rock above our heads. The captain of the company was Mr. Bryce, one, as Dan expressed it, of 'de Debil's own;' he owned the plantation next to his old massa; knew him well. He had gathered, from listening to the sentries' talk, that they were going to stay here for a day or two. 'Dey hab some deviltry in dar heads,' he concluded, 'for I hard 'em talk ob de widow Catlett and someting her daughters war tu du. She libs near Varnel's Station, and is a rebel all ober, and mighty cute, too, de darkies say.'

"We made up our minds to keep earthed until night. I emptied my pockets of crackers, with which I had fortunately filled them, and Dan produced a bag of parched corn, and we ate our breakfast. He then proceeded to stop the opening; he scratched up a few pieces of rock from under the leaves and placed them in the hole, thrusting sticks and leaves about them to make them look natural, and as though they had drifted there, saying to us in a whisper, 'Most on 'em will be gone derectly, and den t'others will go ter poking round tu pars de time and see what dey can see.' He placed himself close to the chink he had left for light, and with his penknife began working on a piece of sapling he had in his hand.

"I lay down among the leaves, and listened to the horses snorting and pawing above me, and at last fell asleep. When I awoke he was on his knees, Captain Phil beside him, looking intently through the little crevice, his rifle grasped in his hand; he heard me move, and made a quick motion for me to be silent. I seized my rifle and quietly crept to his side; he drew his head back that I might see out. There, within five feet of us, stood a Grayback, poking with the butt end of his musket in a hole. I drew back, and was instinctively about to sight my piece and fire, when Dan seized my arm, his eyes speaking plainer than any eyes I ever saw. We sat perfectly still and watched him. He left the hole, and seizing a bush to steady himself, swung down beside us, and stood leaning against the icy barrier, breaking off icicles with the end of his piece, separated from my hands only by the rock and leaves Dan had put there, his body keeping out all the light that had come through the crevice. He must hear us breathe, I thought.

"When satisfied with his amusement, he went on climbing down to the creek. We heard him swearing at the steepness of the cliff, and found he was after water ; and also discovered a guard was stationed below us on the bank of the creek, for its bed was the only road through the gorge.

"''Twould hab been all ober wid us ef you'd hab fired,' said Dan, still in a whisper: 'he hab us like rats in a trap.' I saw our only safety was in keeping quiet, for we could not put our heads out without being seen by the guard below. I slept as much as I could, but it was a terribly long day. The negro whittled, and now and then cocked his eyes and put his ear to the opening, listening to the conversations which were occasionally heard between the guard above and the one pacing below.

"Just at nightfall there was a clattering of horses' hoofs, and the man above us called to the one below, 'They made a fine haul, Sam!' which was replied to by complaints of the cold. After dark, Dan crawled out on a tour of observation. 'Dey'l be keen,' he said. 'tu har what t'others got tu say, and won't keep good watch. Now, Captain Phil, and you, massa, keep quiet.'

"He was gone some time, and when he returned he told me we must get away. He had made out from their talk that this point was a sort of rendezvous. The party that had left in the morning had brought five or six more with them. 'We must wait a bit,' he said. 'I counted the horses ; there are thirty-five ; we must cut dem loose, 'cept what we ride on. See har, massa'—he produced a tin horn ; 'I cut that from a saddle. How I did want to cut Massa Bryce's froat. I knew whar he was dar was deviltry ; hard him tell how he used a poor nigger to-day, didn't want to be took Souf ; he tied his wrists to his saddle, and cut up his hoss to a gallop, slashing de nigger and de hoss at de same time. De poor nigger fell behind, and de hoss dragged and kicked him, and when he was most nigh dead he cut him loose. He tell it wid a laugh, and say, 'Bound to be quiet now 'bout gwying Souf. Neber mind, de nigger's turn 'll come.'

"The night was very dark, and it had begun to snow. We waited until we thought them sleeping, then got out quietly. Dan had directed me which way to go and what to do; he gave us each a whistle. I found out now what he had been whittling at. 'Now, massa, you and Captain Phil go round yonder, and cut all de hosses loose; I'll go dis side. When youse har my whistle, be sure to mount de best hosses and take right up de creek. I'll jine you.' The wind made so much noise among the trees they could not hear us. Reaching the place where the horses were tethered, I chose one for each, and slipped my bridle on my arm while I unloosed the others. I had some difficulty, and they made considerable fuss. I was nearly through, when I heard a reb call out, 'There is something to pay among the horses.' The next minute I heard a shot, followed by the whistle and a long blast on the tin horn. We blew the whistles we had, jumped on our horses, and were about starting them down the steep side of the ridge to the creek, when I heard voices: 'The Yanks are on us!' I could hear, rather than see, a half dozen men advancing towards us. We fired, and drew the pistols from the holsters and fired again; there was a groan and a heavy fall. 'We are surrounded,' I heard. Then I blew the whistle loud, and turning to a point that in the gloom appeared less steep than the rest, dashed down it and up the creek. We had gone over about a quarter of a mile, when there was a galloping behind us. I paused and whistled; it was answered, and I knew it was Dan. 'Hurry up, massa,' he said; 'dey are after us,' he chuckled; 'dey tought de Yanks had surrounded dem fust, but I did not git de hosses all loose, and dey seed me.' I heard them coming, and we did not spare horseflesh. Several shots went past us, but we kept on over the stony road, between two walls as it were. Presently Dan said, 'Git off, massa, and you, Captain Phil, and give dat hoss a cut dat 'll send him flying.'

"I was down in a minute, and we drew under the shadow of a rock, the animals galloping off. As we crouched here unseen, nine rebels, urging their horses to their utmost speed, went by. Before they were out of hearing, we hastily crossed the creek and went a little distance below, where there was a cleft or gorge made by a small mountain stream. We began to mount the cliff by following the stream, and had just got in when five of the party went spurring by to join the others, having caught their horses. Their imprecations on 'that nigger' were loud and deep, as they passed the place where we lay. After a toilsome climb, we reached the top of the ridge, and sat down for a while. 'Safe now, massa, dis chile know dis country; was up har at Coosa Springs free summers wid old massa. I guess Colonel Bryce won't tie a nigger soon; ef he ar'n't dead he mighty nigh it. You see, I had trouble wid de hosses, and he warn't asleep; he come ter see what was de matter, and I couldn't stand to see him right dar, and I put a ball into him; dis roused dem all, and dey saw 'twas me. I tought one time I most gone, but de whistles and de horn dumbflustered dem; dey tought de Yankees all 'bout.'

"We heard no more of that party and about daylight reached the pickets in safety." Bill ended; I said nothing, but I felt he had stolen my thunder.

The men were kept as busy as possible, but there was not much to do, and they were ready for a hand at anything to pass the time. Going round the camps you might see them engaged in all sorts of occupations; every kind of game was resorted to. Often men would gamble away in an hour a whole year's pay. There was also preaching and exhorting. Among the more serious prayer meetings were held, and not unfrequently the sound of a hymn and a profane song would go up within a few feet of each other.

Officers were absent on furlough, and late in the winter, Captain Loomis, who always had thought for the men, returned from Cincinnati and brought with him several hundred little newspapers called the *Knapsack*, published at the Sanitary Fair which had been held in Cincinnati. These were distributed among the men and caused much satisfaction, as they told what the women and men at home thought of, and what they were doing for the soldiers in the field. They had heard of the Chicago and New York fairs and the wonders they had done, and now read with interest of this. They liked to know they were remembered. Often I have heard a veteran say to a new arrival: "What do they say of us at home?" They had a personal interest in the Sanitary and Christian Commissions. Once when some wagon trains were attacked, and stores belonging to these associations were lost, I heard a number of men swear (in a way that would have been anything but pleasant for the gentlemen of the Christian Commission to hear), that they did not care if Uncle Sam lost all his stores, he had money enough to get more and to pay men to take care of them, but it was a burning shame that these associations should lose what they had collected for the sick and wounded ; they hoped in addition that the rebels who did it would suffer for everything in the hospital.

Spring was beginning to come, the spring of the South, while it was yet midwinter at home. I spent much time going round the country. I went out to Huntsville, in

Alabama, and to Stevenson. John was always willing I should go anywhere if it was safe. I was several times up at the "Suck" in the river, which is ten or twelve miles from Chattanooga. After sweeping round the bend where the town stands, the Tennessee runs almost straight North, then makes another sudden curve to the South between Waldron's Ridge and Raccoon Ridge. At this point the river is full of rocks, is very deep and nearly three hundred yards wide, the current is so strong it carries everything before it. Waldron's Ridge rises perpendicularly almost; its face shaded with large trees and appearing like a great wall put there to keep the water back, which in revenge lashes itself in a rage on the other side, foaming and sputtering, and sending wreaths and flakes high in the air. The boats could make no headway at this point; they were helpless amid the whirls and eddies formed by the boiling and foaming water, which dashes along at the rate of eighty miles an hour over the huge rocks.

As this had been the great channel through which we procured supplies, several windlasses were placed along the shore and manned by the men, a detachment under officers being always kept there for the purpose. The boat would put on all the steam it could carry, the men exert all their strength, and foot by foot it would be drawn through the whirling rapids past a certain point, when another windlass and another set of men would take hold of it. After two or three hours of such toil less than a quarter of a mile of the river was accomplished, and the meat and bread of the army went on its way in smooth water. It was hard work, but there was excitement in it, and the men did not dislike it. Those working the windlass on the boat shouted and "heaved ho" to those on shore; the lookers on cheered and encouraged, and sprung to the spokes with a helping hand when help was needed.

There are more twists and turns in the Tennessee river, between Bridgeport and Chattanooga, than in any river I ever saw, and both the "Suck" and the Narrows have to be encountered in that short distance.

The army began to be impatient for a move; the weather was getting warm and they were very tired of being cooped up in the mountains. The rebel pickets extended to Ringgold, and they were pressing on our lines. General Grant, somewhere about the 7th of March, I think, was made commander of the whole army, and had left for the Potomac; General Sherman was appointed commander of the Department of the Mississippi, embracing the Departments of Ohio, Cumberland, Tennessee and Arkansas. Great preparations were making for a campaign. General Sherman was back and forth from Nashville, and finally made his headquarters there.

We had advanced somewhat. General Palmer occupied the Chickamauga battle-field; and the ridges in the neighborhood were fortified. The rebels were at Tunnel Hill and Dalton.

As soon as we had possession of the ground, the First Ohio sharpshooters were sent out to bury the dead of that battlefield, who for nearly five months had lain where they had fallen, exposed to sun and wind and storm, rotting above the earth. Captain Barber preserved every relic for the friends, and tried to identify the corpses by every means in his power. He buried eight hundred and seventy-four bodies, which the rebels had let decay in their sight. They would not bury them nor permit us to do it. I went over the battle-field with John, and down to Crawfish Springs, where we were told we should find the grave of Captain Thomas Murdoch. He was buried by our surgeons, who remained with the wounded when the hospital was captured by the rebels. In a field near the Widow Glenn's were some twenty or thirty graves, and among them was his; the name written on a board at the head. The body was taken up and sent home for burial.

They showed us the ambrotype of a lady which had been picked up in the field. Several of the kind had been found; also letters, envelopes, knapsacks, cups, etc., all of which were taken care of for loved ones away. Most of these articles had names or initials on them, by which they could be known. The command which occupied the spot where they were found was carefully noted down to help to identify the parties to whom they belonged.

When about a mile and a half from Crawfish Springs, we came upon a party as they were going to bury the body of an officer found there; he could not have been recognized by his best and dearest, except through his clothing and hair; he had on no trousers, but white cotton drawers and shirt, and a frock coat; his hair and beard were brown. They measured him and he was nearly six feet in height.

This sight, more than anything else, made me feel bitter to the rebels; it seemed so horrible to let their poor victims lie out like beasts.

A few days after this I was cleaning my gun, while John was lying under a tree reading. A prisoner, who had been brought in the day before, stood with a group under guard quite near me. I put down the piece to get something from our quarters; he took it up. As I returned he was showing it to another, and said, when I drew near: "This is Colonel L——'s gun; he lost it at Bull Run." The guard ordered him to let it alone.

"It might have been his gun," I said, taking it from his hand, "but I captured it, and it is mine now."

"Be you the chap that wounded him thar? I hern him say he'd enermost give its weight in silver to git it back. His father fetched it from France and thar's the family arms on it. I lived on his place you see, and seed him many a time shoot with it."

"I don't know whether I wounded him or no; don't think I did, but I picked up this piece there, and he shall not have it for his weight in gold."

I spoke earnestly and short. The man stood still a moment, then said: "Wal, both sides run that ar' day, they did; neither know'd how bad t'other was hurt, but think you'se run the fastest."

I made no reply; only scowled at him and walked away.

"Phil," said John, after a moment, "I think you forget that man is a prisoner."

"No, I do not," was my reply, "but I was thinking of the poor fellows out there," pointing in the direction of the Chickamauga battle-field, "and I hate their outlandish talk."

"That was the fault of his superiors," John pointed as I had done; "and, as to his talk, I advise you, if your ears are so delicate, to avoid Yorkshire should you ever visit England."

John's tone was cold, and, rather crestfallen, I rubbed away in silence.

Deserters came in every day, often in parties of thirty and fifty. Hundreds would join us in the course of a month. They all expressed themselves tired of the war, and railed at the hardships they had to endure and the scarcity of food. All through the winter our quartermasters gave out rations to the destitute at Chattanooga.

It was in the army of the Tennessee that I first saw negro soldiers. I had heard them talked of, and some of our men who had seen them told me they were the funniest looking troops they had ever seen. So I went out to look at the first company that arrived, expecting to have a good laugh. I was never more surprised in my life. They marched like one man; not, as John said, with the independent, go-ahead tread of the white volunteer soldier, but with the regularity of a machine. Each man seemed intent upon what he was doing and upon doing it well.

They held themselves and their arms beautifully; along the whole line there was scarce a hair's variation in the level of their guns. Their dress was neat, and when they went through the exercise they were perfect in drill.

I afterwards stood by John's side, amid a group of officers who were talking of these soldiers. One officer said they would drill all day long until the white officers were tired out, and they would drill by themselves half the night; that they were more particular about their equipments than most of the whites; more precise, and fought like wild cats.

They also spoke of their truth and fidelity to the cause. A gallant officer, who was their warm friend, stated that when at Memphis he had been ordered with his command, only a remnant, to march some distance from the city, and camp at a certain place. He did so. On his arrival there a soldier informed him that a negro woman, who was hiding in the bushes, desired to see him. He ordered the man to bring the woman to him. She was brought, and told the officer that the rebels had information that he was to be there, and would soon surround him; she had heard her master talking of it the evening before, and had walked through the woods, at night, a distance of eighteen miles, to warn him. He heeded the warning and moved off, having only twenty minutes the start of a detachment of twice his number, who reached the spot to find him gone. He afterward captured the officer in command of that detachment, who asked him how he had received information of his approach at that time, stating that he was certain he had trapped him.

The negroes who followed our army in its march all through, dug and spaded, and corduroyed and laid bridges, in swamps and on dry land, under orders, late and early, with cheerfulness and alacrity.

As John and I talked about the negro soldiers, he said: " Their soldierly bearing is all the result of obedience, Phil. They neither ask why or wherefore. Their duty has been to hear and obey. This has been the whole of their education."

" The better slave the better soldier," I said, laughing.

Some of the men looked at their black comrades in the most curious way; they could not understand that "a nigger" could make a soldier; others received them kindly, but the Irish jeered and laughed at them on all occasions.

I often went to the Provost Marshal's office, where there was always a crowd waiting for orders to get provisions; negroes and white people, young and old; those who had always been poor, and those who had always been rich, and were now ruined, standing side by side waiting their turns—beggars at the door of the government they were trying to ruin. Between five and six thousand persons got their daily rations there, and had nowhere else to turn for bread. I pitied the women I saw; sometimes two or three little children, who had evidently been accustomed to being petted and waited on, clung to their mother and cried for the salt pork and hard tack which the mother patiently and gladly waited for permission to get.

Yet our men all said the women were a great deal worse than the men. Kiler said it was the old story, of "Satan finding some mischief still for idle hands to do," for the Southern women had never put their hands to the use God intended they should, and were now frantic at the idea of losing their slaves, and being compelled to do something.

Katie, a bright mulatto girl, who did washing about the camp, was a runaway slave—free now. On one of the officers asking her what her work was on the plantation, she said : " I did nuffing but wait on young missus, and when she got married I went to her home. I had to fotch her things and dress her, and put on her shoes and wash her feet, and comb her har, and scratch her back, and put on her stockings, and fotch and carry for her."

" Was she good to you ? "

"Yes ; sometimes she would fotch me a box on de head dat enermost would knock me over, and if I did not git her har right would pull my years ; but mainly she was purty good. I allays had a good place to sleep in her room on de floor, and a big piece ob carpet for de cober. It was mighty warm by de fire."

This scratching of the back appeared to be a luxury peculiar to the South. I have heard one man ask another to scratch his back, and ladies who visited the South said it was a common thing for a young lady, when going to bed, to call a negro girl to scratch her back for her, and she would keep her at it sometimes for half an hour while she sat in her night dress and talked.

March had gone. The weather was becoming very warm. The country around looked beautiful, flowers new and strange bloomed on the hills, and beside the little streams in the valleys. The men were busy, and the bustle and din of preparation was on all sides. Our winter quarters at Chattanooga were fairly broken up, and the hot summer of the Southern country was before us.

"This campaign will make or mar us, Captain Phil, and put us to our mettle," said a gallant son of Indiana, as he wiped from his brow the drops that an overhauling of boxes had brought there. And it did, and it showed the enemy what metal there was in the West, and in the whole country.

The men spent much time carving pipes, and cane heads, and little figures out of laurel root. Kiler had a set of chess men he had carved and inlaid with red cedar. He called them Joe Hooker's men, because the roots were dug on Lookout Mountain. Thimbles, and cups, and pipes were sent home in numbers by the boys when they had an opportunity. I saw a great big Pennsylvanian, with his spectacles on his nose, busily engaged carving a doll for his little girl at home. John said he loved him for it. All liked the brave Pennsylvania troops.

CHAPTER XXVI.

ROCKY FACE—RESACA.

"HURRAH," I shouted when John told me General Sherman had taken up his quarters with the army, "now we know there is something on hand."

"Yes, we have a summer's fighting before us," was John's reply.

It was the first of May. Some time before this the giving out of rations to the destitute had stopped by order ; everything was wanted for the army. This looked like business, the veterans said. The railroad had been bringing in barrels of pork, coffee and sugar, and boxes of hard tack ; these provisions stood in great piles ready for distribution to the several divisions, which were coming up and massing about Ringgold. The weather was fine, and the men eager to get on ; they were packing their knapsacks, putting things in the smallest possible space. Orders had been issued that no baggage that could possibly be done without, would be allowed, as the men must be unincumbered.

Now the whole army was in motion and the fighting began. After the battle of Stone River, I had remonstrated with John about being sent to the rear; I felt mean and it looked cowardly.—I was no coward—to be put back with the teamsters and non-combatants, "the tail end" as the boys called them.

Kiler took my part, told John he was making a baby of me—said that lads no older than I did duty every day in the service, and that he was glad Phil had more spirit than to desire to be among that crew, often made up of skulkers and bummers, the scum of the army. He had known them to play poker and brag while the greatest battles were fought, and hardly stop the game to ask which side was victorious.

Kiler had great influence with John. They had been at school together, and although John was only a merchant's clerk and Kiler was the son of a rich and a fashionable man, they liked each other. Kiler had enlisted in John's company, but, as he told me himself, it had been terribly hard for him to get into harness, and learn to obey orders. One day John instructed a sergeant to take men and perform some duty, and told Kiler he wished him to be of the number. Kiler was seated comfortably reading at the time. " Pshaw, Wharton," he said, " what is the use." " The colonel wishes it done," was John's reply. " Ridiculous, perfect nonsense, always disturbing a fellow just when he happens to be a little at ease." He continued his grumbling, though he prepared to obey the order, and John walked away.

" Now you see, Phil," said Kiler, when telling me this, " any other man ' dressed in a little brief authority ' would have given me very serious trouble for this. It was almost insubordination, and in the presence of others too. I forgot John was my commanding officer, and instead of obeying the order without a word, as a private should, remonstrated in rather contemptuous tones as man to man. Wharton had too much good sense to notice it, and I suddenly saw my own error—I know no officer in the service who is so readily and cheerfully obeyed as he."

We had Taylor's Ridge and Tunnel Hill, and the rebels had fallen back to Buzzard's Roost Gap. This is a great chasm or opening in the Range of mountains between Tunnel Hill and Dalton. On one side of this chasm rises Buzzard's Roost, to the height of some seventeen or eighteen hundred feet, a sugar loaf shaped hill. I was told it took its name from the number of buzzards always seen hovering around its top, as though waiting to make a meal of us. On the other side of the gorge is Rocky Face Ridge, which got its name from the fact that it presents an almost straight face of fifty feet in some places, not a crag or bush for a bird to light on, or shrub for a man to cling to. The railroad and the common dirt road, and a creek called Mill Creek, all pass through this gap in the mountains, of which the rebels had possession. They had dammed the creek, thereby making a large lake, and had fortified the dam, while all the ridge in the vicinity bristled with cannon, covering the railroad and every approach.

It seemed as impossible to take the gap as to take the moon, yet the men were going to try. It stood in their path, and it must be taken or they must give way.

On the seventeenth of May we had gained a hill on one of these ridges, and after night some of the men proceeded to draw artillery up there. They fastened ropes to the gun carriages, and clung to roots and pointed rocks, hauling the heavy cannon after them. They would slip back, halt, take breath, and at it again. They were drawn down by the weight of the cannon and those in the rear were unable to bolster up. They would regain their footing, cling to a projection, and slowly mount again. After incredible labor, with bruised limbs and heavy with weariness, they reached the top, planted their pieces, and in the hazy moonlight threw themselves on the rocks to sleep.

The next morning the attack was renewed all along

our line, upon Buzzard's Roost and Rocky Face. General Geary's men fought their way up ridge by ridge. Every step was bloodily won. From rock and crevice, and concealed rifle pits, a deadly fire was kept upon them by the foe, while cannon rent their ranks. But on they went, taking advantage of each projection and making every tree and bit of rock do duty as a breastwork. Crash would come the huge stones, rolled down among them by the foe, crushing and mangling the poor fellows, dashing them from their insecure foothold to the ledge beneath, leaving them a shapeless mass of flesh. With hardly a look, their comrades pressed to the top, springing over deep gorges which opened in their path.

At the top the cliff shelved back, and there arose from it palisades of rocks almost like a built wall; above this lay the smooth surface of the crest, spreading out in a broad space, thronged with rebels. Scrambling, springing, dashing, our men gained the palisades, and went rushing over. Face to face, hand to hand, they grappled with the foe, struggled and tugged. Some gained a footing, some were thrown back down the mountain. Others hugged their opponents and together they went down to death. All the while a battery from a neighboring ledge was sending its bullets among them. Five times on that day did they force this spot from the rebels, and each time was it retaken. At length our men remained the victors, yet only for a little, for that night it was decided to be untenable, and our force was withdrawn. So ended the eighth of May.

All this John told me, and his face glowed as he spoke of the deeds of the New Jersey men, who had been among the storming party. Every step of the way, he said, had cost a life, for we had been but a few days from Chattanooga, and our loss was reckoned at nearly a thousand men. "And what is going to be done now," I said, when he told me we had retired from Rocky Face Ridge.

"Nobody knows," interrupted Kiler, who was present; "if we cannot get through Buzzard's Roost Gap we can get through some other way. Old Billy, instead of looking after Johnston, I guess, will make Johnston look after him."

I had just fallen into a doze that night, when I was roused by Kiler's voice.

"Wharton! Captain!" John was on his feet in a moment. "There is a poor fellow on a ledge over here, who must be desperately wounded. I cannot sleep for his groans. I think if you will help me I can reach him."

"Bring the canteen, Phil; it is full of water," John said, as he started with Kiler. I followed to a place about three hundred yards off, where a cliff arose abruptly, and for ten or twelve feet presented a smooth surface of rock jutting out above in ledges, on which some stout shrubs grew. Our men lay all about sleeping.

"Oh, God!"

"Do you hear that?" said Kiler, as we reached the cliff. "It is but one of many, but somehow those groans came home to me to-night. I could not rest without an effort to relieve the poor fellow, and he is just out of reach."

"I think we can manage it," was John's reply; "here," he turned and stood with his back to the cliff, "sling this canteen over your shoulder, then climb up me to my shoulders or head, and I think you can reach that sapling that shoots out this side. You used to be the best athlete in the class." John braced himself against the rock, and Kiler climbed to his shoulders. "Stand firm," he said, as he reached there, and raised himself on tip-toe to gain the sapling. His first effort failed ; another, he could not touch it.

"Take to my head," said John.

"I am too heavy."

"No, no," was the reply, as a groan as of one in mortal agony reached us ; "make haste."

Kiler cautiously mounted to his head, with the aid of a stick I handed him, settled himself a moment, stooped, gave a spring, and caught the shrub in one hand. Bracing his knees against the cliff, he drew himself up and we lost sight of him.

There was a silence of some moments, then we heard him exclaim: "Good Heavens ! Bob, is it you?" Then there was a confused murmur of talking. In a few minutes he put his head over the ledge.

"Phil, run to that cluster of shrubs and bring the flask from the pocket of my overcoat. Stay," as I was moving ; "bring the overcoat and my blanket too, and rifle. Captain, you can manage to get them to me on the end of the piece.' It was a few feet to where he had been lying, and I was back in a moment with the articles. John put them on the end of the bayonet, and holding by the sapling Kiler leaned over and got them.

Five minutes passed and again he bent over the ledge. "Wharton, don't wait for me ; there is nothing to be done ; I shall stay here until morning."

Early next day he came to John ; the poor fellow we had heard groaning was his cousin, Bob Anderson, a rebel. "Blood is thicker than water," he said ; "that is the reason I was so drawn to help him ; he had grappled with one of our boys near the top there, and together they had rolled down the steep ascent, bounding from ledge to ledge, in each other's grip. Both had been wounded, and when they reached a resting place our man died, but in death held tight to his foe. The suffering and horror of his stark, cold enemy locked to him was greater than any suffering from his wounds," Kiler continued, "for when, by main force, I had relieved him of that he was easy. I would like to bury him, captain. I always liked him, poor fellow. He was kind-hearted and would not have put one of his negroes under ground with as little ceremony as we must put him. I have his watch and message for his mother and the girl he was to marry. He was an only son, and my aunt is a widow."

John ordered some men to assist him, and the two bodies were lowered and buried side by side under the cliff.

Some fighting was going on about Buzzard's Roost, but the troops were moving off. A cold rain set in which continued for several days, and as no fires were allowed to tell tales to the enemy, the situation was rather uncomfortable. On the night of the eleventh we lay without shelter, and the rain coming down on us, when suddenly a man, not far from where we were, began singing:

"Dark was the night and cold the ground."

The aptness of the words called forth some dry jokes from those lying about; but before the hymn was through there was a full choir of voices singing it. I could not but laugh the next morning when the storm was over to hear the same voice burst forth:

"The rosy light is dawning
Upon the mountain brow."

Looking around, I saw the voice belonged to a tall, thin backwoodsman, who was engaged in folding and strapping his blanket.

"He keeps his mind in unison with the elements," said John, smiling.

"And his hymns, too," I remarked.

"What! Long Tom?"

"We call him the barometer," said a private standing near. "He has tunes for all weathers and circumstances, songs for victory and defeat, and he is powerful in prayer."

Sherman did make Johnston look after him, for the best part of our army had gone further South, passed through Snake Creek Gap, where they had a smart skirmish with the enemy, and now were marching before Resaca, a little town on a bend of the Oostanula River, about fifteen miles from Dalton, which Johnston had fortified. The next news we had was that Johnston had withdrawn from Rocky Face, and with his whole force was at Resaca, determined here to check our further advance. Our men had torn up the railroad tracks, and the bulk of them were in the neighborhood of the Oostanula River, where there were plenty of hills, swamps, and ravines. It appeared to me that an ax had never been among these forests, the tangled undergrowth of which concealed hundreds of rebels; and every hill about this little village bristled with cannon. The sharp-shooters had their rifle pits artfully covered with brushwood, through which they could pick off our men without being seen.

On Saturday, the fourteenth, the skirmishing was general; a brisk fire was kept up all along our line, which extended much further than that of the rebels. We took their first line of rifle-pits, but on Sunday, as it had so often happened in this war, the battle was fought. One of the approaches to the town was up a steep hill, commanded by the rebels alone. It was a stirring sight to see our men charge upon the double quick, and the artillery thundering up, each piece drawn by six horses, the animals white with foam, with a driver to each pair, lashing them to fury.

The men talked much of an encounter which some of General Hooker's men, I believe, had with the rebels for a battery in a kind of fortification on the side of a hill, where the enemy's rifle-pits were thick above ; from these they kept a never-ceasing fire, hot and fast, on our boys as they approached. Several attempts to take it had been unsuccessful, but the Blues were determined to have the guns. They took breath, then made a rush, and succeeded in getting so close to the wall of the fortification that the guns could not be used against them, and they made sure they were not used at all by keeping a sharp lookout, and putting a bullet into any Gray who dared to show his head, while they were protected by the wall ; as one of them said, " a regular dog in the manger affair, we could not fire the cannon, and would not let them fire them." Here they stayed for some time. Night came on, but have the guns they would. The Pioneer Corps came to their aid, and amid showers of bullets, which fell like hail, undermined and broke in the sides of the fortification. The boys rushed in, fastened ropes to the gun carriages, and drew them out, while batteries on both sides sent shell and shot hurling through the night, making a noise I never heard equaled.

The next morning it was discovered that the enemy had retreated and crossed the Oostanula. I stood on a hill later in the day and saw the troops of Generals Hooker's, Palmer's and Logan's divisions march into Resaca.

We had lost many men ; hundreds of our maimed and dying lay in the valleys and along the mountains. Several of our generals were wounded, among them Generals Kilpatrick and Willeck ; but the enemy's loss was also great; they had suffered both in officers and men. We had taken a thousand prisoners and had beaten Johnston, and this was compensation to the army for all. Early in the morning we were in pursuit. Our forces came up with the rebels at Adairsville and Cassville; we drove them out, and for several days they ran and we followed, fighting. At length Johnston crossed the Etowah, burning the bridges after he had done with them. Our men lay at Cassville, Kingston and Rome, the latter a pretty place on the Etowah, near where the Coosa and Oostanula join and form the Etowah river. It is some seventy miles from Chattanooga. Here we made a halt to wait for supplies. The weather was bright, the country beautiful, large plantations and fine houses were scattered all along the banks of the river, but the owners had almost all run away. A few negro women and children alone were left in the great mansions. These had no fear of Linkum's men, but the white women shook with terror at our approach, believing we were capable of committing all kinds of atrocities, and would do so.

I was glad to get into a country not quite so mountainous. We were only some eighty miles at farthest from Chattanooga. Lookout Mountain, Missionary Ridge, Pigeon Mountains, Chickamauga Hill, Taylor and White Oak Ridges, John's Mountain and other ridges or spurs lay between Kingston and the river at that point.

We had a beautiful camp here, and I enjoyed every moment of the halt. The men were in the wildest spirits. We had plenty to eat, poultry and fresh meat, potatoes, hot cakes and honey. The negroes were capital cooks, and after the day's work were ready to dance or sing, or hold meetings. The men lay round the camp fires, and joked and told stories, each trying to outdo the other in the wonderful adventures he related. Often the glare of some burning house, found deserted by its owners, and so considered rebel property and lawful spoil, added brilliancy to the scene; yet no one ever knew who applied the fire, for if inquiry was made there was profound ignorance on the subject.

The first thing to be done, ere we could eat, drink and make merry, was to fortify; this was always the next thing after a halt, even for the night. Each company made its own fortifications.

The engineers drew the line, to mark where they were to run, the men scattering all along it, as posts, to keep the boundary; up hill and down dale, through swamps and over ravines. A detachment would start for rails; logs, rocks, trees, anything that would help to resist bullets, would be brought in by cart loads. In fifteen minutes the whole line would be bristling breast high; ofttimes trenches would be dug the entire length, the earth, thrown up between the sticks and stones, making a formidable breastwork behind which, in the trenches, the boys lay at their ease, ready to fight the enemy should he appear. I never knew the adage of "many hands make light work" so truly verified as I have seen it by an army fortifying.

I took great delight in the cavalry. It was a grand sight to see Little Kil, or Generals Garrard, Wilder or Stanley start out on an expedition; there was so much that was stirring and exciting in it, and they seemed so interested and alive to everything. I knew several of them—among others, Captain Lester Taylor, of General Stanley's staff, another gallant Ohio boy. They were kept moving on this march, but enlivened the leisure time they sometimes had in camp by races, which greatly excited and amused the men. While we were here on the Etowah, we had some fine races; a regular course was laid out, and animals entered for each heat.

I heard one man say to another at the track one day: "I say, Jack, that horse makes almost as good time as the deer that scart you so the day you took the back track at Chickamauga." "With the captain ahead," said the one addressed, hitching up his trousers as he answered; "we were only trying to catch up with him, to play a game of marbles on his coat tails." This was the first I had heard of a frightened deer that broke through the disorganized ranks that day, terrifying the men.

John and I had left camp early one morning and gone into Kingston. We were walking down the street when suddenly I was startled by the sound of a church bell pealing loudly quite near us.

"What does that mean, John?"

"It means that there is preaching in this church right before us, and we will go."

As he finished speaking we saw a guard enter the church and come out, having in custody a man in his shirt sleeves without a hat, and wearing a pair of trousers which were much torn; they marched him into General Sherman's quarters which were near.

We took our seats in the church and waited some little time for the preacher. When he arrived I was astonished to see he was the person who had been walked off by the guard; he gave us a fine sermon, and when the service was over we heard he had spent the morning cleaning the church and getting it ready for worship. In doing this he had torn his trousers; then he had rung the bell, for which offense he had been taken to the general's quarters, as the general had forbidden all bell-ringing. When he had informed the general it was Sunday, and he was ringing to let the soldiers know there was service, the general dismissed him saying, " he was not aware it was the Sabbath."

CHAPTER XXVII.

KENESAW MOUNTAIN.

ON the 23d of May we broke up our camp on the Etowah, and the whole army began to move towards Allatoona which was about twenty miles further South on the Western and Atlantic Railroad. We had rested ourselves and received plenty of supplies, so all were in good humor, ready to scale the Allatoona Mountains if it was necessary to do so, in order to dislodge General Johnston who had possession of the Allatoona pass and was fortified there. We moved in a southwesterly direction, and if I had been asked our destination I should have named almost any other place before Allatoona. Indeed the movements of the army were generally Greek to me until John explained them. We usually took a wide sweep and pounced down on the enemy when they thought us miles away.

As soon as we had crossed the river and were fairly *en route*, the fighting began and we fought all the time. Strange that I, who at home would have been horror-struck at the sight of a dead body covered with blood and wounds, here daily passed hundreds with scarcely a look.

"The rebs have the best of it now up there in their nests in the mountains," I heard one man say, "but wait 'till old Flanker gets on their track."

All day long the men fought—skirmishing they called it, but it was all a battle to me, yet not a battle in order; and at night when it was too dark to see to fight longer, they would fortify and lie down to sleep. All kinds of reports reached one column respecting the other. Now one would assert that our advance was engaged—another that Hooker's column was having a hot time—a third that Thomas was in trouble at Burnt Hickory, etc.

The country was not like that we had left behind. There were no fine houses and but few cultivated fields, but we passed through dense forests, thick with matted underbrush, and over rocky hills through the wilds of Georgia.

There came news of the engagement at Pumpkin Vine Creek, where General Hooker's column was hotly pressed. Then that General McPherson had reached Dallas, below which the rebels were strongly intrenched. Here there was a battle, and for a little time General Sherman had his headquarters in the town. Next our cavalry under Generals Garrard and Stoneman took Allatoona pass, and the enemy departed in the night. We had fought round the Allatoona Mountains, and now we had to fight over and around Kenesaw and Lost Mountains, for General Johnston was in position there, trying if possible to save Marietta. He was fortified south of the town, and his signal stations could be seen on the mountains, whose sides were bristling with cannon and crowded with men ready to meet us.

Rain, rain, rain—such rain as I never saw anywhere else, had set in. The sky was like a dull sheet of lead and the driving stream came down without ceasing. Sleeping in pools at night, to spring up begrimed with dirt and mud in the morning, and shake the water from one like a wet dog, by way of making a toilet, was now the order of the day. I went with John and Colonel —— to see the deserted rebel works, which were indeed very strong. The pits and holes they had made in the hillsides were as thick as, and reminded me of, the burrows of prairie dogs. So the days went by; we were in front of Kenesaw. There had been an attack upon our communications in our rear, and some of our supply trains had been captured, but we had plenty to eat for man and beast, and so far were all right. Our lines and the enemy's were not a quarter of a mile apart.

One of our batteries sent a shell to the top of Pine Mountain and killed the rebel General Polk who was standing there with some others taking observations. The enemy had retired—or been driven rather—from Lost Mountain by General Hooker, and now were in force at Kenesaw, which they had fortified, and made impregnable. So General Sherman besieged Kenesaw.

"You ole fool," said Jim, the captain's man, one day, shaking his head at the mountain, "you might as well have sum sens' like Davy Crocket's coon; he seed his marster and comed down, and you've seed yourn."

Kenesaw Mountain consists of two peaks, Big and Little Kenesaw. On the top of Big Kenesaw could be seen the rebel signal station, while their Bars floated from some works on the brow of the lesser mountain. Eight hundred feet high, and very steep, the peaks nearly joined at the top. The sides were covered with thick woods having a tangled undergrowth of dwarf shrubs, where whole regiments could be sheltered. Almost every foot of it was fortified; rifle pits and breast-works, and huge rocks, protected the foe; there were batteries on the top, and felled trees and entrenchments at the base. It was only three miles from Marietta, and was considered the citadel of the town. Negroes had been employed for months on its defenses, and it was thought impossible that the Yankees could take it. For two weeks we lay around its base. We had Pine and Lost Mountains, but this was right in our path, so with fire and shot and shell we besieged it. We would attack a point, gain an advantage or lose one, then pause for a day or two, perhaps, to pick out some more assailable place.

On the 24th, about six hundred conscripts from a camp near Marietta escaped, and came into our lines. They had a fight for it, and some two hundred of their number were killed and taken prisoners, but these others managed to get in. "Tired of the war," they said, "and did not want to fight."

On the 27th General Sherman determined to attack the mountain, and it was done by General McPherson's and General Thomas's commands. In this assault we were unsuccessful, and were driven back with great loss. Among the killed were General Harker and Colonel McCook.

The next day there was a truce to bury the dead, that lay decaying on the neutral ground between the two armies in front of Generals Newton's and Davis's divisions. It was a strange sight to see the armies meet. There were two regiments from Kentucky, one Union and the other rebel. They rushed in among each other, shook hands, called each other their first names, "Bill" and "Bob," inquired after friends at home, and were apparently as friendly and kind as brothers meeting after a long absence. I heard one boy about my own age inquire of a great six-foot Union soldier, "How the governor was?" then laugh at the way he had stolen his best horse and galloped off with Bragg. "Tell him," he said, "if you live to get home, that I am all right, and I wish he was, and give my love to mother." The work done, and the truce over, they returned to their lines, and we to ours, ready to take each other's lives at any moment.

The next night an attack was made upon a working party sent out by General Davis to entrench. A large force suddenly pounced upon them; the fight became general along the whole line of that division, but they were repulsed, losing, it was said, some two hundred, while our loss was only five or six men.

Our troops were again in motion. All night long on the 1st and 2d of July was the army moving, turning completely round as quietly as possible in order to cross the Chattahoochie and get between Johnston and Atlanta. The rebels were wide awake, they saw what General Sherman was after, and determined we should not cross the river before them; so on the night of the 2d they did just what General Sherman wanted them to do, evacuated Kenesaw, and started for the river ahead of us. On the 3d of July the Stars and Stripes waved from their stronghold on the mountain, was carried to the town of Marietta, and shook its free folds in the breeze from the roof of the Kenesaw House—and in the hands of our men was still pursuing them toward the Chattahoochie River.

CHAPTER XXVIII.

CROSSING THE CHATTAHOOCHIE.

THERE we were at the beautiful town of Marietta, on the railroad, eleven miles from the Chattahoochie river. As I stopped at a well, nicely roofed over, in the public square, where some negroes were drawing water for our troops, I thought how I should like to have lived there. The houses were large, the gardens fine, and all looked as though they had been occupied by well-to-do people. The Kenesaw House fronted on the square; it was a fine hotel, with a wide gallery running the whole length of it above and below. There were factories and a paper mill, and, outside of the town, on a little hill, was Marietta Military Academy, where General Sherman had once taught military tactics.

"Arrah," said Pat, as he stood guard over the prisoners in the enclosure, "you were a stupid set. Jest to think, 'Old Billy' himself taught you how to beat him, and you couldn't do it!"

It was the "Fourth of July," and I determined to have a good dinner to celebrate the day, so we sat down to fried chicken, sweet potatoes, honey, roast apples, a cup of coffee, and blackberries well powdered with sugar.

Our troops were in pursuit towards the Chattahoochie, and the rebels were trying to keep them back until their wagons had crossed. There was a battle near Nickajack Creek, which somewhat hastened their movements. Our boys gained one bank of the river ere they had well reached the other. I had heard so much of the Chattahoochie that I was glad to see it; everything seemed to depend upon our gaining and crossing it. Rebel prisoners at Chattanooga had scoffed at the idea of our reaching its banks, for then we should have Atlanta. The boys fairly shouted at sight of its waters; even the weariest wished to push ahead and camp in the "Gate City," little dreaming of the long, hot days, red with blood, which must be passed ere the Stars and Stripes would float over Atlanta.

We had a fine time resting while waiting for bridges to be laid and supply trains to come up. It was dreadfully warm, and we bathed, fished, and blackberried to our heart's content. The men had plenty of everything, even to new clothes, which some indulged in.

"This is much better," I heard one say, "than eating steaks from Colonel Starkweather's horse, or devouring raw, green corn while we filled the ambulances." First we had to fortify, and when this was done we were ready to take our ease. Some of the men never finished fortifying; they tried to excel each other in making each individual position the strongest. They liked to have their work shapely and neat, too. I have seen men work for hours at their breast-works and intrenchments, and then sit down to smoke with their eyes on them. But presently they would knock the ashes out of their pipes and begin again, and pull down and put up, until they were satisfied. Perhaps every day, while we occupied the trenches, they would add or take away something. This was only when there was plenty of time, though, and in places where we would hold the position for a season. When merely for a night tenantry, or in front of the enemy expecting an attack, all that was thought of was to get the work done quickly and have it strong, the finishing touches were after considerations.

While near here I saw a negro man have a narrow escape. He was making coffee and one of the men called to him from the trenches to bring him a cup. They had their earthworks pretty well done, and the shot and shell of the opposite party were falling fast, but passing some distance beyond where they were digging. The cooks had also raised a sort of fortification, in the shelter of which they broiled and fried, and they did not care to pass the open space over which the balls whizzed.

Blacky expressed his fears that he might be hit. The soldier insisted on having his coffee, however, and called to him to dodge the bullets.

At length, spurred by the laughing of those around him, Pomp seized the tin cup, and darted from under cover, the men hurrahing and cheering him on. He dodged a piece of shell that plowed the ground before him, and incited by the cheers which followed his escape, plunged forward, when the enemy's artillery opened and the shrapnel showered the iron rain by the pailful. A ball struck the cup he held, and with a yell he fell to the ground. All supposed him dead; but after a few moments, when there was a lull, he started up and sprung in great leaps to the trenches, knocking a man down as he gained their edge.

"Where's my coffee, you black rascal?" was his salutation from the man who had brought him into peril.

"God knows, massa, and he won't tell. I tought dis nigger gone sure enuf; tought my hole arm tored off—reckon youse not git any coffee dis time."

There he stayed, and did good service, too; neither threats nor persuasions could get him back to "Bummers' Roost" again.

The weather was terribly warm, and it was impossible

to make long marches had this been desired, for the men were very weary.

The commissary wagons were dragging along slowly, bringing up the rations of the army, piles of bags of coffee, beans, etc., barrels of pork and crackers were accumulating.

We heard all sorts of rumors from Atlanta. I saw the *Atlanta Appeal* one day, a newspaper John had borrowed from Colonel —— for a few moments, and it was rejoicing at our having reached the river, as it would be so easy to destroy us there. Prisoners told us if we got too near the citizens intended to burn the city; that they were preparing for this by removing their valuables and families to a distance.

Meantime we kept on our way. The men asked few questions. I heard one man say to another, who inquired the cause of some movement, "I don't know. I made up my mind when I joined the army I must go it blind, and keep my mouth shut, and I do."

Our pickets were posted along the north bank of the river, while the rebels were on the south. With no shade, in the hot sun, it was terribly warm, and pop, pop, would go the rifles if a man but showed a finger from behind his defenses. The men had to keep so close they were almost sick from the intense heat, and thought they must be sun-struck if it continued. The river was narrow at that point, and presently they heard, with secret delight, from the other side: "Halloo! I say, Yank!"

"Well, Johnny?"

"Suppose we stop awhile, take a swim and have a talk, while we get some boughs for shade."

"Agreed, Johnny, honor bright."

"Honor bright it is."

The time was fixed and the truce faithfully kept on

both sides. In ten minutes after it was settled, Yanks and Johnnies were laughing, talking, and bathing together. Indeed, the pickets became so friendly, that finally they agreed not to fire at each other at all.

Our cavalry took Roswell and laid a bridge over the river there. I heard a man telling of the destruction of the factories in that town. Some four or five hundred girls were employed in them, and it was their only means of subsistence. In a half hour they were laid waste and they had nowhere to get bread. "I don't know what they are to do," said he. "I suppose Government knows what it is about. It would not do to let them manufacture clothes and flour for the rebels; but it looks mighty hard. Some of them were just the size of my own little girls at home; they cried and wrung their hands, and lamented in a way that made my heart ache."

The boys made a regular frolic of crossing the Chattahoochie; some waded it where it was shallow, some took off their clothes and so crossed, while others—whole regiments—went through it in soldierly order, just as they marched through the streets.

They laughed and joked, and threw water on each other, playing like children, dipping their heads in and shaking the streams from them like water dogs.

The man known among us as the "Barometer" began singing "On Jordan's stormy banks I stand," while we stood waiting for the word "forward," and as we reached the opposite bank he struck up, "We have passed over Jordan —Hallelujah," but his voice was lost in the music of the band which accompanied us across, and to which some of the men tried to dance in the middle of the river.

On the 17th we left the Chattahoochie behind us, and pushed forward towards Atlanta. The rebel works near the river were the strongest we had yet seen, but we were told Atlanta was trebly fortified and impregnable. The different corps marched on different roads. The 4th was on the Roswell and Atlanta. General McPherson, accompanied by Garrard's cavalry, went towards Augusta. I always felt proud of Generals Kennar and Israel Garrard; they to me looked and acted like true chevaliers. When I saw them I gave longer and louder shouts for the Ohio generals.

I climbed a hill and had a view of "Our Mecca" as John called Atlanta, which was only six miles distant, and appeared right within our grasp. We kept on fighting at almost every step, and reached Peach Tree Creek, a stream which would be thought a considerable river in Europe; it was deep and wide, and we had to wait for it to be bridged. General Johnston had been removed, and General Hood now commanded the rebels. We might be said to be besieging Atlanta, for our whole army was round it in a semicircle. On the 20th of July General Hood came out of his fortifications, and attacked us while near Peach Tree Creek. Part of the men were engaged making breast-works, when the pickets ran in—the enemy following close upon their heels.

It was a bloody day. The rebels fought desperately, but at length were repulsed with great loss. I heard John say General Hooker's column was totally unprepared for it, but the men fought like heroes, and " The Head of the Family," for General Hooker called his corps " his family," had the dead piled in heaps on his front.

The surgeons were busy, for the wounded were borne to their quarters in a continuous procession. It was dreadful to see the little streams of blood trickling down from the stretchers as they were carried along, always leaving a red track behind them. The next day there was but little fighting. We had taken hundreds of prisoners. Some of them were sullen, but almost all were disposed to make the best of the circumstances ; said they were glad they were taken, they were tired of the war, etc. Almost the first things they expressed a wish for were tobacco and coffee. In conversation they said "we had to go into it—we never believed you'ns would stand up to it so, or git so far down as the Chattahoochie."

All my school-boy ideas of an army with bright uniforms, gold lace, feathers, new and gay banners tossing in the wind, and looking as fresh as the fancy volunteer companies do at home, when they turn out on a holiday to show themselves for a few hours and be admired, were put to flight by the actual looks of men in service. In reality the soldiers' clothes were worn, faded, and torn, from marching through the hot sun and dust, and forcing their way through briers and underbrush, discolored from the rains that had beaten upon them, or the dampness of the ground, where they had made their beds. Their faces were bronzed, their hair and beard uncut, their shoes worn,—in many cases they were ragged, in some barefoot.

The officers, particularly the older ones, wore shabby uniforms, and were unshaven ; a white shirt was a luxury only worn on particular occasions. Yet the men bathed and washed and kept their bodies clean, and made ludicrous attempts at hair cutting, and their arms were always bright and in good order. Indeed the veterans rather prided themselves on their worn appearance. They jeered at a new recruit, called him green, and informed him on his arrival, that a few months' service would take the "*fancy*" out of him. As for their colors, the more battle worn, ragged and jagged and bullet holed they were, the dearer they were to the hearts of the men. When, after a hard day's march, their tattered ensign blazoned with battles won was unfurled, I have seen them straighten their weary limbs, raise their drooping heads, and step out as erect and proud as so many kings.

I heard a veteran color sergeant call to another who bore the bright colors of a new regiment :

"Take your knife and rip her up, man, and put a few shots through her. I would not walk under such a new rag as that—why you are blazoning to the whole army and the enemy, too, that you have never done anything for your country before."

If our army so little resembled the army of my imagination, still less did the enemy's look like it. To begin with their rank and file, I must say they were very inferior men to ours in all respects. Then they had been put to such straits, that in dress and accoutrements whole regiments looked like what we familiarly call "rag-tag and bobtail." The officers were much more showily uniformed than with us ; they wore more tinsel and braiding and gold lace, but generally this was weather-beaten and tarnished, and did not present a very brilliant appearance.

The affection the men had for their guns was curious. In one of the fights before Atlanta we recaptured the guns belonging to Captain Loomis's battery, and I saw an artilleryman go up to one of them, stoop down, look in its mouth, pat its sides, as gently as he would have patted a woman's cheek ; I observed that they always spoke of them as "she" and "her."

We were still in the neighborhood of Peach Tree Creek, when on the morning of the 22d General Hood again attacked us. He got into the rear of the Army of the Tennessee, and fell on our right, at a time when it was reported he had evacuated his works on our front. The attack was so sudden they were near defeating us, but our men fought dauntlessly and, in the enemy, had foemen worthy of their steel. At length beneath the persevering courage of our army the rebels faltered—and, after a few moments, turned and fled.

General McPherson was killed by a sharpshooter while reconnoitering in the early part of the day. General Logan took command, and McPherson's death was concealed from his men, for fear of its depressing influence on them. General McPherson was greatly beloved both by officers and army. They mourned him as a man and regretted him as a general.

"Another Ohio general wounded," said John, coming to where we stood talking of General McPherson. "General Force has, I hear, received a severe wound in the face and head, which, it is feared, will prove mortal, and Capt. Bryant Walker has been badly wounded in the leg."

"They take our best," said Kiler. "Force is a good soldier, an excellent commander—gentlemanly—brave—and as cool in danger as if he had all his life been seasoning in the service. I hear Captain Walker is one of our most talented and promising young men. His father was a great lawyer, and a liberal and true man. Ohio may well be proud of her sons."

"You and I and John, for instance"—I said laughing. On Saturday we were burying the dead, which on account of the heat must be done quickly; there was still some fighting going on. Atlanta was in a state of siege, and our works almost as strong as the enemy's.

There was another battle on the afternoon of the 28th, principally with the Army of the Tennessee, commanded by General Howard, in which the rebels were beaten with great loss. John told me they had an Atlanta paper at headquarters, in which was the statement that, at the rate they had lost lately, the Confederate army would be annihilated in three weeks.

Our men fought without defenses; for, having moved from their former position, they had not time to throw others up before the attack, so had no breast-works save those they hastily pitched together in the pauses. The rebels had several generals wounded.

This battle was called the battle of Ezra's Church, as it was fought in the woods round a country church of that name. A little creek ran near. The strife was severe on its banks; the bodies fell into the stream, the blood reddening its waters. This stream was called Dead Man's Creek.

As soon as the assault ceased, and the rebels retired to their works, our men sallied out to bury their dead, who, with the wounded, literally covered the ground.

They talked much of a soldier of the Forty-sixth Ohio regiment, named Davis. Brave and daring, he had determined to have a trophy of the fight, and so persistently hewed his way to the front rank of our army, and while the enemy's artillery rained shot and shell, stretched over the breastworks and seized the colors—of the Thirtieth Louisiana, I think—from the hand of the color sergeant, and unhurt bore it back in triumph.

The August heats were now upon us; still there was fighting of some sort each day. Our troops were moving, changing their position, and getting to the west and south of Atlanta. They had become dexterous in dodging shell and shot. A missile would be heard screeching through the air; if it came their way they turned their heads, and if inconveniently near, would evade it, and call to their comrades to look out; if otherwise, they kept on their course unheeding.

It was a long time before I understood the difference between the various kinds of shot. Canister is shot placed in a tin can or box in four rows, the box having iron plates top and bottom, and a handle. The spaces between the balls are filled with sawdust, and the case is made to fit the gun from which it is to be projected. Howitzer canister has forty-eight balls, common canister twenty-seven.

Shrapnel is a shell which varies in size, according to the gun in which it is used, sometimes containing one hundred and seventy-five musket balls, and again having but thirty-nine. When several batteries were going at once, I have seen the balls from shrapnel fall as thick as hail stones. The spaces between the balls in the shells are filled with sulphur, which is poured in hot, and when cool makes a compact mass, in which a hole is made for the powder necessary to explode the shell. It was invented by General Shrapnel, and is called by his name. Grape shot consists generally of nine balls in three layers between plates, having a pin running through the middle of the plates fastened with a nut at the top, and a handle across the whole. It is called grape shot from its supposed resemblance to a bunch of grapes.

A shell is a thick iron globe filled with powder and ball.

The siege continued until the last of August, when wagons and horses and all indispensable articles were sent back across the Chattahoochie with a large number of troops to guard them.

The whole army, then, leaving the strong works that had been erected in front of Atlanta, moved round to the west and south, in the direction of "Rough and Ready," Fairburn and Jonesboro', breaking up the West Point and Macon Railroad.

General Sherman completely deceived the enemy. They supposed they had gained a victory, and that on finding we could not take their works, we were running away from them. Our scouts told us there was great rejoicing in Atlanta ; that hundreds of citizens went out to see our old camps, laughing and jeering at the " Yankees."

On the 31st they came up to and attacked the Army of the Tennessee, near Jonesboro', and were completely beaten. The slaughter was fearful. The battle was renewed on the next day, the 1st of September, and continued until night. We drew up around Atlanta, and in the night the enemy retreated to Lovejoy's Station, some thirty miles below. Next day we followed them but they were strongly entrenched. We had what we wanted, Atlanta, and General Sherman thought it would not pay to molest them, so we marched slowly back, encamping some eight miles from the town. Through the night we were startled by frequent and loud explosions. It was General Hood blowing up his ammunition, locomotives, cars, etc. The next day, September 2d, our army entered the " Gate City," and we moved to our camps.

The boys could hardly realize that Atlanta was ours.

CHAPTER XXIX.

BEFORE ATLANTA.

OUR army being in camp around the city I prepared to see all that could be seen. John no longer required me to ask permission to go and come, unless it was on a dangerous expedition, or one which would take me to a distance. Kiler and I were great friends. I had been in all the late battles by his side, and he generally told me what was going on, if he knew. We heard some ludicrous stories of the consternation which prevailed when the rebels were evacuating the town, and sad ones also of the terror of the citizens, and their frenzied efforts to get away. The noise made by the explosion of the ammunition, with the glare from the flames of the burning cars, added to their fears of the "Yankees" dashing in among them every moment, almost took away their senses, and made them run about like insane people.

"I cannot but think, Phil," said John, "how much they must have suffered, with night to add double horror to it all, and the women and children as innocent perhaps as our own at home."

First of all I went to the scene of the explosion. Long rows of wheels told where the cars had stood, and were all that remained of nearly one hundred destroyed; they were filled with ammunition stores, set in train one after the other, with the locomotives at the head, and thus blown up; the chimney pipes of the latter were still standing, as were also some chimneys of the rolling mill which had stood near the track. No wonder there was such a din carrying destruction with it.

Our shells had made sad havoc. I saw many houses which were torn to pieces by them, and others having windows and doors shattered and great holes in their sides or roofs. Many stories were told of sudden deaths and marvelous escapes. Fear of the shells drove the women and children to the caves, which they had compelled their slaves to excavate with much time and labor. I went into several of them; they were quite large, and dug deep in the earth, supported by beams and roofed with logs over which a hill of earth was raised; the entrances were zigzag apertures; some had ladders and trap doors.

Taking their servants, chairs, tables, etc., whole families sought refuge in these places, for they were shell proof, and some remained there pursuing their usual occupations. Many of the caves were in the gardens adjoining the dwellings and were only used when the city was under heavy fire. When a brisk bombardment took place at night and continued, the female population and children, aroused from their slumbers, could be seen retreating to these dens. Some families retired to their cellars, but these were considered unsafe, for should anything befall the house they were liable to be entombed alive, instances of which were known.

I read the signs as I went along with great interest. I was known at home as a reader of signs, and although often laughed at for my inquiring mind, was frequently able to give needful information of places of business, etc., when asked.

I remember the signs, "J. J. Lynch," "Atlanta Hotel," "Washington Hall," "A. J. Witgenstine," "Atlanta Oil Factory," "Slave Auction" and on one shanty in rudely printed letters, "Niggers bought and sold here." These signs fascinated me; I gazed on them with a sort of wonder. I had seen places placarded "horse auctions, cattle bought and sold here," and they were nicer in appearance than these slave markets. I had heard my mother tell of such things, for she was a Southern woman, and had owned slaves. Before the war John had thought the Government had no right to meddle with this peculiar institution. It had been entailed on the South by those who had gone before; but now what a revolution! I saw the blood mount to his face at the sight of these human shambles.

There were some very pretty houses in Atlanta; they were cleaner in appearance, and the city had not the decayed, dilapidated look of most Southern towns. It was built during the past twenty years, having become a great railroad center. Almost all the dwellings had piazzas in front; indeed this was a prominent feature in all Southern houses. General Sherman's headquarters was a handsome house, with a broad piazza supported by columns, and surrounded by a garden. A sentinel stood at the gate beside the American flag. At least this was called his headquarters, but when I saw him he was sitting in a common little fly tent also called his quarters. There were some handsome buildings, the City Hall, several churches, a medical college, hotels, etc.

I went to the jail, quite a large square building, where some prisoners were; a "mixed set," as Private Jones who was with me remarked. There were gray-haired feeble old men, and boys of from ten to twelve years of age, who had helped to man the works. These works were a wonder to me; we could never have taken them. The forts were surrounded by *chevaux-de-frise* so strongly built that it would have been impossible for our men to have stormed and taken them under fire.

There was a truce of ten days commencing on the 12th

REFUGEES.

of September. General Sherman had decided to burn the city, leaving only sufficient of it to make a military post. He issued an order that all citizens should depart either North or South in a given time. Those who wished to go North were assisted by Government, and their houses were protected. Those who went South took what they could with them, and that which remained was considered lawful spoil by the soldiers; being rebel property, it was confiscated. Rough and Ready, a station on the railroad just ten miles South of Atlanta was the place to which the rebels made their exodus. A detachment from each army was ordered to that point, and their lines designated. The rebel women and children, with their household goods, were sent there, and dropped between the lines, their friends meeting and receiving them with cheers and shouts.

"The flitting" was one of the strangest sights I ever saw. Sidewalks and streets were filled with bedding, furniture, clothes, and crockery. I heard one young lady berating a negro girl for not taking care of her hoop. People ran here and there, searching for conveyances, wagons, carts, anything on wheels, which could take their things away. Children lay in the streets on beds, or were running under feet and getting hurt; women, young and old, sat in chairs rocking themselves, in a sort of despair, or stood beside tables, or on portions of the sidewalk, keeping guard over their plates and dishes. Vehicles were being loaded, or were jostling each other in their passage; men were swearing, children fighting, babies screaming. I saw several girls with pairs of chickens in their arms, trying to hold them until ready to start; every now and then the chickens would flap and peck, and almost get away, when the young ladies would stoop down and secure them between their knees until they could get a firmer hold, or dive in the crowd after them when they got loose.

I was not feeling at all well, but I made the most of my time while our army was at Decatur and Eastpoint. I managed to get among them, and was back and forth all the while, and heard and saw much that was going on.

When General Hood started for the Chattahoochie, thinking to cut our communications, and General Sherman followed with most of the army, leaving General Slocum in command at Atlanta, we had dull days—dull for me, for I was for several weeks sick with a fever. We had news of the victory at Allatoona, and of the enemy attacking the garrisons all along our line of march.

I heard a veteran, with a wise shake of his head, say: "'Old Billy' knows what he is about; he is driving Hood out of his way, where others can take care of him; but Hood don't know it."

Next we heard of "our boys" in Alabama having a good time; then, that Hood was over the Tennessee, and our army was back again.

The first of November came, and the troops began to leave the line of the railroad and center at Atlanta. To my great joy I was well again, my illness had not been sufficient to send me to bed, only to make me good for nothing.

There was talk of a great move. All sorts of surmises and rumors were afloat as to what was to be done next. The few people left in the city were making every effort to get away, for it was known that Atlanta was to be destroyed. All was bustle, confusion and preparation. A bomb was going to burst somewhere, but where, none could tell. Every night there was a fire, and many dwellings were destroyed. The troops who came in burnt up the towns in the rear, along their whole line of march, and tore up the railroad. It reminded me of the Spaniards burning their ships that they might have nothing to retreat to—they must go on or die.

At last the order was given, Atlanta must burn. Foundries, machine shops, factories, refineries, warehouses, depots, and stores were set on fire, and plundered while burning. Everything that could add fuel to the fire was pitched in amid shrieks, jest and laughter, song and wild dance. At night you could see men bearing boxes and bales and throwing them into the flames. Here a group formed a ring, and with fantastic step danced around a bonfire made of Confederate stores; there another stripped the house of a noted rebel, smashed his furniture, and threw the wrecks with the rest.

So it went on, and amid it all the army passed on and out, into the very heart of the enemy's country, surrounded by the foe, with no succor near, and no dependence but on itself and Providence. Going about, seeing what this and that detachment were doing, I lost John and "our company." I knew they were ordered on, but could not find them. I was sent first to one place, then to another, in answer to my inquiries, and came near getting into one or two fights, owing to my persistency in insisting upon being answered. At last, when I was almost ready to give up, I happened to see our colonel, who directed me where to go, giving me two or three sharp words of reprimand for always straying, ordering me to keep closer to our company.

In a couple of hours' time I found John, and went immediately to getting my things together; but Jim, John's servant, had done this for me. John's orders were that I should always help myself.

CHAPTER XXX.

FROM ATLANTA TO SAVANNAH.

A THRUST in the side capsized me as I stooped to strap my blanket closer, and the new order was shouted in my ear, "All surplus servants, non-combatants and refugees should move to the rear."

"I belong to the captain, and that order does not apply to me," was my retort, as I gathered myself up.

"Is that so! Then lend a hand here, my arm is not of much account since the hurt it got crossing the Chattahoochie. 'Old Lightning' is on the rampage, and means work by that order. I am ready for one, to follow wheresoever he may lead. Halloo! Snowball, what are you going to do with yourself?"

This last was addressed to Cæsar, a negro who was passing, dragging one leg after him as he limped by.

"Nuffin, Massa Kiler, I's jest gwyne along."

"You had better 'tote' some of this then;" Kiler kicked at a box of hard tack. "I intend to live off the country, and good living I mean it shall be, you can bet on that. I hope we have plenty of salt along, Captain Phil; the rebs are likely to be short of that article. There, shoulder this, you grinning monkey."

He attempted to put a box on the black's back, but he slid from under, and it fell to the ground and broke open, the contents scattering around.

"Yah, yah, yah, no, tank you, Massa Kiler; dis nigger no tar his ole gums chawing dat stuff, when he knows whar de sweet taters and t'odder good tings bees hid—dis chile need no dogs tu find dem."

"They will find you before long, you hoary old sinner."

"Dey gone done dat ready, sah. Look har now"—and he tore a bandage of his leg, and showed where a piece of the flesh had been taken out to the bone; a terrible wound, inflamed and swollen. "Dey scented me out, but de bit ob ole scythe I sharpened ob nights, and put a handle tu, went right down his froat. Yah, yah, he neber trouble nigger agin. Ole massa swore awful, when he found him best hound dead and dis chile off. Yah, yah."

"The devil will have you yet if you don't take care of that leg."

"Guess he won't git needer ob us 'fore our time, massa."

"Off with you, but harkee: if I catch you treating another white child as you did that boy yesterday, I will take the pay out of your skin."

"Dat's nuffin, Massa Kiler," with a look of astonishment and contempt; "he's only poor white trash; he can't do nuffin, and he don't know nuffin. Why, he won't eben sell like de nigger; nobody giv nuffin for him, he's no account nohow."

"Off with you, I say, you black rascal you! What do you mean by talking of white people in that way?"

He aimed a blow at him which the black dexterously dodged; then, drawing nearer, he said in a low tone, with a knowing leer and expressive gesture:

"Plenty ob poor white trash in this army, tu; dis nigger knows quality when he sees 'em—dis chile 'customed tu lib wid 'stocracy—dem low Irish and mean whites neber used tu nuffin. Cæsar knows dat—all de poor white trash not Souf."

"You had better hold your tongue, or you will get a bullet through that wool of yours."

"Yah, tink, massa, a nigger don't know what folks tu talk tu—quiet as a mole tu dem! Youse better be a nigger slabe, Massa Kiler, ef youse want tu larn tu keep a still tongue b'tween your teef."

"Well, Captain Phil," said Kiler, as Cæsar left us with a leer in his eye, and his finger behind his nose, "I hope the negroes will all get their freedom. I did not wish it when the war began, though, but I want them kept away from me. What a profound contempt they have for the poor whites, and no wonder; there is nothing like them to be found East or West, save in the slave states. I have often been surprised at my mother's description of the North Carolina clay eaters, whom she had been among in her youth, but these 'no-account poor white trash,' as the negroes call them, living in such a Goshen as this, beat all."

"There—I am ready for the word—weary of destroying and seeing destroyed to-day; besides my arm pains dreadfully. Let us go over there a little out of the din and smoke and sit down. I wonder if I shall ever be able to do anything away from the rat-tat-tat of that drum."

John was busy somewhere, so Kiler and I went aside and waited for John's word of command.

"Yes," said Kiler when we had seated ourselves, "the negroes understand character; they have been obliged to study their masters; but these poor whites! I was at some distance from the column one day, when we were in the neighborhood of Marietta, and came upon a miserable shed, not much larger than our great pig-sties at home, and not half so well built, nor so clean. Well, this shed was the home of nine human beings, who were all hanging over the fence in front of it as I came in sight, and stared at me as I approached, half in wonder, half in fear, their rags literally fluttering in the breeze.

"I stepped up and spoke to them. They continued to stare for several minutes without answering; finally the old woman among them said:

"'You bees a Yank, been't you?'

"I replied that I was.

"Then she wanted to know, 'Ef thar bees any critter soldiers coming this way? Wes uns was afeard of critter soldiers.'

"The dull sound of our column moving on the roads could be distinctly heard.

"I replied they were passing on.

"I tried to enter into conversation, and found none of them could either read or write. The father and their oldest brother were in the army, but they had not heard from them for eighteen months. They lived as they could, and seemed half starved. Three of them were girls between sixteen and twenty, with yellow matted hair which hung in strands about their clayey faces, begrimed with dirt. They talked in a drawling tone, with the usual number of w's and r's in every third or fourth word. As I took my pipe from my mouth to speak to them, and whiffed the smoke aside, the old woman snuffed it in such an eager, hungry way, that I drew the remainder of the paper of tobacco from my pocket and gave it to her. She snatched eagerly at it, hugged it to her breast, and started on a trot for the shanty, followed by the three oldest girls and myself, for I was curious to see the inside of that dwelling. She had already filled her pipe, and was on her knees at the tumble-down fireplace, trying to blow a coal into life, at the same time shoving back and keeping off the girls, who were making efforts to get at the paper tightly clutched in her old hand. I looked round while

I questioned the mother, for the old woman was the granny.

"A rickety pine table, and a half-dozen sections of sawed logs, about a foot in height, were all the furniture. On one side of the room were two ledges, raised about a foot and a half from the floor, and filled with straw and dirty rags, which served as beds, in one of which a starving dog lay sleeping. Two or three pewter plates and a broken iron pot was all the house contained.

"Baffled in her attempt to get at the tobacco, the eldest girl went to the wall, and from one of the chinks took a slender stick with a piece of dirty rag wound around one end; this she put into her mouth, when another girl ran up and claimed it; they tussled for its possession, the struggle ending in the elder seeing and seizing another dip, which was also between the chinks, then both dropped on the clay floor, rubbed and stared at me.

"The mother, with whom I was talking, chewed and expectorated like a man. She told me they had not seen tobacco for months, but used the leaves of a vine found in the woods in its place. The clay floor was worn in ruts and hollows by the rain, and covered with refuse of all sorts, among which a yellow cur was snuffing and scratching; a stench came from the room that was almost unbearable; the bare knees of the girls protruded from their clothes as they sat on the floor, and the woman who stood beside me had her nakedness hardly covered; their dirt was only equaled by their ignorance. They believed the most monstrous stories of us, even asked 'if Linkin wasn't a nigger.' Glad to get outside, I left the cabin, followed by them all, and when I looked back after I had gone a few rods, saw them hanging over the fence just as I had found them."

"You came near paying dear for that visit," said Jones, who had come up a few minutes before.

"Yes, it cured me of straggling; I came within one of capture."

"How?" I asked.

"I had hardly got out of sight when some rebel cavalry reached the place, and they told of my visit. I heard them after me and hid."

"The nigger does it," said Jones. "The rich have their slaves, and they are taught to make and mend, as well as sow and reap; why, some of the niggers on the sugar and rice plantations are splendid mechanics. There is our colonel's man; now he is a great deal better millwright than I am, although I was raised to it. The planters, who never lived by the sweat of their brows, think hard work 'nigger's' work, and despise a white man who does it, and call him a mudsill—a good name for these yellow, clayey looking people. They won't employ them, because their niggers save them the expense. The poor whites think it's a disgrace, and even if they were not too proud, never have a chance to work beside the nigger. The rich hate them because they are poor, and the niggers hate them because they are white, ignorant, and more of slaves than they are. Hark! what is that? hear how the boys yell! they have come upon something." He listened a moment, then remarked: "They will not leave much in Atlanta."

"It seems to me the poor white women do all the work that is done," I said, as Jones seated himself again.

"There are no men now to do it, Captain Phil; but you are right; the men lie about, or ride about if they can get a horse, chew, smoke, swear, and do nothing, so are ready for any deviltry that turns up. The women must do the work, if it is done, and a mother won't let her child starve. Besides, such womenkind like a man the better the less he does for them; they think he is a kind of lord, then, and a little above them. I tell you what it is, let alone the country, the right, and all that, I would not have missed this campaign for a snug little fortune. Wait until it is over; the plodding Yankee and thrifty Western man, to whom this whole country will be open, and who had never dreamed of its richness, will buy, and possess and work it, until it will become a second Eden."

"Yes, Jones; I believe it is a part of their punishment that their fair inheritance is to pass from them. They will no longer be Southern men, on Southern soil; the despised Northern mudsill will go in when the negro goes out. Look at Tennessee! she has everything in her borders to make her great, but energy, and we will furnish her that. This whole—" Kiler paused.

"Fall in—forward there."

We sprung to our feet and were soon in our places, ready for our "grand promenade" through Georgia.

It was the fifteenth of November. Atlanta was behind us in flames. The men had permission to take what they wished before the fire seized it. With shout and hurrah they darted to and fro, loaded like pack horses, with things they could not possibly take on a march. The confusion was such, I thought at one time they had got into a fight among themselves; explosion followed explosion, and yells rang on the lurid air.

Amid it all we marched slowly out, the band playing and the men singing and shouting. I wish I could describe it, but I cannot. John's company was among the last which left that evening, and it was night when we turned our faces from Atlanta, whither we did not know. The day had been clear and warm, but smoke and flame filled the atmosphere and almost stifled us. As the sun set red and angry amid this black pall, the noises of the city we were leaving in its ruins behind us mingled with the music of the bands. The rat-tat-tat of the drums, the yells and shouts of the soldiers, who had left and were burning houses and fences in front, dancing, jumping, leaping in their wild joy at the onward move, the cries of the teamsters to their mules, the heavy tramp of the column, the clatter of horses; all went to make up a sound that almost deafened us.

As it grew later, and the stars peeped out, and all was so still and beautiful in the heavens, you could trace one long line far ahead by the fires marking its path. Then the men began to weary; the march was quieter, the tramp, tramp, tramp more distinct, and in the frequent halts, caused by the stalling of the wagon trains, they sat upon the ground and slept, or leaned upon their arms, talking or joking, in a more subdued way. Occasionally a restless spirit would call to the band, which could not hear: "Give us the 'Wandering Jew,' that fellow that's always 'marching on,'" and somebody else would start up, "Wait for the wagon."

Where were we bound? None knew, few cared, so that it was to victory. I heard one veteran declare, "the Ocean would bring us up;" another, "that we would see sights between this and the Gulf;" while a third insisted, "Augusta was our goal." All had as much faith as the negroes, who invariably, when they heard these speculations, shook their heads wisely with: "Git along now, Massa Sherman know what he 'bout; jest trabel on."

Almost all the black skins, finding they would not be permitted to accompany us, had set their faces North from Kingston and Atlanta towards "God's country," afraid to remain after we had left. Those with us were such as were employed as servants, and a few others who managed to hang on despite orders to the contrary. There was little sleep that night. The remainder of the army was to follow next day. The weather was beautiful, the road good, the country fine. Should I live to be as old as Methuselah, I shall never forget that campaign. It was something to live for, something, John said, to tell of winter nights to my grandchildren. On we crept ; now waiting the movement of the supply trains which had the road, and catching a little sleep as we might until daylight came, and we could take rest, which we did, dropping right down where we were.

The country appeared almost uninhabited. We saw no enemy, the houses we passed were deserted, and consequently were fired as soon as reached ; indeed, so many dwellings were burnt in our course that, should the panic-stricken people return, they would have nowhere to lay their heads.

Out of Atlanta—but we did not feel fully started until the sixteenth, when, between seven and eight in the morning, we again took the road. Passing through one or two villages, we destroyed the railroad depôts and tore up the tracks, seizing everything eatable that came within our reach. The boys were certain they were "bound for Augusta."

On Friday, November 18th, we reached Rutledge, a town on the railroad, in the midst of a beautiful and fertile country. Here the men foraged to their heart's content. Many negroes had joined us and eagerly gave information where horses, mules and valuables were hidden. Parties went out in all directions and returned laden with luxuries as well as necessaries. I saw a stalwart fellow with a tin kettle slung over one shoulder filled with honey, a couple of live geese over the other, a young porker squealing and kicking on his back, and his pockets bulging with all kinds of green vegetables.

John had lost his horse and was riding a miserable animal; a grinning black came up to him.

"Marcy, massa, I tell yuse whar yuse git a finer critter than that ar nag yuse on—I helped to hide dem myself, I did."

We went with him to a little thicket in a hollow and found picketed, with plenty of food to keep them quiet, two beautiful animals, a black and a gray, of which we took undisturbed possession.

"We've cleaned out this country," said Kiler; "the rebs will know the Yanks have been about. That pile of brush over yonder looks suspicious though."

He made great strides towards it, followed by several others, plunging his bayonet into what appeared to be the clearings of the field brush, cornstalks, etc., piled in a stack; a great bellowing followed. The rubbish was thrown aside, a thong cut, and a fine cow and calf appeared.

"Milk for our coffee, boys; you drive her ahead while I put fire to the stuff."

Across some fields came a family of blacks, the mother tottering under the weight of an immense bundle she carried on her head, while several small children hung to her skirts, dressed in the one dirty garment universal with black children of this class and age in the South. With their whole attention upon the soldiers, every now and then one or another of the small ones would stumble over the stubble and fall, nearly pulling the mother down; then she would stoop and aim a blow at the youngster, which it almost invariably dexterously dodged.

When they reached the place where we stood, I saw that the huge bundle was a feather bed, tied up in a ragged quilt, protruding from which was a bonnet and several pieces of bright finery.

"Dar," she dropped the bed on the earth, seated herself upon it, and wiped her face with the skirt of her dress. "Dat's safe, any how. Stan' back, got no manners tu git afore de gemmen dat ere way," she thrust one of the boys behind her.

"What are you going to do with it, aunty?" asked Kiler.

"Jest tote it along." She laughed and shook her head, "Miss Fanny guv me de goose afore she was marrid, 'cause she done b'lieve 'twas gwyne tu die; I put it in my bed and nussed it, and when it git well I sot it on de eggs; got fifteen young goslings, den she swar Chloe stole 'em. Keep de feathers till git enough ter make dis bed; not gwyne to left it 'hind for nudder nigger. Ketch dis weasel asleep."

"Where are you going?"

"Don't know, massa, reckon yuse do; least ways, I jist kitch on, any how."

There was a pretty-looking girl, almost white, dressed up evidently in stolen finery.

"Look there," said Kiler. "It reminds me of the Israelites borrowing from the Egyptians when they made their exodus."

"It is almost a parallel in history. The Southerners are the taskmasters, who feel to the negroes as the Egyptians felt to the Jews," said John.

Colonel F—— had a couple of fine blooded horses, and his man Harry, a good-looking negro, black and shiny, dressed in the blue, with the smallest of military caps set on the top of his glossy wool, rode one of them. White and black took him for an officer. It was amusing to hear the comments of the former as they pointed him out to each other. The indignation and scorn with which they spoke of the mudsill Yankees, led by a nigger, was only equaled by the admiration with which the negroes gazed upon him as, pompous and full of airs, he curveted his horse among them, ordering them out of the way.

I went out with a foraging party some six or eight miles from the column, to the home of a rich planter, who had fled at our approach. As we made our appearance the negroes left everything, and stood to gaze at us, trying to hide their delight. The white women and children came out upon the gallery, and when the officer in command rode up, scowled upon him, and the women haughtily demanded what he wanted.

"Everything, madame," was the reply, as he raised his hat in salutation, while the boys proceeded to help themselves from barns and outhouses.

No whit alarmed, the women used their tongues briskly and cuttingly. Two of them were very handsome, although dressed in homespun.

"See," said the youngest of these, taking hold of her coarse dress with her white, dainty fingers, "to what your rapacity has already reduced a Southern lady." "Don't, Maria," the other interrupted, with the utmost contempt in her voice, "*he* cannot understand. *His* women are accustomed to nothing better." Taking the children by the hand, they swept into the house and up stairs.

"I did not intend to enter the dwelling," said the officer, with a flushed cheek, "but if they will let their tongues wag, they shall pay for it." So saying, followed by some dozen others, he stalked through the wide hall into the dining-room, and summoning the cook there, ordered her to prepare a good dinner.

Black as jet, the cook stood twisting a rag in her hands, while he gave his commands; a broad smile broke over her face as he said: "See that the meal is of the best the house affords, and let it be well cooked and well set, and, harkee, be careful that I do not have to search for what we want."

We took possession of the house below, but did not venture above stairs, where the ladies and children were. We sauntered through the rooms, examined the furniture and ornaments, and opened the book cases, and looked at the books. The floors were covered with Brussels carpets, pictures hung upon the walls, and in one room there was a marble bust and a grand piano. The latter Lieutenant B—— opened, and played and sang "Yankee Doodle" and "Hail Columbia," etc., with spirit.

After looking at everything, we went out on the gallery, as they call the porches about Southern houses, and the men smoked.

After a while we were called to our meal. The table was nicely set, and there were fried chicken, hot biscuits, corn bread, honey and molasses upon it in abundance. We enjoyed everything hugely, then quit the premises, leaving things inside the house just as we found them. Outside the place was stripped of everything; the cotton gin and a lot of cotton, out-houses, fodder, and fences, burnt, the stock driven off, the hogs and sheep slaughtered, geese, ducks, and hens appropriated. Now squads of men were driving into thickets and wandering round emptying the sweet potato *caches*, corn cribs, etc., and searching for hidden treasures. I could scarcely believe my senses that in one short hour a prosperous plantation could be made such a smoking, barren waste.

As we crossed the barn-yard, a fine-looking mulatto stood by the remains of a corn stack, moving the blades about with his feet. He turned his back to us and faced the house as we neared him, and busied himself tying straw in a wisp, at the same time saying: "Better look under de gal'ry, massa; house sarvants know, but they 'ceitful; dese niggers try tu git wid yuse tu-night. Massa tell de sentry not to fire on de poor black folks." Then with the same look and manner, he walked toward the house, stopping every few minutes, as if intent on tying the straw.

We took up our line of march for the column, driving the stock before us, almost every man with a living necklace strung about him, or adorning his bayonet. Along they went, cracking jokes and picking their poultry on the road, green garden stuff protruding from their pockets. Not a blade of anything had been left, as the place was known to belong to a noted rebel.

Passing down the fine avenue we saw the ladies at the windows, and pausing made them a low bow, which I need hardly say was not returned.

When a little distance from the house, numbers of the field hands started up where they had hid themselves, and accompanied us on the road, singing, dancing, and shouting "We bees guying along too." They kept up for a good way, then we lost them; but the next morning I recognized most of them in camp.

Having finished Rutledge, we kept on our march, camping near Madison that evening. We visited it next morning, and literally sacked it. When we entered, the boys had already broken into stores, appropriating and scattering their contents in all directions. John had advised me to keep out of this sort of thing, but I could not resist the fun, particularly when I saw Kiler foremost in it. So I plunged into the midst of them. "Good for you, captain," yelled one of us, as he wrapped me in a mantilla, and put a cap on my head. I was soon decked in all sorts of finery, and emulating the rest, began throwing things to the winds.

"There are some neckties, Joe," and a parcel of bright ribbons were sent over our heads. "Some skeeter net for you," and pieces of lace were cast under foot. Men strutted round dressed in bonnets and scarfs, trailing bits of finery after them, and with their affected airs making the lookers-on roar with laughter.

I saw one chap with a bonnet on wrong side before, and any quantity of women's wear on his person. He had a big syringe he had seized from some shop, with which he went round squirting upon the crowd. Another had strapped himself in a harness, and wore a string of onions for a necklace, and an earthenware pot for a hat, while a number of bright tins hung down his back. A third went about with an armful of brooms, with which he swept all he met in the face, and sang loudly, "Buy a broom; buy a broom." They threw crockery at each other, dusted each other with salt, sugar, and flour, until there was nothing left to put a hand to; then they seized the letters which had been cast forth from the Post-office, and in merry mockery read aloud their contents.

One man stood on a horse-block reading aloud a letter from a soldier in the rebel army to his sweetheart. I laughed until I felt weak, and the men shouted. It was a funny letter, and he had a very comical way of drawing down his face, and putting his cap in his eyes at the pathetic parts.

At length we were ordered out, and took the road to Eatonton, the men dancing, singing, and shouting, while the bands played their merriest tunes. As usual, we left flame and destruction behind us. The negroes joined us by hundreds in a day, bringing their best clothes with them. The men were willing to lend a hand to anything, and took the curses and hard words of the soldiers in good part. One of them said to Kiler: "Yuse like my

SACKING OF MADISON.

old dog, massa ; mighty good to bark and scar folks ; but yuse got no teef, yuse can't bite." They knew the boys were their best friends, always ready in a rough way to do them a kindness.

We had some "falling" weather now. It began to rain, the air was cold and penetrating, and the negroes felt it. Their voices were less frequently heard, but they trudged steadily along.

Among the groups who kept particularly close, was one in which was a girl of about twenty, with very black wool, thick lips and broad nostrils, but extremely thin and scrawny, with that ashy look a sick negro always has. Evidently she had but little strength, yet she managed to keep up, although appearing anxious and worn. The change in the weather made her cough, her head drooped, and she kept one hand on her back.

John observed her hanging on one of the wagons, and asked her mother what was the matter with her.

"She's allys mighty poorly, sah, has de mis'ry in her back, pears like she could hardly git along."

One of the teamsters was ungearing a broken-down mule to put another in its place, and drawing her attention to it, John told her she might have it. A good-hearted fellow, who heard what was said, called out, "I will fix it for her, captain." In a few minutes he had twisted her a kind of bridle, given her a blanket to put around her, and she was seated on the animal's back. It did her small service, however, for she fell from it, and was drowned at the crossing of the Oconee.

The country we were passing through was beautiful, but the towns were no more like the towns I had been accustomed to see than the people were like our people. The buildings looked old and tumble-down ; almost all of them were frame, and appeared to have been painted but once, some of them not at all. Things seemed to be broken and never mended; made, never repaired. The people, even those who lived in fine houses, and had lands and negroes, were more ignorant than any people I had ever seen.

At one of the plantations, a woman who owned scores of slaves asked me, "Ef that was the Yanks critter company passing by; she had hearn they bees coming?" Well might the "boys" call this the "dark region," Egypt, etc.

The soldiers had no mercy on the plantation owners, but, as far as I saw, were generally kind to the "shiftless, no account, poor white trash." When they plundered a town they would let them have a share with the negro, and on the road I have often seen them give the half-starved children their rations.

Every night when we halted John and I talked over the day, what we had seen and heard. So far we had had no fighting and had advanced without molestation. "It is dreadful, Phil," said John, "but it is the fortune of war. My heart aches for the helpless children; all this misery from wrong doing, Phil."

As we neared Milledgeville the rain ceased, and the roads, which had been slippery and wet, quickly dried. Foraging parties, which the men called the "locusts," went out and returned with everything eatable the country afforded; we reveled in sorghum, molasses, butter, fresh bread, beef, mutton, poultry, sweet potatoes, honey, peanuts. Fresh horses and mules were driven in in great numbers by the "mule brigade."

The capital was formally surrendered to us, and the Stars and Stripes planted on the State House. The band played national airs, during which performance I saw one lady stick her fingers in her ears. Those who could, wandered round, seeking what they might lawfully devour, for it was strictly forbidden to enter dwellings or destroy private property. We remained one day at the rebel capital. Some of the boys had the run of the State House; they poked among the books, and captured lots of Confederate money, which they pocketed as trophies. They fired the penitentiary and some other buildings, foraged the country far and near, getting the usual amount of good things, including some silver which had been buried for safety, then we crossed the Oconee, and betook ourselves in the direction of Sandersville. I had been sick two days, and lost all this, but now was as bright and well as ever.

Our army of contrabands steadily increased. It was useless trying to keep them in the rear, they crowded between the wagons, before, behind, everywhere, and were only kept back by the bayonet. The men for amusement would tell them terrible stories of what they intended to do with them, at which they only shook their heads and laughed, or uttered some odd joke. Trudging on to liberty without a shoe or stocking to their feet, with but little to wear and nothing to eat but what the soldiers gave them, they evidently thought themselves much better off than the "poor whites," whom they despised and pitied. Every night during the journey the religious darkies held their meetings, prayed, exhorted, sang, shouted, told their experiences and blessed God for delivering them from bondage. They were mostly Methodists. "Massa Linkum" was particularly mentioned in their prayers, and the Yankee army supplicated for with agony and tears. Some of their petitions were very touching, although they would ask God "to give Massa Linkum a tin cup full ob bressings—bress him from de crown ob his head to de sole ob him foot." One of their favorite hymns was:

"Jesus up ter heben hab gwyne,
    I'm mos' dar;
Bids de pilgrims follow on,
    I'm mos' dar.
Ole companions far' you well,
Hobbling down ter def and hell—
I wid Jesus Christ ter dwell—
    I'm mos' dar.
No more sorrow, no more sin,
    I'm mos' dar.
Come, my Jesus, let me in,
    I'm mos' dar.
O! de angels bright as day,
Welcome, brudder, hear them say,
Glory! glory! cl'ar de way,
    I'm mos' dar."

A ring of soldiers always surrounded these meetings, and they sometimes joined in the singing. Often one of the "brudders" would start up and clap his hands and shout "Glory! glory! glory! Massa Sherman hab come," whereupon the whole assembly would go almost wild.

The officers said the world had never before seen anything like the sight our camp presented at night. These poor creatures, particularly the women and children, who had tramped all day, keeping up with the column, were at night ever ready for worship or jollity. Getting a violin they would play, sing, and dance, with soul and effect, to the great gratification of the crowds looking on.

"Mars'r had a big black cat,
    Go in, go in.
Mars'r had a fine wool hat;
    Go in, go in.
Darkey hab some 'possum fat,
    Next go in.
Yellow gal as sweet as honey,
    Go in, go in,
Nigger do de work, and mars'r spend de money,
    Next go in."

While singing this they would caper, slap their sides, and shake their heads in the most comical way. Those who were too old to dance sat on the ground and kept time with their knees, knocking them together, while the lookers on slapped each other on the backs in chorus.

We were now in a different country, traveling through the "grand old woods." Our route lay amid the pine forests; great tall trees growing like the cocoanut tree, with high straight shafts, surrounded with a coronal of green leaves. In and out, in and out, we wound, our line of march nearly eight miles; and ever far ahead and far behind could be seen the dark coats and the white wagons winding beneath the trees. I told John it made me think of "Thanatopsis," which I had recited at a school exhibition just before the war broke out. He smiled and bade me repeat it for him, which I did, and he enjoyed it also.

I often went to the rear to see the blacks, for, force or drive them back as we would, they came up in a little while all the stronger. Hourly they received reinforcements, and had really got to be an army of themselves. Officers told them they must wait, we would come again, there was no subsistence for them, etc. They shook their heads and still came on, feeling perhaps that the denial was not heartily given, only considered necessary.

Passing a large plantation, the negroes told of the dogs kept by the owner which were a terror to the blacks for many miles around. The boys had killed every dog on the route, mongrel curs suffering with the pure of blood.

Hearing of their whereabouts, a squad of men went in search of the beasts, but they were not to be found. When this was reported, an old woman exclaimed: "I'se knows whar dey ar," and described the place where they were hidden. There they were sure enough, muzzled,—Kiler, who had been one of the searchers, returned, dragging the gasping body of a hound after him, a clean limbed, beautifully formed creature, which he threw among the negroes.

They gathered around it exulting, their white teeth gleaming, and their faces wrinkled all over with joy and inward laughter. They kicked and beat the carcass. "Yah, yah, youse neber track nigger any more, youse done for now, yah."

"I feel savage enough to tear that beast to atoms," said Kiler, between his shut teeth. "To think my brother was once pursued by a thing like that."

As we neared Sandersville we heard firing in front. At Buffalo Creek, where there was a great swamp, and many bridges, the enemy had burnt all the latter, and we had to halt, while the pioneer corps made arrangements for crossing. The shooting was brisk, but we gained little information of what was going on. All were eager and excited. Three or four hours passed in this way. Then the column advanced, the firing still continued, and we momentarily expected a general engagement. We kept marching on, however, and so quietly entered the village, without further trouble. We there learned that the enemy's cavalry had attacked our front, they had been skirmishing all the way, but now they were driven off, and we saw nothing more of them.

We halted one day at Sandersville, destroyed the railroads in the neighborhood, burnt the depôts, and visited the plantations, laying them under contribution, and keeping the negro women steadily employed cooking for us. Some of the men had been very fortunate in finding, by the aid of the negroes, valuable articles which had been buried. Some sported gold watches, and other pieces of jewelry. The wagon trains were more carefully guarded, and we began to travel faster, for the enemy's cavalry were hanging about us, and might attack us at any time.

On the 27th we reached Davisboro'. Our cattle trains were so large they were getting unruly. They had plenty of corn, while we reveled on sweet potatoes, and fresh bread, for the men made the mills fly, had sorghum syrup, honey, and even fresh eggs for breakfast.

We were nearing the Ogeechee River, and wished ourselves safely across, for it was one of the miserable swampy streams common hereabout. Our destination was still all conjecture; some of the boys insisting it was Augusta, and that after the passage of the river, we would take a direct course towards that city. The roads were good, and the men laid waste the bordering plantations without halting. You could constantly see parties of stragglers coming up laden with plunder, slaughtered and quartered sheep and pork dripping from their bayonets, and their pockets bulging with money and valuables they had "lit on."

At length we reached the Ogeechee, and halted, for the bridges were all gone, a road had to be made, and pontoons put down for the passage of the wagons. When these were completed, all wended their way over, the wagons on the pontoons, the men on a foot bridge they had constructed. It was with difficulty the negroes were kept to the rear. They made every effort to evade the guard, frantic with the thought of the enemy's cavalry coming down upon them.

I never in my life saw such a sight as this army of contrabands presented. One would have to see it to believe it. On blind horses, on lame and halt mules, and in crazy carts, children on the backs of their parents, and in the arms of their sisters, broken down old men, and decrepit old women, yet with life enough left in them to join in the march to freedom, and to keep up with the army. This "keeping up" was what I could not understand, for they did it, day by day they were there marching on. "The largest part of them were women and children, the little ones half naked, their elders dressed in their best," toting what they could not get on their backs, but always good humored and cheerful, and ready with a quick retort for any jest flung at them. Many were tidy pretty mulattoes, with bright handerchiefs pinned upon their heads after their own peculiar fashion of wearing this article. They depended entirely upon the army for subsistence and had the manner of receiving it of a dog that knows he is a favorite with his master. They have always depended upon the white man for food and clothes, I heard a veteran say one day. "They don't know what freedom means, don't know it is liberty to work for their daily bread, and provide it as they please."

The river passed, we hastened on to Louisville, where we rested for a day. We kept Thanksgiving royally, had all the good things of the season, I am not sure that some of the boys did not have pumpkin pies. After we left Louisville, the country was very fine, and although the weather was now warm, making marching very fatiguing, we made good headway. We went out of our way as usual, to pay our respects to the plantations in passing, but this was beginning to be an old story with us now.

Nearing Millen, many of the men dropped from the ranks to visit the prison pen, which lay about two miles from our line of march. I was anxious to go, but John would not consent; he reminded me that two of our company had strayed from the column a few days before, and hadn't been seen since. There was little doubt that they had been killed or taken prisoners by lurking rebels.

When Kiler, who was among those who went, returned,

he described the dismal coop, in the midst of a dreary pine forest, over which vultures hovered, waiting their prey. There our poor men had been obliged to burrow like rabbits, to keep themselves from cold wind and weather, with no covering above their heads, and almost naked, while they were systematically starved, until some of them, unable to bear their wretchedness longer, deliberately trusted their souls to the mercy of God, and walked to the dead line, where they did not have to wait their doom. The men ground their teeth in indignation and hate, and rushed to the destruction of the depôts and houses on the way with an eagerness of retaliation that was fearful to see.

"When I was a prisoner among them," said a man of about forty, with iron-gray hair, "I witnessed a scene which it makes my heart sore to think of. There was with us a young lad of about seventeen, as delicate as any girl; his mother was a widow, and the boy had a fortune, and had been tenderly raised. When the cry for men swept over the North, he insisted upon going, but his guardian and his mother would not permit it. Time passed; the boy's patriotism waxed hotter and hotter; he implored, and his mother yielded, as she had always done to him, and he went. Three months afterwards he was taken prisoner. At first, although he had to shut his eyes when he ate his food, he resolutely made the best of it, and kept up the spirits of us all. Then, as days, and weeks, and months wore away, he pined for his mother's voice and his home. He could not hear from her. He became thin and weak, and took a fever from exposure. The men nursed him as though he had been a babe—carrying him in their arms, and saving the best bits of their food for him; but he turned from it; he could not eat such food, although he was starving. He would lie for hours and talk in a half delirious way of his home, his mother, the garden, the birds, and the watermelons. One day he was lying with his eyes shut in the sunshine, when a prison officer came along, and, saying he was in the way, brutally kicked him. It broke the boy's heart. That night he raved in delirium, he prayed, he sang, he talked to his mother and his schoolmates; one moment he was with Jesus and the angels, the next he was on the battle-field where he had been taken prisoner.

"We sat round him and watched, and wet his lips and forehead with water we had procured for him at the risk of our lives, and we took turns and rocked him in our arms, that his emaciated little body might not touch the hard bare earth. We saw the end coming, and hoped he might know us ere he died. He did know us. Day was just breaking when he opened his blue eyes wide and looked into our faces. 'I've been dreaming of mother,' he said, 'and now I am going to Jesus.'

"We could say no word.

"'You have been very kind to me,' he went on. 'If ever you get away from here, you must tell mother not to grieve for me; God has shown me that it is best.'

"He turned his face against my breast, as though to sleep. When I looked he was gone. I hope, I pray that God will forgive me for the deadly bitterness that sprung up in my heart then, in the very presence of the holy mystery of such a death."

He stopped, and no one spoke for several moments. At length one struck up "Rally Round the Flag, Boys," and all joined in.

I have tried to tell this story in the man's own words, but I cannot tell it as he did.

John was present at the time, and he held my hand tightly. I saw he was much moved.

Afterwards I asked him who the man was. "I do not know his name," was the reply, "but I think he is from Michigan. I have noticed him several times. He is a brave soldier, and I believe a good man. Phil," he said, after a pause, "do you know what I thought when he spoke of that boy? I thought you might have the same fate; think of this when you would run recklessly into danger to which no duty calls you."

I heard some of the officers talking with John one day; they spoke of the morals of the army. One of them had served in Mexico, and in the Crimea, and he said he had not believed it possible that in an army the standard could be so high; he had known of no insult offered, or act of violence committed upon any woman or child; on the contrary, he thought the women on the plantations carried things with a high hand.

Dwellings had been entered and private property taken, but when done without orders this was promptly punished. He spoke of the case of two men who had been caught stealing women's clothing; they had been sentenced to wear the clothes they had pilfered, and were now trudging along, each tied to the tail of a wagon, dressed in the frocks they had coveted—the laughing-stock and scorn of the army. So it was now; although burning with indignation at the sight of Millen prison pen, they destroyed no inhabited private dwelling, and were guilty of no outrage.

The weather was still very warm, but we kept steadily on. The men began to talk of the seaboard being their destination, and to crack their jokes about Savannah. We were among the pines; birds were singing in the green tops over our heads, while under our feet it was splash, splash, through creeks and swamps, most of which had to be pontooned for the wagons to pass over.

"It was trying to the flesh and trying to the temper," Jones said, as he drew himself heavily from a sort of quicksand, where he had gone in almost to his knees in an attempt to force a passage. It was slow work. The teams plunged along, the drivers straining every nerve to keep them right, using hard whips, and harder words, bawling at the top of their lungs; officers were screeching orders, riders sinking into ditches and foaming and sweating in their attempts to get out. The men were passing on now over shoe-tops, now to the ankle in the slough, some swearing, others laughing and cracking jokes about finding the bottom. In this way we marched on to Springfield. On crossing a creek some one asked its name. A bluff Indianian shouted out: "Ebenezer. They are fond of the name. We have little Ebenezer, big Ebenezer, and Ebenezer proper here, and up country they have Ebenezers too. Their 'stones of help' do not seem to do them much good."

Whereupon "The Barometer" sang out:

"Here I raise my Ebenezer!"

and they traveled on, singing it at the top of their lungs.

On another occasion, when we were going on quietly, at the close of the day, just before reaching our camping ground, he burst out with:

"How tedious and tasteless the hours,
When Jesus no longer I see!
Sweet prospects, sweet birds and sweet flowers
Have all lost their sweetness for me."

When another voice, in a rough but hearty tone, was heard:

"Lookee yonder! Just put rebels in that second line and we will all join in."

There was a cheering laugh, followed by rebuke for the speaker's want of reverence.

"Do you think," was the reply, "that I would throw dirt at my own mother by making fun of such things. I just thought the words suited our case exactly, and spoke out in meeting. Bless you, I have sung that many a time in the Methodist chapel, where the old woman belongs, and if I get through this war it is her prayers will take me."

At length we were over Ebenezer Creek, its branches, swamps, and all. Begrimed and with clothes torn, some of the men presented a sorry spectacle. Our lines were narrowing, the army drawing closer together, for we were nearing Savannah. It was about the 10th, I think, for I had almost lost the track of the days of the month, that a gun-boat made its appearance on the Savannah, and shelled us, but did no harm. We had come upon the obstructions they had planted in our path, as we neared the outer line of their defenses. The road passing over swamp and morass was piled with logs, through which a squirrel could hardly creep. The men were jubilant, and no longer asked "What is that?" when a roar met their ears. They knew what it was—expected it—longed for it—rejoiced at its coming and worked the harder to get nearer and have their share.

I listened now for the sound of the sea waves which came faintly to my ear, and trod beneath the live oak and palmetto, where the earth never seemed so beautiful to me as it did then. Strange luxuriant vines, festooned with their dark and bright green, the trees already draped by the hoary gray moss, which swung to and fro on the branches, making these giants of the wood look wild and weird. The air was soft, the sun bright, and when the music of the band was heard in the distance, I did not wonder that the men felt exultant and impatient to meet those who kept them from what they already deemed their own. John's company was now in the front, and I kept pretty close to them. If there was anything going on I wanted to see it.

We had carried the first line, taken the enemy's redoubts, which commanded the road through the swamp over which we were advancing, and they, in full tilt on a double quick, were making their way back to Savannah.

I was standing looking at a prisoner who had been brought in, when suddenly I heard one close beside me exclaim : " Laws a marcy, ef yonder aint young mars ! " and a negro who had been working in front hustled back among the men, who laughed at his terror. Another, who was an officer's servant, and had been with us some time, looked at the man defiantly, almost insolently, and said : " 'Pears like these here cullard pussons never git no sense. I'd like to see my ole mars make me back out like dat." His eyes flashed viciously.

The negroes told terrible stories of cruelties practiced upon those of their color who had again fallen into the hands of their former masters. Here, for the first time, I heard the account, which has since been published, of their treatment by the enemy's cavalry at Ebenezer Creek, the driving them into the water, where they perished by hundreds. The blacks believed they would be tortured in every possible way if caught, and placed entire confidence in these tales. They would shake their heads knowingly, if you appeared to doubt, with : " Dis nigger knows."

Our lines were so connected that the divisions could support each other, and although the enemy constantly contested the roads by which we advanced, as yet they had done it but little to our damage. We heard of

"OLE MARS."

strong fortifications in our way, of torpedoes and obstructions of all kinds; but, no whit alarmed, the army steadily approached the coast. "The Old Tycoon," the boys said, "had made up his mind to have the city, and have it he would." So if Hardee were wise he would give in handsomely, for you might as well try to turn a river up stream as turn old Billy back when he meant forward.

In a few hours more Savannah was invested, and preparations were making to storm Fort McAllister, which stands with two sides to the land, on a spot of dry earth upon a peninsula formed by the Ogeechee river, and is surrounded by a dense swamp.

John told me one evening that a reconnoissance had been made, and that the fort would probably be attacked next day. We were out on the road at the time, standing talking, when a body of our cavalry came dashing along. I moved quickly to get out of the way, caught my foot in a vine and fell. Ere I could gain my feet again they were on us. One moment I felt as though something was grinding me to atoms; then I knew nothing until I opened my eyes and found myself in the surgeon's hands, and John bending over me. My ankle was sprained and a rib was broken. It appeared to me impossible to bear it, not the pain, but the being compelled to lie quietly while so much was going on. Then, too, the hurt was so inglorious. Had it been a bullet or bayonet wound I would have been proud to have had it—but to be rendered helpless by a tangled vine and the hoof of a horse —it was too much, too unheroic.

I almost put myself in a fever thinking of it. John listened quietly to all my complaints on this head, and when I paused for breath, said:

"And so you think, Phil, the hundreds and thousands

of soldiers who have been stricken down by disease, and had to lie in camps and hospitals suffering from their maladies are not heroes! To my mind there has been more true heroism among them than was displayed by their brothers on the battle-field. Thirsting for action, they have been compelled to curb their eager spirits, calm their tempest-tossed souls, bear patiently agonies of body which brought no glory, yet have exulted heartily in the victories achieved by their comrades, while burning to achieve such themselves."

I did not answer, for it was very bitter to me.

"My poor boy," John said after a moment, drawing his hand across my brow, "you must learn that 'God knows best.'"

John gave me full details of the entry of the army into the city, and everything that was done. I lay in bed and heard all about Fort McAllister. Trying to possess my soul in patience, I rejoiced heartily, and was *so* proud that Savannah was taken by the Western army, and presented as a Christmas gift to the nation.

CHAPTER XXXI.

THE CAROLINAS—HOME.

I DID not see the rest, but Fort McAllister was taken, and Savannah came into our possession after a siege of eleven days. Hardee evacuated on the night of the 20th of December and General Geary pushed in after him.

It was gray dawn when the troops entered the city, the mayor and council going out to meet the general, and surrendering it unconditionally.

I went in a couple of days afterwards in an ambulance, and had to keep my bed two weeks. John insisted upon it, only reconciling me to the confinement by pointing out that if orders came to leave, and my ankle was not better, I must stay behind.

It was a sorry Christmas for me, but a great one for the nation. I could imagine "Father Abraham's" satisfaction. The forts he had promised the people that they should again possess, were gradually coming into their hands.

A beautiful city is Savannah. It was founded (as Tom Doolan said, when asked the question at an examination, by General O-leg-athorp (Oglethorpe) and he bore the name O-leg-athorp, ever after) in 1732.

I saw but little of it until just before we left, when I mounted my horse and rode about. I had some curiosity to see Pulaski's monument, which is mentioned in our geographies as among the beauties of Savannah. The citizens must have venerated the memory of this heroic Pole, for they have erected several monuments to his memory. They have given his name to an hotel, and a fort, and a square, and, I think, a street as well. He was a nobleman banished from his country, who volunteered in our Revolutionary war, and when the city was attacked by the British, was killed while gallantly defending it.

One of the monuments raised in his honor is in Chippewa Square; another, jointly commemorating his deeds and those of General Greene, stands in Monument Square. It is a beautiful column, rising like a pyramid. The corner stone of this last was laid by General Lafayette, when he visited the United States in 1825, and the ceremony was conducted with much pomp and parade.

Many of the houses in Savannah are palaces. General Sherman's headquarters was in a house owned by Mr. Greene. It was a two story dwelling which stood in a garden facing a park. A wide gallery ran all round the outside, the ascent to which was by marble steps, flanked on each side by tall pillars holding lamps. A sentinel paced this gallery. I knew the man, and contrived while holding converse with him, to get a glimpse of the hall inside. It was broad and long, and flagged with marble; there were four doors on each side of it, with heavy moldings and carved cornices; a large chandelier hung from the center and sconces protruded from the walls. At the farther end, before a door opening on a garden, stood several pedestals ornamented with statues, and brackets holding pictures hung here and there. Large tubs containing tropical plants stood on the marble pavement, their branches almost touching the ceiling. I was told that the drawing-room and the inside of this dwelling corresponded with what I had seen.

The streets of Savannah are very wide. Broad Street and West Broad Street are on opposite sides of the city; then there are South Broad and Liberty Street running through the center; and Bay Street near the river. Broad street is beautiful; it has a grassy walk through the middle, shaded with trees, for foot passengers, with a carriage way each side. The streets are not paved, they are covered with sand instead. The city is regularly laid out, and has handsome public buildings. Every square, or two, I have forgotten which, there is a small park, of an oval shape, planted with shade trees; there are twenty-four of these parks altogether.

The Southern trees are the handsomest I ever saw. The pines and oaks with their draperies of moss are solemn and funereal looking, but the magnolia is gay and bright, as is also the orange when in fruit and blossom. I saw the bay, and another tree called the Pride of India, with which the streets of Savannah are planted.

The people seemed very poor. I observed several boys in the streets dressed in suits of patched bedticking, one who wore a coat made of a worn patch-work quilt, and negro women in dresses made of gunny bags. I went to church one Sunday, and saw many gentlemen there in homespun suits—others in old, shiny, long-tailed coats, and hats of a by-gone era.

The ladies had evidently not seen the last Paris fashions. Although it was some time since I had visited stylish places, these were some years behind the last I had seen. Many of their bonnets had, no doubt, been taken from closets or garrets, where they had been thrown with other rubbish, and "done up" by the owners—their faded ribbons being renovated as far as possible. A great many of the ladies wore black. I think any taste in head-gear might have been suited in that assemblage.

Secretary Stanton paid a visit to Savannah, on which occasion General Sherman reviewed the cavalry on Bay Street, in front of the Exchange. There was a great crowd, and much cheering for Mr. Lincoln.

I went to the hospital to try to find a man of John's company who was ill. I saw and talked with many of our men there; they were very enthusiastic and impatient to get out. One of them described to me General Sherman's making the rebel prisoners take up the torpedoes.

"There is no getting round 'Old Billy,'" he said. "He had information that the roads to Savannah were filled with concealed torpedoes to destroy our men. He placed the rebel prisoners in front of our advance columns, and compelled them to dig up the infernal machines, a work they did not like at all, 'but the fox was the finder.'"

This hospital was a large, low, two story building with trees about it; the men were very comfortable, and were well taken care of.

I had but little time to go about the city. I should like to have visited some of the forts, but had not the opportunity. The city was quiet and orderly; the people looked listless and sad. Preparations were making for a march through the Carolinas, it proved. John was afraid I would have the fever again, and tried to persuade me to remain at Savannah. My ankle was well, only a little weak, and I had my horse; so, as the left wing was likely, as rumor said, to plunge into the swamps, I prevailed on him to let me accompany his old friend, Mr. D—— of Bull Run memory, who was going with the right wing.

No doubt some of my readers think that when an army moves it does so in a body. If so this is a mistake. It moves by corps and divisions, each having its own wagon, ammunition, ordnance and ambulance trains, pack mules, etc., carrying all it needs on the route. Each division has also its own badge by which it is known to others.

Thus in the Army of the Tennessee, the badge of the Seventeenth Corps was an arrow; a red one for the First Division, a white one for the Second, a blue one for the Third. For the Fifteenth Corps it was a cartridge-box; red, white and blue for the divisions. In General Slocum's army, the Twentieth Corps had a star, red, white and blue for the divisions; the Fourteenth an acorn, red, white and blue for the divisions.

General Sherman had reviewed the troops. The whole army had been inspected, and there was a getting together of stores preparatory to the new march. The quartermasters had a busy time. Think of having to furnish nearly two million rations of bread, twice as much coffee, besides sugar, salt and bacon. For although the order was published to subsist on the country, no general would have felt justified in starting without providing rations for his men in case of emergency.

It was estimated that General Sherman's wagon-train was forty miles in length, the train of each wing covering twenty miles; the ammunition wagons were one thousand in number, and required twelve miles of road to move on; then the batteries covered seven miles, the ambulances were one thousand in number and covered five miles. I got these particulars from the officers or men, and put them down in my note book.

I knew one or two of the war correspondents, and I liked to go about with them, for they found out everything. John told me he saw an estimate, which said it required over eight hundred wagons to transport the bread alone; and that, exclusive of the ambulances, there were six thousand wagons in the army, carrying provisions, tents, baggage, ammunition, etc., and they were drawn by thirty-six thousand horses. From Atlanta through to Savannah we did not lose a wagon. Besides the wagons, two thousand pack mules followed the army. Shovels, spades, pickaxes, materials for building, pontooning instruments and tools must go with the column for use on the way.

All the horses of the wagon trains and ambulances, as well as those belonging to the officers had to be kept shod; and men, materials and tools must be on hand to do it. The cavalry had their own blacksmiths. These horses must be fed, and it being impossible to carry forage, the country had to furnish it. To the foragers or bummers, therefore, was assigned the duty of providing entertainment for man and beast. I heard a general say that General Sherman could no more have moved his army without the bummers, than he could move a wagon without wheels. There was nothing the rebels were so afraid of as Sherman's Bummers.

Sixty men from each division were set aside for this work, making in themselves a little army of from seven to eight hundred men, mounted on horses and mules. They cared for nobody, were afraid of nothing, and tried to make themselves look as terrible as possible. "Come boys, it is time to bum," or "We must be off to market." And they would start while the stars were in the sky, and ride the country for miles in the front and flank of the army. They unearthed everything that was hidden, and loading their animals with pigs, geese, turkeys and chickens, they seized any vehicles at hand, coaches or dung carts, and filling them until they could hold no more, then impressed the negroes to drive them.

In our march through Georgia, I more than once saw a medley of hams, eggs, cheese, honey, potatoes, pickles, preserves, live poultry, and dead hogs, taken from a handsome carriage. They seemed to be up to every trick and artifice of the people to hide their provisions or silver. The more they protested they had nothing the more the bummers believed they had everything; they left no place unsearched, and if they found anything, destroyed what they could not take away, in revenge for the trouble they had in finding it. They made the negroes dig the sweet potatoes, and load the vehicles, as well as drive them, which they were very willing to do.

At night, as the tired column approached its camping ground, the bummers would be seen planted along the line of march, beside hills of fodder and provisions, each squad keeping watch over that allotted to its company. Their presence always told of good cheer, and they were received by the men with shouts of welcome.

After the night's arrangements were made, they would collect around the fires, and tell their adventures. One night I saw a tall, raw-boned fellow exhibiting a pretty little French watch, and a pair of earrings which he declared were for his "girl." He had smelled them, and unearthed them, he said. The boys laughed at that, and insisted he had been robbing the women, and some not very complimentary remarks were made by one or two present, as to the courage of a man who would take a woman's traps, even though she was a rebel woman.

"Now you hold on there," was the reply; "you had better not be passing your opinion until you know what you are talking about. I'll tell you how it was. The captain ordered us not to enter that house, but to take what we pleased from the outside premises; we had taken everything and were going to leave, when a pile of manure near the barn caught my eye; it had been newly turned over, and it was early in the day for that work. I asked a nigger who stood by what was hidden there and he said

"Nuffin, massa." But there was a look out of the corner of his eye such as I had seen in niggers' eyes before, when things were under cover, so I began to turn the pile over; and the boys smelling a rat, ran back to help. In a few minutes it was scattered and a box full of gimcracks brought to view. These were my part of the spoil, and lawful spoil, too, for we had orders to take all we could get or wanted outside the doors."

There were some terrible stories told of the bummers. They defended themselves by saying they had to provide for the army, and their orders were to live off the country; this they did by taking from rich and poor alike. Let those who brought on the war reap the reward, was their feeling.

About the middle of January, the right wing went by sea to Beaufort. I enjoyed the sight of the great deep. I never wearied looking at it. The army went into camp at Beaufort and Pocotaligo.

The left wing began its line of march up both sides of the Savannah River. A few days after, we heard of it floundering in the swamps, trying to force its way through the flood, for the rain had deluged the country and covered the swamp roads. In three or four days it had made but seven miles. It was impossible to proceed; the roads were impassable, the boys walked in water, stood in water, worked in water, slept in water, with alligators for company; but they made a frolic of it, and jest and laughter rang through the dismal marshes. The roads were obstructed by trees felled across them, their branches interlaced, making a barrier through which the men had to force their way with guns on their shoulders, and hatchets in hand.

About the 29th or 30th, we broke up our camp at Pocotaligo and Beaufort, one column moving towards the

River Cambahee, the other on the road to McPhersonville. This was a pretty little village, with handsome shade trees. We left it in ruins.

"We are in South Carolina, boys," said a huge Wisconsin man, as he fired the last house ; "don't leave them a rope to hang by."

"Ay, ay," said another ; "as they have made their bed, so they must lie in it."

They burned and destroyed with twice the zest they did in Georgia. As we marched along the road the people stood and gazed in wonder. The boys sang out and shouted and danced as though we celebrated a festival.

We found most of the houses vacant, the owners having run off, consequently they were fired and burned.

The country was poor about the Coosawatchie, with great swamps which had to be crossed, and through the swamps ran many deep wide streams and shallow and treacherous creeks, in which the wagons would stick fast, and which must be bridged. This the men did, at the same time keeping on and skirmishing with the enemy until we reached Hickory Hill. Scarce pausing, we crossed Coosawatchie Swamp and camped on Duck Creek. Our way was lighted by burning dwellings, fences and trees ; sometimes we marched between lines of fire.

The weather had been bright and beautiful ; now a cold rain fell. The enemy were at work trying to impede our progress ; we could hear them cutting down trees. The other column was in Whippy Swamp, pulling down almost as fast as the enemy put up ; working and fighting by turns. Indeed, they seemed to be amphibious, and almost as much at home and as jolly, when up to their waists fighting in the green slimy water, as when marching on the sandy roads. They rebuilt the bridges, made the roads, and drove the rebels at the same time, till at length they were through the swamp; and after a fight at Rivers Bridge, where the rebels thought themselves impregnable, (and where we should have been impregnable) were over the Big Salkehatchie, the ugliest river I ever saw, with its horrible swamps, and treacherous roads, and were pushing on ahead.

About the 4th of February we left Duck Creek, where we had been soaked, and started for Beaufort Bridge, by way of Angleseys. The causeway through the swamp was broken up and the bridges—over a dozen—destroyed. Nothing daunted, the boys set to work and pulled down a frame church near, repairing the roads and building the bridges with the timber, and likewise crossed over the Big Salkehatchie.

Passing a tree near the roadside I saw General Sherman was under it, writing on his hat for a desk, an orderly beside him.

"There's old Billy now," some one remarked.

An aged negro toddling along as near the column as he dared, approached and said eagerly: "Whar, massa, whar? Please tell me whar?"

"There, look well at him; he is your best friend," said a soldier, pointing him out.

The negro stood and gazed intently, and drawing nearer looked again.

"Well, what do you think of him?" said the soldier who had pointed him out, for the column had halted.

"Why, massa," as the general crushed his old soft felt hat on his head and rode on, "he's not much to look at, but I reckon he's powerful to do."

A shout of laughter greeted the reply.

There was some little skirmishing between the rivers, but the enemy generally managed to keep out of the way, yet as we neared the little Salkehatchie they seemed determined to dispute the crossing and there was some sharp fighting.

At night there were beautiful scenes, the fires lit up the sky, and wreathed the trees, having a grand effect. I saw a pine wood on fire; it cracked and hissed and spluttered, and the light was like the brightest day. The moss and vines which hung from the branches were festoons of flames. One moment it looked like a great cathedral burning, with columns and arches and all kinds of fretted work. Then the limbs would fall, the vines give way, and it would take some other form, weird, wild, or fantastic.

The houses on the plantations all along our route were destroyed, and the provisions in them seized.

It was cold, but the Little Salkehatchie had to be crossed; the order had been given. A swamp, as usual, ran all along its banks, and the causeway over it was held by the foe, and strongly obstructed. Our men waded to their necks in the water, holding their guns and ammunition in their hands above their heads; thus they charged through the swamp, right up to the breastwork, behind which the foe was sheltered, and took it, the rebels running at their approach. On the 7th we struck the Charleston and Augusta Railroad, and began to destroy the track. It rained, and was so cold I thought I should freeze in the saddle, until we reached Hamburg, where I warmed myself by the burning cotton, nearly a thousand bales of which had been found and set on fire.

We had news from the left wing, which was out of camp at Sister's Ferry, and making its way through the swamps under almost impassable difficulties, and building the roads as they marched. They were beyond Danielton.

Some of the men who had been out on a reconnoissance to Cannon's Bridge returned well laden with books, which they enjoyed at the camp fires. Some "big rebel" had been moving his library and a wagon had broken down ; the men coming upon it helped themselves, removing the books for him.

On the 11th of February, the whole Army of the Tennessee crossed the South Edisto, and the next day proceeded to cross the North Edisto, which was a more difficult matter, as the water was waist deep, and the causeways were fortified and defended by the rebels. It was done, however, the causeway gained, and the Army of the Tennessee marched to the North Edisto, accompanied not by a pillar of fire but by walls of fire. The dry grass had caught, or been ignited, and the flames were on every side lighting up the long line of march, for it was gray dawn ere the whole army had crossed over.

Mr. D—— and I rode into what remained of Orangeburg, which had been given to the flames. It must have been a beautiful little place, but now it was but black and charred ruins. The people young and old sat in the streets beside the little, and it was very little, they had saved from their burning homes. Many of them had not a garment but what they wore, and were without food. My heart ached for them, for it seemed as though they must die of want. I saw an old, gray-haired man of seventy, his long locks on his shoulders, begging from the soldiers for his grandchildren, who sat among the cinders crying for bread. The men gave him all they had, which he seized and carried off with trembling hands, that were white and small, and never could have done any rough labor.

Leaving Orangeburg, we marched in the direction of Columbia and entered the pine district. The air was heavy with smoke and sickening with turpentine, for the men found large quantities which they fired, and then burned the trees which yielded it. The atmosphere was so heavy and thick that it was with difficulty that one could breathe. Objects could not, while in the forest, be distinguished at any distance for the smoke, which, black and thick, hung like a pall in the heavens. I felt as though I should faint, and became so dizzy while in the Pines I could hardly sit upon my horse.

Keeping on through Caw-caw Swamp, we reached Sandy Run, the boys finding and burning much turpentine on the way, so we were accompanied as usual with smoke and flames.

As we drew near Columbia the men uttered many a threat, and spoke through their shut teeth of this home of the South Carolina aristocrats, in a way that made me afraid to hear. The weather was cold ; a "Scotch mist," as we called the fine rain which fell, carrying a chill to one's very heart. Keeping on, we reached Congaree Creek, where there was quite a battle for the bridge. The rebels defended it with a cannon at one end, and set fire to it at the other, but our men rushed up to the cannon's mouth and put out the fire.

The people along the road were terribly alarmed. Women in groups besought the officers, almost on their knees, for protection, and when assured of safety, could hardly believe they were not to be murdered on the spot, the bummers, and rowdies from the army who had strayed and pretended to be bummers, had inspired them with such horror.

It was near here I saw a fight among the bummers. They could not agree about the division of the spoil they had taken, and drew arms on each other. But for the orders of an officer, who happened to witness it, there would have been a regular battle.

Riding through a swamp Mr. D—— and I heard a noise in the bushes, and suspecting a hidden foe, turned to see what it was, and caught the flutter of a woman's dress. We pushed after, and when we came up, found three terrified women clinging to each other's drabbled dresses, one a black and the other two white. They begged piteously for mercy. We dismounted and went to them. The white and black women were each about fifty years of age, the other was a girl of about sixteen. They were wet to the skin, half famished and in such terror that they shook as though they had the ague. It was with difficulty we could make them believe we intended no evil.

A little reassured, they told us the bummers had visited their place and stripped them of everything, the half-dozen negroes the lady had owned going off with them.

The old negro woman, who had been the playmate of her mistress in her youth, had refused to leave her, and, hearing the army coming, they together had fled to the swamp, taking the young girl, who was the lady's only child, with them. Ere they reached it they saw their home in flames. They had made a little shelter at some distance with boughs and grass, and had ventured from it to try and find something to eat.

There was that in the lady's face and manner which took a strong hold of both Mr. D—— and myself. We lighted a fire, which they had been afraid to do, assuring them there was no danger of discovery with smoke all round them, and gave them the contents of our haversacks, for we happened to have two days' rations with us. They were particularly glad of the coffee, of which we had nearly a pound; we gave them our blankets, and the tin cups which hung upon our saddles.

This warmed the old negro's heart, and she told us in confidence that she had hidden some taters and bacon for missus, in a place where Satan himself could not find them, and where she could get them when the army had gone.

Seeing them a little more comfortable we went our way heavy at heart.

Columbia, which we were approaching, stands on the Congaree River, at the junction of the Saluda and the Broad. There were expensive and beautiful bridges over the rivers, but the rebels burnt that over the Saluda at our appearance. The Saluda factory, which like the Roswell factory gave employment to many women, stood near this bridge and was destroyed by our troops. The sight of Sorghum Camp, where our men who were prisoners had been confined, and which was passed on the way to Saluda, roused the indignation of the army and intensified the bitterness of the feelings with which they regarded Columbia.

There was some skirmishing and fighting, in the midst of which the Saluda was pontooned; the men crossed and made a sharp attack on the rebels, who tried with their artillery to defend the bridge over the Broad, but finding themselves driven back, they set fire to and burnt it. Every effort was made to save it, but in vain; they had covered it with rosin and piled pine kindlings upon it.

We could plainly see the city. It appeared deserted; the doors and windows of the houses were shut, and there were no persons in the streets. Some of our men swam the river, others went over in boats and hastily constructed rafts to protect the pontooners, who were at work all night bridging the Broad.

The men spent the time, while waiting, in getting ready to enter, putting on their best clothes, burnishing their arms, etc. They were determined to make as fine a show as they could in this center of rebeldom, which they hated little less than Charleston itself.

At length the word "forward" was given, and with every token of victory, and "Hail Columbia" and the "Star Spangled Banner" ringing on the breeze, with shout and dance, and "God bless you" from negro and white in welcome, we entered the city, which had been evacuated by the rebels and most of the secesh inhabitants, and surrendered by the mayor.

The negroes in their joy tore open the cotton bales in the streets, and scattered the contents by handfuls in the air, as a salutation to the troops, who in passing assisted them in the work of destruction by thrusting their bayonets in the white piles, and casting it abroad.

Every man had more or less cotton upon him. One poor fellow came near being burnt up; the cotton he had on him, by some means, took fire. I was attracted by his cries: "Put me out! Put me out!" He was more frightened than hurt, however, for his clothes were only a little scorched.

That night I witnessed the most terrible scene I ever saw in my life; the like of which I hope I may never see again. I thought the burning of Atlanta dreadful, but John explained that it was a military necessity. The burning of Columbia was the horror of horrors. The city in flames; aged women, young women, children and infants in arms, decrepit old men, and sick and infirm old women huddled together by hundreds—with no food, no clothes, no shelter. Their tears, and prayers, and lamentations were almost unheard amid the shouts of the pillagers, the oaths of the drunken soldiers, the crackling and hissing of the flames which were destroying their homes.

In the parks and sheltered corners, half dressed and clinging to each other, were frightened groups, who again and again were obliged by the approach of the fire to move from even those poor retreats.

The sky looked an ocean of flame, and the earth was as light as it was ever made by the brightest sun.

Columbia was a handsome city; everything showed that wealthy people had lived there. The houses were large, the gardens beautiful, and there was, as is usual in Southern cities, a great number of shade trees.

General Preston, Mr. Rhett and Wade Hampton lived there; I heard some of our cavalry talking, while standing in front of Hampton's house, a palace of a place. They had lately had a skirmish with him and his band, but did not appear to be much afraid of him.

"A pretty good fighter, but the most overbearing of all the Southern crew," I heard one say.

They looked as though they longed to clang through his splendid mansion and turn their horses into his paradise of a garden. The soldiers did burn the house and lay waste the garden before we left.

Passing the park I saw a number of women and girls surrounded by our officers and men, who appeared to be guarding them. They were dreadfully terrified. I found they were young ladies who had been at school at the Convent. The Convent was burning and they had been compelled to leave it with the sisters, and had nowhere to go. Everywhere our officers and men were working, trying to protect the helpless people, and save their homes: but many of the soldiers were drunk and ungovernable. They ransacked houses and dived into the cellars for liquors, drinking costly wine like water and quarreling over the spoil, even shooting at each other.

The streets were strewed with everything. The frantic people had tried to save some little of their household goods, and furniture, beds, crockery, pictures, books and statuary could be seen cumbering the ground, the half crazed people sitting among them.

The public buildings of Columbia were very handsome. There was Christ Church, the Baptist Church and Methodist, all fine buildings, the Town Hall and market, the Court House and the hotels, Congaree and Columbia House, with the new Capitol, said to be one of the finest buildings to be seen anywhere. The Capitol was not finished and not burnt.

Columbia stands on a hill, but there are many swamps about it. The Columbia and Kingsville Railroad reaches the city through a gloomy cypress swamp on its edge. In entering we crossed the Spartanburg Railroad, also the Saluda Canal. The whole ground appeared saturated with water.

It would be impossible to give any idea of things the next day. The ruins were still burning; the half-clothed people were begging for bread and crowding the churches for shelter, startled and affrighted every now and then by explosions that shook the buildings they were in to their foundations.

The army was destroying the ammunition and arms they had found.

Our commissaries were ordered to give food to the people, of whom hundreds had nothing to eat.

We left Columbia February the 20th, I think it was, and I for one was glad to get away from so much misery. The houseless, homeless, destitute people begged piteously to go with us; and having permission so to do, they seized every kind of article, and followed after. Aristocrats, negroes and "poor whites" made a long line of refugees, the like of which was never seen with an army before. The negroes and poor whites had generally the best conveyances—the former often traveled in the family coach, while the mistress and children came behind in a cart or carry-all. The animals attached to these vehicles made one laugh in spite of one's self; broken-down cart horses, mules and oxen, and in one case even a cow assisted to drag them along. Besides this caravan, there was a large number on foot, who preferred picking the crumbs that fell from the army to remaining behind.

Mr. D—— and I rode several times along the line of people, and always found the negroes cheerful and full of jokes, no matter what the difficulties to be encountered. The soldiers had a kindly feeling for them, and scarcely ever refused to help them. They remembered that the slaves had always been the friends of the Federal soldier, and had assisted the poor prisoners when they could.

The first night out from Columbia we camped on a high ridge which ran along a creek some nine or ten miles from the Wateree River. The soldiers were full of fun and frolic; they built fires, around which they sang and danced. The bugles sounded, the drums beat, and drunk with their success in humbling South Carolina, they sang "Hail Columbia" and "Yankee Doodle," boasting that they had crushed the head of the serpent. At the same time they gave those with them bread, and were really kind to the refugees.

We kept on, fording the creeks with difficulty, for the rains had swollen them much beyond their banks. We had some skirmishing, took some wagons and quite a number of prisoners. The rebels also seized several of our wagons.

We crossed the Wateree on pontoons, and kept on in the direction of Liberty Hill, another aristocratic locality, having handsome mansions and costly furniture, and negroes in abundance. The boys visited the larders and carried off what they wanted, to the great disgust of the owners, who talked to them of "their rights."

We turned for some purpose off into the interior, burning cotton, of which we found a large quantity, seizing horses and cattle, and making bonfires of houses.

Nearing Camden it began to rain. All night long the water came down. We were thoroughly soaked, and could scarcely find a road.

In one of our halts for the night I saw a lady and two children who had been out in the wet in a wagon without a cover, with only boards for a bed, and no sides, but drawn by a tolerably good horse. The lady looked the picture of despair. One child was in her arms, another at her feet, its face hidden in her lap. The train had halted, and other vehicles were pushing on her, yet she made no effort to get out of the way, but sat with the reins lying listless in her lap. A negro man of about fifty, strong and well built, was pushing his way through, dragging a mule; he turned, saw the lady, went a few steps further, halted, then went back, and going up to the wagon, said: "Bress me, Miss Ann, be's this youse and the little chilers, tu?"

She looked at him, but made no answer. The child at her feet raised her face and said:

"I am so cold and hungry, Uncle Dick," and began to cry.

The man threw the mule's halter over his arm, seized the bridle of the horse, applied the whip, and with some exertion drew the wagon from the mud, where it had stuck, and drove it on one side in the bushes.

"Don't cry, little miss, wait a bit, Uncle Dick will come back," he said, and starting off, he returned in a few moments with some hard tack and salt pork, which he gave the children. The lady shook her head when he offered it to her.

Going up to the negro, I asked him who they were.

"My ole massa's daughter," he said; "she's done lost her father, and her husband, and her brudder in dis war; and she's got nuffin, and no one tu care for her ef Uncle Dick don't. Her house was burnt, her provender all took, and her niggers left her, but, please God, Uncle Dick 'ill do for her."

I went to one of the officers, and told him what I had seen; he gave me bread, meat and a blanket; I begged some coffee and sugar from the men, got another blanket and went back. The old negro had gathered a quantity of moss and leaves, and laid them upon the boards of the wagon, and made a fire, at which he was holding the youngest child in his arms. He blessed me over and over when I gave him the food, spread one of the blankets carefully over the lady, who was now lying in the wagon, drew the other round the children, then untying an old, battered tin quart-cup from a string which held a motley collection of things on the mule's back, proceeded to make some coffee.

"Bress God, Miss Ann should have sumfin tu du her good."

I went off, but silently promised myself to keep an eye on that old negro and his charge, and I did. My conscience told me I had not been faithful to an injunction solemnly given me by John. "Phil, you will have many opportunities of helping others on this march without its conflicting with your duty, for your own sake don't neglect one."

The next day I saw "Uncle Dick" with the mule and horse harnessed together in the wagon. He had made a rough seat in the wagon, over which he had put a framework of brushwood, and on this stretched one of the blankets, under which cover sat Miss Ann and the children, while he drove.

I complimented him on the improvement.

"Yes, massa," he replied with pride, " I was not in tother army for nuffin ; not gwyne tu be caught in the woods again wid not so much as a knife tu cut a stick ; tried him once wid de seceshes and liked tu perished. When I'se made up my mind to come, I'se put all my fixins together on de ole mule's back."

It rained terribly. If anything could have depressed the army the weather would. We could find no roads and the wagons could hardly get along at all ; they would stick fast, and the teamsters would swear and beat the horses and mules in a way it made one shudder to see. I often wondered that the soldiers were as humane and kind-hearted as they were, for they got accustomed to the suffering they saw constantly.

At length we reached Camden, where a battle was fought in the Revolution. It was a pretty little place, and had an iron statue of some Indian chief in the market square.

We continued on to Lynch Creek where we had a terrible time ; it rained in streams for three days and nights ; all the while the boys worked in the water, sometimes waist deep, to make the bridge. The enemy's cavalry attacked us several times, but was driven back. I was sick and kept in camp. As we crossed I saw an Irishman frightened almost into fits. The boys had become so accustomed to snakes in the swamps, they did not mind them at all, but considered them a part of the ceremony. A don't-care backwoodsman trod on a long, greenish brown one, and, seizing it by the head and taking good aim, threw it over Paddy's shoulders. The first he knew of it, the slimy thing was round his neck. I never heard such shrieks of horror as the man gave, as he tried frantically to shake it off, his comrades laughing and shouting at him the while. At length one went to his assistance and threw it away; the poor fellow was of an ash color. "Sure," he said, "I'd rather been a prisoner with the rebel devils than had that thing on me."

I could sympathize with him, for nothing gives me such a shuddering horror as the touch of a snake. He did not hear the last of that soon, for they joked him about it on all occasions.

We kept on through rain and mud, building bridges over the swamps and streams, until the third of March, when we reached the pretty little village of Cheraw on the great Pedee river. There we remained two days, captured a great deal of ammunition, and, when we were about to leave, burned the public buildings, business houses, etc. We had a terrible explosion there, caused by the blowing up of the powder magazine, and some of the refugees in our train were killed. The noise was terrific, the earth shook under our feet.

At Cheraw I saw John, and right glad was I to be with him again. He gave me a history of what he had gone through since we parted, spoke of the men of the right wing in the highest terms; no men could do more than they had done. He thought it best I should keep my horse and go on, as I had begun. I would rather have been with him, for I liked marching with "our company" best, but he saw I was not very well. The wings kept close together now, and I could easily see him.

After crossing the Great Pedee we were soon in North Carolina; it rained all the time. The first place where we camped was at Laurel Hill. Leaving this we kept on towards Fayetteville, trying to reach there before the rebel army entered. We had to stop at night in a swamp, camp we could not; the rain fell pitilessly, and the ground was covered with water. Some of the officers kept on horseback all night, sleeping there if they could. The train of poor people who followed us must have suffered every possible privation. I found a wagon stalled, and not quite full, and creeping into it slept well.

The soldiers were kind to the people all along the way. "Stay your hand, we are in the North State now," they would say. The country was miserable, interminable pine forests after you left the swamps. The people seemed very poor, and were sickly looking.

The rebel cavalry and ours had a battle just before we reached Fayetteville, but General Kilpatrick drove them after a hard fight with great loss through the streets of Fayetteville, and beyond to the river, and our army took possession of this poor little place. General Sherman had his quarters at the United States Arsenal, which was a magnificent building, but was destroyed when we left. The whole army brought up at Fayetteville, and lay camped around it. There the eyes and hearts of the men were gladdened by the sight of the tug Davidson, which came up the river with dispatches to General Sherman. When they saw her they cheered and cheered again, until hoarse with hurrahing, and many of them cried. It was hearing from home.

I wish some of our stay at home boys, who think an army must be all glare and glitter, fuss and feathers, who read in the papers of General Sherman's Grand Army, and pictured it going through the pine forests and dismal swamps, with music playing and banners flying and bright blue uniforms, could have seen it entering Fayetteville. In the first place an army does not always have music to march by, and on this campaign they had only the "stirring drum" on occasions. Then they did not go tramp,

tramp through the forests and make their way through swamps, removing barricades with a gun in one hand, a hatchet in the other, with the flag unfurled—if they had, in all probability it would have trailed in swampy mud. It was only when they entered a place like Columbia, or wished to make a display for some purpose, that they gave every banner to the breeze and let the rebels read Vicksburg, Chickamauga, Chattanooga, Atlanta and Savannah on their torn folds.

Many of them were barefooted; they had plunged in mud, worked in water, and marched over the sands of the high lands without shoes. They were ragged and their clothes were grimed with mud and discolored with stains of a darker hue. No longer Boys in Blue, they wore clothes of any color and fashion; here and there you might see a swallow-tailed or frock coat of the finest quality, its fit showing the wearer had not been measured for it, mixed with garments of the coarsest homespun made in the strangest fashions and worn-out officers' coats, while suits of rebel gray and butternut cloth abounded.

The greatest scarcity seemed to be in trowsers; all were torn; some came but to the knees, others did not come so far; some men had none at all, and marched in their drawers. The head coverings were as varied as the clothes—military caps, oil skin caps, cloth caps, black, blue, gray and brown, with fronts and without fronts, soft hats and straw hats, high crowned and low crowned, some with no crowns, others with no brims. Some carried patchwork quilts, blanket shawls, or squares of Brussels carpets for blankets, while others had them of the finest and costliest wool, and others again had those which were supplied to the army. One man would pass with a pet coon on his back, or a cat, or a bird; another would have some household article for his comfort or convenience—it might be a pot or a chair. Following these could be seen the poor miserable mules, mud bespattered, with their hair matted together, and laden with pots, pans, kettles, dishes, chairs, shovels, spades, picks, axes and hoes.

"Don't you think I would cut a figure in Miss G——'s drawing-room, Phil?" said Kiler, standing before me, his arms akimbo. "Would not she turn up her aristocratic nose at the sight? See my hands"—he held them out—"brown, scratched, hard and warty, and my 'pedestrian digits,'" he stuck out first one foot, then another; they were cased in what had once been expensive alligator hide boots, now broken and worn, his bare toes protruding, "and these pants, and this blouse, and this beard, and hair," passing his hand over them. "I could make my fortune sitting to artists for a 'rough.' I think it an outrage to have no photographer here to take the 'Grand Army' just as it is; people at home will never believe we looked as we do."

On the morning of the 14th of March we left Fayetteville *en route* for Goldsboro'. The left wing had a battle with Hardee on Black River, at Averysboro', on the 16th, and defeated them with great loss to him and considerable to ourselves. I heard some of the men describe the part they had in the fight. The enemy's works were in a pine forest, and our boys took to the trees, Indian fashion, the trunks affording them fine protection from the balls. It was a bloody battle fought in the rain with the mud ankle deep. The enemy made off in the night, leaving dead, wounded and dying behind them. John was in the battle, and had his arm grazed by a bullet. I saw a detachment from General Kilpatrick's cavalry come back from the field, and each man carried a dead comrade before him on his saddle.

"A FIGURE."

Crossing Black River we kept on as well as the roads would let us, but they were dreadful, all swamp and morass. I came very near leaving myself in a North Carolina swamp. I had taken to horseback again, and wanting to get to John's side, took a short cut through a pine wood which edged a swamp. I felt myself sinking, my horse floundered and tried to get loose, and looking round I saw I was in a quicksand; fortunately a couple of the boys came to my assistance, and I got out and did not trust that treacherous green-looking earth again.

About the 19th, when we were near the pretty little town of Bentonville, in Johnston County, a report came from the front that the enemy were in force and well fortified, our foragers had been skirmishing with them. Then and there began the battle of Bentonville, the last battle fought by Sherman's army; I cannot tell anything about it. I only know that I was in it; that we whipped the rebels handsomely; that, as usual, they departed during the night; and that Kiler saved my life.

The fight began on Sunday, the rebels fought long and well, but the rest of the army marched all day and night, and came to our aid. We were in the Pine Woods. I did not know anything, except that the enemy was before us; all was confusion around. I did not know what any one else was doing; I only know I wished to kill rebels, and was doing all I could, when suddenly I was jerked to the ground; a bullet whizzed where my head had been, and I heard Kiler, who stood over me, say:

"I gave him as good as he sent."

"'Some in rags, some in tags, some in velvet gowns,'" I heard a veteran singing as we were on the road to Goldsboro' again. "I tell you what it is, Jim, I have heard of an army fighting in armor, but I never before heard of an army fighting in drawers." Hundreds of our army had no shoes, and one-twelfth of them no trowsers.

"If I was a Johnny," he continued, "I should not like to be whipped by a man in his drawers."

"They couldn't help it, they did their best. I tell you what it is, when Uncle Sam is in the right, he cannot be beat; they fought like tigers."

General Scofield's army was at Goldsboro' and the men swarmed out to meet their old comrades. Such singing and dancing, hurrahing, shouting, and clapping of hands as they made. They rushed at and hugged each other in their enthusiasm. The flags waved, the bands played, the batteries thundered in welcome. Late in the night groups sat about the camp fires, telling each other what they had gone through, and inquiring for this and that comrade, who rested beneath the sward of Georgia or the Carolinas.

At Goldsboro' we went into camp to rest and wait for supplies of food and clothing. There was some laughter at the appearance of the men as they filed in review before Generals Sherman, Slocum and Schofield, with their free, don't care air and heterogeneous accoutrements, but it was reported General Sherman said, "He did not care what they carried, so they carried plenty of ammunition."

"Yes," said one. "The old Tycoon tells us what he wants done. He knows we will do it, and he don't fuss to have it done by the regulations. If he did he never would have got through Georgia."

Goldsboro' is a pretty place, with a handsome Courthouse, Hotel, Academy and other public buildings. We stayed around it until the 10th of April; the men made themselves at home; some of them to while away time and make a little money, turned peddlers and sold tobacco, coffee and other things in the streets, driving quite a trade.

Finally the army was again equipped and on the road to Raleigh, the capital of North Carolina. "The Great Flanker" was chasing the "Great Retreater." The roads were dreadful, and had most of the way to be corduroyed, but the country was cleared and we saw fine farms and good houses.

On the 12th the news came that General Lee had surrendered. The men were crazy with joy when it was announced. Their shouts were deafening. They leaped and danced, and embraced and swung each other round in the wildest way ; threw their hats in the air and spread their banners and had their bands playing.

Reaching Raleigh the army marched through the city in front of the State House, where Generals Sherman, Howard and Logan were posted.

It began to be whispered that General Johnston was negotiating with General Sherman for the surrender of the rebel army ; meantime there was a truce, and during this all were horrified by the intelligence of Mr. Lincoln's murder.

The troops received it as if every man had lost a near relation. They did not want peace now ; they would not have it. What they wished was to be led against Johnston, and they told their officers so. Vengeance they wanted. Vengeance. "Oh !" said a cavalryman, "if I only had the leaders of the rebellion here," he ground his iron heel in the earth, "I could crush the life out of them."

"I hope," said another, "I may never see wife or child again if I ever spare a rebel," and the tears dropped from his bearded chin. All was gloom.

"He was ours, and we loved him," said a gray-bearded old man from Illinois. "Pray God He keep our hearts right, and let us have malice to none."

For my part, I just leaned my head against John and cried. I thought of the time when I had seen him at the White House, when he laid his hand upon my head and said: "You look like a brave one." I put my hand where his had been and felt so proud his had been there.

John told me he thought those words of Mr. Lincoln's in his message, when he spoke of having malice to none, had done much to calm the men. At least he found it so, in quoting them to men of his command; but if there had been a battle after this news, the slaughter would have been terrible. The poor negroes looked utterly miserable. One could see the white streaks made by the tears on their cheeks. Some of them held a prayer meeting, and I never heard anything as touching, as the way they sang amid their sobs: "Take us to Abraham's bosom."

Our camps were around Raleigh, which was filled with our soldiers. It has beautifully shaded streets, fine gardens and good public buildings. Fearing an outbreak when the army should hear of Mr. Lincoln's death, large detachments were ordered to the city. The weather was fine, the flowers in bloom, the trees green, and here, where no plundering was allowed, we waited for peace, and peace came in Johnston's surrender. Yet, though the men longed for peace, they were ready to go on with the war, and when the truce expired, and the word "forward" came, they marched with alacrity over roads such as we never saw North, and through rain from which we would be careful to shelter our cattle. When orders met them to retrace their steps and go into camp again, they knew it was peace, and with many a "hurrah for Billy; he's all right!" they turned their backs upon the enemy for the first time in the campaign.

It was funny to hear the Bummers bemoaning the peace

prospect. "To think," said one, "I cannot take a man's horse when I want it."

"Yes," said another, "and instead of helping myself to the best a house affords if I wish it, and then burning it over the owner's head because he had nothing better to give, I shall have to wait at the door, hat in hand, and be thankful for any crust he will throw me.' He cut a caper and burst out with "When this cruel war is over."

"I'll tell you what; it's my opinion," said a squirrel shooter from Ohio, "a good many of you will be guests of the State before you are a month out of this. You've had your hand in too long, and stealing will come natural."

"O, you dry up; you are only jealous; Sherman's Bummers and their deeds will be remembered long after you are forgotten. We shall be the bug-bears for the children and grandchildren of future generations."

The surrender was proclaimed to the army, then the *one* thought was to get home.

I went about a little to take a look at things. John told me to go down and see Bennet's house, where Generals Sherman and Johnston had met to talk of terms, as it would be historical. It was on the railroad, about three miles from Durham, half-way between the picket lines of the two armies. It was a small one story frame building with a few trees around it. The house below consisted of but one good sized room, which held a bed, table and chairs; the walls were bare, the floor bare. There was a covered stairway in the room, running to a half-story above.

We started for home, impatient, joyous; the people met us with shout and gladness. Ruin no longer was in our track. We passed through Richmond; the men were eager to see Libby prison and Castle Thunder—where so many of their comrades had suffered martyrdom.

Reaching the battle fields of the army of the Potomac, shout after shout went up—one brave army acknowledging the deeds of the other.

Keeping on, the spires of Alexandria and Washington were seen in the distance. Four years before some of us, fugitives, in mud and rain, worn in body and almost crushed in spirit, had wearily trodden that road—O, but we remembered it now! I strode closer to John, and looked in his face and he understood me, and smiled. "You were a boy then, Phil," he said, "you are almost a man now!"

"See." I pointed to my little flag, in shreds, but blazoned all over with our victories. "I had hoped to have given this to Mr. Lincoln," my voice was husky, John took my hand, and squeezed it: "It is the sting that is in every thing here, Phil."

Then followed the review—there was no sting in that to me—I thought not how blood-bought had been our victories. It was all joy—triumph.

I went into Washington and with Mrs. Leavit saw the glorious army of the Potomac pass in review, saw the people almost worshiping those heroes, while shouts of gratitude filled the air—I thought I could not feel prouder.

But the next day—when General Sherman's army passed by also, and I with them—my cup was full, I was a part of it—an atom—but yet a part.

When I saw Generals Howard and Slocum and Logan, and "Little Kill," our noble good Governor Dennison, Senator Wilson, and our gallant commander in Virginia, General Benham, I felt at home. When I read Vicksburg and Shiloh, Stone River and Chickamauga, and saw among all, and high above all, "The poor officer with the large family," and heard the acclamations that rent the air, I felt a hero among heroes. I waved my flag and looked at the bronzed faces round me, and thanked God I had been permitted to be with Sherman's army.

I sat one night during that summer in Mrs. Leavit's parlor, and marked John's quiet modest manner, and as she talked in her enthusiastic way of our victories, I heard him repeat softly :

> "Not with Te Deums loud and high Hosannas,
> Greet we the awful victory we have won,
> But with our arms reversed and lowered banners
> We stand—Our work is done !
> * * * * * * *
> At whose defeat we may not raise our voice
> Save in the deep thanksgiving of our prayers,
> Lord, we have fought the fight. But to rejoice
> Is curs no more than theirs."

THE END.

CHAMPLIN'S BOOKS FOR YOUNG FOLKS.

"AN INVALUABLE ADDITION TO THE SCHOOL LIBRARY."—*Baltimore Gazette.*

TO PARENTS:

YOUNG FOLKS' CYCLOPÆDIA OF COMMON THINGS.

Large 12mo, pp. 690, with a very full index, $3.

The writer has attempted to furnish in simple language, aided by pictorial illustrations, where thought necessary, a knowledge of things in Nature, Science, and the Arts which are apt to awaken a child's curiosity. Such features of Astronomy, Chemistry, Physics, Natural History, and Physiology as can easily be made intelligible are explained, special attention being given to the natural objects which most immediately affect human happiness—such as air, light, heat, and electricity, and those parts of the human system whose health is influenced by our habits. Much attention has been given, too, to explanation of the manufacture of articles in common use, and to all the animals interesting from their domestic relation or as objects of curiosity.

The arrangement is the same as in the cyclopædias for adults, as the work is but a stepping-stone to them, and it is deemed of importance to accustom the child early to the forms and methods which experience has shown to be the best.

What prominent Journals say of it:

"It is a thoroughly excellent thing, thoroughly well done, and there can be no doubt whatever that in every household into which it shall come the book will go far to educate children in that skillful and profitable use of books which distinguishes scholarly bookowners from those who are not scholars. . . . In every way, we regard the publication of this 'Young Folks' Cyclopædia' as an occasion of rejoicing, and in the interest of education we commend it with all possible earnestness to every parent."—*N. Y. Evening Post.*

"Just to test the quality and to see whether those for whom it was made would care for it, the writer left this book on the study table, about which these children gather. There was a fight for this cyclopædia every night until parental authority decided 'thirteen years' should read it aloud. On the other side, time and again, has the parent pointed to this invaluable book. To the parent it is a boon, to the child a blessing."—*Cincinnati Times.*

"An occasional pertinent anecdote is introduced, and a bit of folk-lore is not rejected. The interest is continually aroused. The work will fill a gap long vacant. Should be placed wherever children meet for lessons and reading."—*Boston Advertiser.*

"Teachers and parents should see that this cyclopædia is in every library where children can have access to it."—*N. E. Journal of Education.*

"Clearly printed and freely illustrated with woodcuts. The definitions and descriptions are carefully accommodated both as regards length and clearness, to the childish mind. The compiler more or less consciously plays the part of a wise parent who is not restrained from enlivening his instruction with poetry (as in the case of Tennyson and the dragon-fly) and with familiar anecdotes, of which the index contains an imposing alphabetic grouping. There can be no doubt that at the ordinary cyclopædia repels the child by its fulness and technical obscurity; and such an abstract as this ought, as the compiler anticipates, to cultivate the habit of reference, besides saving parents the mortification of having questions put to them which they are unable to answer."—*The Nation.*

"The book will be as valuable as a small library to any young person."—*Independent.*

"A very successful embodiment of a very excellent plan. . . . . The

[OVER].

illustrations are numerous and excellent. . . . The information is accurately and judiciously given, and not 'young folks' only, but many adults will find the book constantly useful."—*Literary World.*

"A fountain of instruction and entertainment to those young persons who are so fortunate as to possess it." —*N. Y. Observer.*

"Will be very generally hailed with favor both by the young folks and the parents of the young folks."—*N. Y. World.*

"This book is one of the best ever issued. It cannot fail to prove a vital auxiliary in the education of the children of the present."—*Cincinnati Commercial.*

"Grown folks, judging by the average of human knowledge will have reason to use and respect the handsome volume. . . . The style of the text, while not in the least commonplace, is so clear and sensible, that every young reader and student of ordinary intelligence will comprehend it. The possession of such a book by a youth of inquiring mind is the next thing to a liberal education."—*Phila. Bulletin.*

"Although it is professedly for the young, we are much mistaken if it does not become a favorite book with all in the household. The book, in its completeness, thoroughness and style, is a credit to author and publisher." —*Hartford Courant.*

"The practice of consulting a work of this kind would greatly tend to quicken the power of attention, to stimulate juvenile curiosity, and to strengthen the habit of careful and accurate reading, as well as to enrich the memory with a store of instructive and valuable facts. . . . A model of construction and arrangement. . . . The facility of using the work to advantage is greatly assisted by the indispensable appendage of a copious and accurate index."—*N. Y. Tribune.*

The "Cyclopædia of Common Things" was followed by the

YOUNG FOLKS'
CYCLOPÆDIA OF PERSONS AND PLACES.

Large 12mo, pp. 956, with a very full index, $3.50.

The Press speaks of it as follows:

"When the former work appeared we gave to it the heartiest and most cordial approval, founding our judgment upon a somewhat thorough examination of the scheme, and of the manner of its execution . . . We have no occasion to hesitate in forming a like opinion of Mr. Champlin's second cyclopædia. . . . This opinion, founded as it was solely upon an examination of the book with reference to the known characteristics of childhood, has since been confirmed, and more than confirmed, by observation of the use actually made of the cyclopædia by lads and young maidens who are its owners. We know copies of the work which are in daily use, and to which their young owners turn instantly for information upon every theme about which they have questions to ask. More than this, we know that some of these copies are read daily as well as consulted, that their owners turn the leaves as they might those of a fairy book, reading intently articles of which they had not thought before seeing them, and treating the book simply as one capable of furnishing the rarest entertainment in exhaustless quantities." *N. Y. Evening Post.*

"This is a book that has novelty and wear in it."—*N. Y. Tribune.*

"Opens a new world to the young, introducing them to famous persons, classic scenes and buildings. . . . It is copiously illustrated, and printed admirably."—*N. E. Journal of Education.*

"It makes use of the last census, and it embodies the recent discoveries of Olympia. The volume, in fact, is sufficiently large and altogether commendable."—*Boston Advertiser.*

"We have experimented by numerous references, and find that the material is very judiciously selected, and presented to meet what we believe to be the wants of young persons."—*N. Y. Observer.*

"Mr. Champlin's work fills a gap which no other does. Its sketches of persons are vivacious and in the main accurate. The illustrations are well selected and some are novel."—*Springfield Republican.*

"A book of to-day. . . . An indispensable aid to the parent who would never be 'stumped' by a youngster's questionings."—*Rochester Democrat.*

HENRY HOLT & Co., Publishers,
NEW YORK.

www.ingramcontent.com/pod-product-compliance
Lightning Source LLC
Chambersburg PA
CBHW032017220426
43664CB00006B/273